RHETORIC AND COMPOSITION
AS INTELLECTUAL WORK

RHETORIC AND COMPOSITION AS INTELLECTUAL WORK ∾

Edited by Gary A. Olson

Southern Illinois University Press

Carbondale and Edwardsville

Library of Congress Cataloging-in-Publication Data

Rhetoric and composition as intellectual work / edited by Gary A. Olson.
    p. cm.
Includes bibliographical references and index.
    1. English language—Rhetoric—Study and teaching. 2. English
language—Composition and exercises—Study and teaching. I. Olson,
Gary A., date.
PE1404 .R485 2002
08'.042'071—dc21   2001042057
ISBN 0-8093-2433-4 (paper : alk. paper)

FOR ELVIRA AND OWEN NILES

Contents

Part Two. Historical Inquiry

Part Three. Ideological Inquiry

Part Four. Philosophical Inquiry

Part Five. New Directions

Preface

I T'S NOT ALWAYS APPARENT, but other disciplines have a long tradition of struggling over their intellectual identity. Anthropologists, for example, have debated for decades whether anthropology should be conceived of as a social "science" (in the tradition of Margaret Mead, say) or as a discipline that operates less as a "science" and more as an interpretive, hermeneutic, even rhetorical field (in the tradition of Clifford Geertz and Renato Rosaldo). For Geertz, all texts in the social sciences are in one way or another "fictions," constructions, and he has argued that anthropologists need to treat them as such, not as inviolable, unassailable statements of scientific truth. Treating research reports and the like as "texts" does not diminish their usefulness or even their "truthfulness"; rather, it opens these texts up to a richer, more significant interpretation that leads to broader understanding of the subject at hand. This perspective, however, has caused great anxiety among those anthropologists who understand their task to be not one of interpretation but of objective, scientific data gathering and reporting: taking careful notes in the field (a primitive, aboriginal village, say), applying accepted anthropological principles to this data, and then reporting this factual information to fellow scholars. These are two very different—some might even say opposing—ways of conceptualizing the discipline, and so the debate has often been intense as each group has struggled to position *its* notion of the discipline to be the one accepted by the field as a whole. As a result, some anthropologists have felt that the field has no coherent identity, that, in the words of Geertz, "somehow the field doesn't hold together internally." But to Geertz, an atmosphere of pluralism, diversity, debate, and conflict is productive because it keeps the discipline intellectually vital: "If you want that certainty, and if wobbling around in the water bothers you, then you should go into chem-

istry, not anthropology—and, I have a feeling, not into rhetoric and composition either" (202).

Geertz is correct, of course, that rhetoric and composition, like anthropology, is engaged in disciplinary struggle, in debates over the identity of the
field, and that those who feel uncomfortable with such lack of certainty are
likely to remain very unhappy. While there are several ongoing debates over
our disciplinary identity (and the same is true with anthropology), the one
that is most persistent and, at times, heated is the dispute over whether rhetoric and composition should be an intellectual as well as service discipline.
That is, while many compositionists insist that all research, all inquiry in the
field, should serve the sole purpose of furthering and refining the *teaching* of
composition, many of us contend that although we all desire to learn more
about the teaching of writing or about our own writing processes, these are
not the *only* intellectual concerns we should have as a discipline, that constituting rhetoric and composition as a discipline whose raison d'être is the
teaching of writing is dangerously and unacceptably narrow and even, in
some people's eyes, anti-intellectual. The truth of the matter is that rhetoric
and composition *already is* an intellectual discipline, that for at least a quarter of a century the field has developed an impressive tradition of intellectual
work in a remarkable assortment of subject areas, many of which do not
consider the teaching of writing to be their only or even primary focus or
objective. *Rhetoric and Composition as Intellectual Work* describes, examines,
and critiques some of the intellectual work in the field and proposes new
directions for such work in the future.

A collection of nineteen essays by some of the most distinguished scholars
in the discipline, *Rhetoric and Composition as Intellectual Work* illustrates the
rich diversity of scholarship in the field. Cumulatively, these chapters present
a picture of a vibrant field of substantive scholarship about a formidable
array of academic subjects relevant to the workings of written discourse.

Part One, Disciplinary Concerns, comprises four chapters addressing
issues related to rhetoric and composition's status as a discipline. Jasper Neel
discusses the theory/antitheory debate, arguing that ignorance of theory prevents us from seeing that changing our position on a subject actually changes
what we see and how we see it. He concludes that the discipline only becomes
mature and self-sustaining when it constantly interrogates its theoretical
underpinnings. C. Jan Swearingen provides a historical perspective on our
disciplinary formation, cautioning us that if we are not careful, we may well

undo the progress of the last three decades, reverting back to our predisciplinary service-only days. She fears the return to a situation in which graduate work in the field is discouraged and openly disparaged unless rhetoric is closely associated with literary theory and composition is tied exclusively to the undergraduate writing program. Echoing Swearingen's caution that we stand to destroy what has become an intellectually exciting, rigorous, and productive discipline, Gary Olson addresses both the theory debates and the historical development of rhetoric and composition as an intellectual discipline. He responds to a revitalized backlash against theoretical scholarship, claiming that hegemonic struggle over the discipline's identity is healthy so long as such struggle is not mean spirited. In the final essay in this section, Charles Bazerman makes a case for writing studies as a major intellectual discipline in today's academy. In order to illustrate his broad notion of the discipline, he reviews some of his own scholarship and the three "syntheses"—the historical, theoretical, and practical—that have informed such work. These four chapters provide a context for the discussions that follow.

Part Two, Historical Inquiry, examines the significance of archival and historical scholarship. In the context of arguing that we should all conceive of the field in terms of "writing studies," Susan Miller illustrates the value of archival research. She posits that the descriptor "writing studies"—as both the content of our scholarship and the name of the discipline itself—helps us avoid the often pejorative "composition studies" and can encourage a sense of shared objective among the scholars in disparate subject areas in the field. She then demonstrates how archival research serves as an exemplary mode of intellectual work in writing studies. Drawing on her work as an experienced researcher, Susan Wells also explores the significance—as well as the frustrations—of archival work. She details three "gifts" that archival work offers us: it helps us learn to resist epistemological closure; it offers us the possibility of reconfiguring the discipline itself; and it helps us avoid surrendering to resentment about our low status in the academy, because, in the end, archival work makes substantive contributions to human knowledge. In an attempt to move historical inquiry in new directions, Susan Jarratt discusses how studies in traditional rhetoric can employ an "analytics of space" to confront social difference. Such projects would examine the available documents in order to draw attention to how rhetoric was used in public spaces and, in doing so, would foreground questions of power and participation within those spaces. All three authors in this section survey some of the most important scholarship in their respective areas, providing a taste of the variety and substance of intellectual work emerging from historical inquiry.

Part Three, Ideological Inquiry, considers the role of ideological and institutional critique in the intellectual work of the discipline. Gary Olson posits that ideological critique and the ability to "represent" are central not only to the intellectual work of the discipline but also to our pedagogies. Examining several contributions to the tradition of ideological critique, he maintains that this analytical tool offers the possibility of moving toward substantive change in intellectual and social arenas and that it can also serve as a tool for students to effect real change in their own lives. Tom Fox suggests that the same is true for institutional critique. He claims that a principal achievement of composition scholarship in the last decade has been the examination of how educational institutions use literacy instruction to reinscribe cultural hierarchies. In his own intellectual work, Fox seeks to discover ways to function ethically and politically within institutions while discovering ways to change them from within. Drawing a sharp distinction between "academic" work and "intellectual" work, Lynn Worsham explores the role of theoretical scholarship in the intellectual work of composition and argues that the discipline must engage ideological critique if it is to rise above the status of a service discipline. She claims that an examination of the role of emotion in the workings of ideology is central to such critique and that, consequently, the purpose of the intellectual work of writing is to alter the affective relations that position us in the world. Keith Gilyard surveys the ideological struggle over the "Students' Right to Their Own Language" document and demonstrates why such work is valuable. He takes issue with the field's tepid response to the document's main claim: that judging a particular dialect unacceptable is clearly yet another way that the powers that be exert social dominance over marginalized groups. The four chapters in this section attempt to put into relief the kinds of intellectual work that are informed by ideological critique and to suggest how such work has already become central to the intellectual work of rhetoric and composition.

Part Four, Philosophical Inquiry, illustrates how various kinds of intersections between philosophy and rhetoric have produced substantial contributions to the intellectual work of rhetoric and composition. Analyzing two Supreme Court cases, Steven Mailloux explains how and why rhetorical hermeneutics is a fruitful avenue of inquiry. He describes the project of rhetorical hermeneutics as "the use of rhetoric to practice theory by doing history." Thomas Kent provides an overview of paralogic rhetoric, an understanding of rhetoric that has become the foundation of the post-process movement in composition. Before considering the implications for composition studies of paralogic rhetoric, he outlines its five principal assumptions: that writing is a kind of communicative interaction; that communicative interaction is thoroughly hermeneutic; that writing requires hermeneutic guesswork; that writing requires interaction with others; and that writing is not a process. Barbara Couture describes how philosophical conceptions of truth and truth telling—despite postmodernist pronouncements to the contrary—can have a significant impact both on our own practices and on the teaching of writing. She describes the kind of intellectual work that she and others engage in as an exploration of philosophy's role in rhetorical practice—an apt description of the work of each of the authors in this section. Finally, Victor Vitanza outlines his "third sophistic" way of seeing. He explains that in his theorizing he attempts to resist and even circumvent the constraints of systematic and alienated ways of seeing that are imposed on us by language and language conventions, and he details three "aconceptual starting places" from which he attempts to "see" in new and productive ways. These four chapters illustrate the depth and breadth of a strain of intellectual work in rhetoric and composition that has engaged fruitfully with both the philosophical and rhetorical traditions.

Part Five, New Directions, presents four new and emerging areas of inquiry in the intellectual work of rhetoric and composition. Reviewing some of the recent work in body studies, Sharon Crowley argues that scholars in rhetoric and composition need to grapple with the insights arising from such work. Advocating a posthumanist conception of subjectivity, she charges that the discipline still clings to a modernist conception of self, one that supports a discriminatory and inequitable distribution of intellectual and political power. Similarly, John Trimbur cites work related to visual rhetorics and contends that such scholarship can transform our theoretical and pedagogical notions of literacy. Identifying himself with the post-process movement, he claims that earlier scholarship obscured the materiality of writing, failing to locate the writer in the labor process in relation to the means of production. He argues cogently that if we study and teach typography as the culturally salient means of producing writing, we will be better able to locate writers in the writing process. Cynthia Selfe and Richard Selfe provide a substantive look at the intellectual work emerging from computers and composition studies. They narrow their focus within this burgeoning area to three subareas: work addressing educational issues, social and cultural issues, and issues of representation and identity. Finally, William Covino shows how the current recuperation of the ancient connection between rhetoric and magic provides useful insights for the discipline. After surveying some of the key work in this area, he analyzes the rhetoric pertaining to the 2000 presidential election to suggest how the magic-rhetoric connection manifests itself in popular culture. All four of these chapters indicate that scholars in rhetoric and composition are continuing to push at our disciplinary borders, discovering new and productive sites of investigation.

Together, these nineteen essays examine rhetoric and composition as an intellectual discipline and illustrate some of the new and ongoing kinds of intellectual work that have contributed to the field's emergence as a respectable contributor to the intellectual work of the academy. Of course, these few essays do not represent the entire field of rhetoric and composition or the whole spectrum of intellectual work being done there; that would have necessitated a multivolume set. However, *Rhetoric and Composition as Intellectual Work* does suggest the diversity of intellectual projects that have and will continue to make rhetoric and composition more than a service to the university (though it is certainly that), more than a field devoted solely to improving writing pedagogy (though it is that too), and more than a stepchild to literary studies. As the chapters of this book attest, rhetoric and composition has much to offer to the intellectual milieu of the contemporary university.

Work Cited

Olson, Gary A. "The Social Scientist as Author: Clifford Geertz on Ethnography and
    Social Construction." *(Inter)views: Cross-Disciplinary Perspectives on Rhetoric and
    Literacy*. Ed. Gary A. Olson and Irene Gale. Carbondale: Southern Illinois UP, 1991.
    187–210.

Acknowledgments

I'D LIKE TO THANK Merry Perry and Jennifer Hord for invaluable editorial assistance; Coleen Connolly for her proofreading acumen; Tammy Evans for her hard work on the index; Lynn Worsham for her wit, wisdom, and sage advice, especially in helping me conceptualize this project; Elvira and Owen Niles for moral support; and Karl Kageff for his keen editorial instincts. I am particularly grateful to the contributors to this book and to those like them who have worked hard to build rhetoric and composition into an intellectual as well as a service discipline, one that can and has contributed substantively to our understanding of the complexities of rhetoric and discourse in all its myriad manifestations.

Part One

Disciplinary Concerns

1

Reclaiming Our Theoretical Heritage:
A Big Fish Tale

JASPER NEEL

IT IS AN INTRACTABLE CONUNDRUM, the theory versus praxis split—more intractable and more confusing in rhetoric and composition than in most other disciplines because contemporary rhet/comp grew from the classroom. Homiletics in divinity schools, moot court in law schools, copy writing and reporting in schools of journalism, marketing in schools of business, and similar disciplines share the problem. When praxis is the purpose, must one theorize at all? As with most such conversations, the technical vocabulary and discursive strategies begin with Aristotle. In Aristotle's *Metaphysics,* one is either a metaphysician, and hence an intellectual, or one is not, and hence one is a person of "practical affairs." The metaphysicians regard those of "practical affairs" as less rigorous and, in the world of language teaching, less moral because their very practicality forever traps them in sophistry. Those of practical affairs regard the metaphysicians as elitists—theoreticians who never begin any actual work because they never have their thinking completely straight. For the practitioner, Stanley Fish's old T-shirt with the question, Sure it works in practice, but will it work in theory? is an ironic description, not an in-joke.

The answer to the question *Must* one theorize at all?, of course, is, No. One need not theorize about any praxis. The price, unfortunately, at least since Aristotle, is a mixture of naïveté and self-deception. Let's experiment with an analogy seemingly far from rhetoric and composition—whaling.

Reading Jonah

Robert Sullivan's new book, *A Whale Hunt,* offers an interesting entry into the contemporary state of whaling in the Americas. Five centuries ago (between 1300 and 1600 C.E.) whaling was apparently a rich and satisfying way of life in what we now call the Pacific Northwest. From the perspective of contemporary, web-based global capitalism, the descendants of these now nearly extinct whalers seem poor, downtrodden, and hopeless. But in 1500, when whaling thrived, the Native Americans of the Pacific Northwest not only enjoyed great material prosperity (a fact that archaeologists have recently uncovered) but also developed a sophisticated spiritual life; everything from impressive architecture, interesting art, and healthful diet to cosmology, theology, and spirituality grew from and depended on whaling.

By 1950, however, few Native American tribes of the Northwest were still whaling. The Makah tribe, about whom Sullivan writes, decided in the mid-1990s to resume whale hunting as the only possible hope for restoring their rapidly evaporating culture. Almost immediately, however, they were opposed by a host of animal rights activists, environmentalists, save-the-whale aficionados, and opponents of the Japan-based whale meat industry.

Whales offer an interesting perspective from which to view the theory-praxis conundrum in rhetoric and composition. Centuries ago, whaling "theory," the theology and cosmology of a now nearly lost whale-hunting people, grew out of the practical need to eat coupled with a bountiful supply of whales. Established whaling practice, in other words, created an occasion for theory to justify, regularize, and sustain whaling as a human endeavor. In contrast, the Makah's decision to resume whale hunting in 1995 shows theory driving practice. Makah tribal leaders could easily see their culture dying as their unique identity as whale hunters, the very origin of their self-respect, withered away. They theorized that a return to the practice of whaling — the spirituality of the preparation for the hunt, the death-defying and arduous struggle of the hunt itself, the joyous celebration of victory over one of nature's most formidable foes, and even the money generated by supplying an international demand for whale meat — could reconstitute the Makah as a people with an identity and a way of life. Whereas praxis led to theory in the Pacific Northwest during the second millennium C.E., theory could enable aimless, rootless, nearly identityless Native Americans in the third millennium to resume praxis, thereby reconstituting themselves as a people. The Makah, as Sullivan explains, had lost the praxis almost entirely.

Their first task was to rediscover the traditional ways of whaling, because almost no one in the tribe could remember how the tribe used to hunt whales.

Unfortunately for the Makah—and for all whaling people these days—a nearly hegemonic countertheory reigns, a countertheory that glorifies animal rights, that sees the ecosystem threatened by the extinction of whales, and that uses anticapitalist economic theory to oppose the whale-meat industry. In this theory, whaling is an evil and primitive practice that must be eradicated from the world. The praxis that derives from this countertheory uses national and international legal systems, a massive public relations apparatus, and high-risk civil disobedience both onshore and especially on the high seas to impede any effort to resume or expand whaling. And the story grows ever more complex. The early, primitive practice of whaling led to sophisticated, theologically sanctioned whaling theory. After the death of established whaling practice, sophisticated sociological, anthropological, psychological, and economic theory led the Makah to try to rediscover practice. But by the time such a practice could be demonstrated theoretically as socially desirable, the countertheory already ruled the day. This countertheory has led to very effective practices through which all whalers are revealed as evil, rapacious murderers of a highly intelligent mammalian relative of human beings.

So, which takes precedence? The whale's right to live a full and satisfying life free from predatory, harpoon-bearing carnivores? The moralist's right to prevent evil behavior because, to the moralist, the behavior *is* evil? The whale eater's right to enjoy a good meal? Native American whaling-based culture, which, without the whale hunt, has about the same chance of survival as would the United States if Christianity were outlawed and free enterprise abolished? And does it matter if the Native Americans re-create the whale hunt using modern technology? Radar and sonar to find the whales? Motorized boats to catch them? Harpoon canons that are much more accurate and have far greater range and power than harpoons thrown by hand? Modern materials for lines, hooks, and fishing paraphernalia? Must the hunt be conducted exactly as it was with exactly the same ritual and equipment as those used in 1500? Would 1900 equipment be acceptable? If the Makah forego everything but a twenty-first-century harpoon gun, is that acceptable?

Like it or not, this is a theory-praxis problem, undeniably an intractable conundrum, but one made much worse if the parties involved cannot foreground their theoretical assumptions and trace the origin, history, and invisibility of those assumptions. Let's expand the whaling analogy just slightly to include all extremely large sea animals. This will allow us to look at the ancient Hebrew story of Jonah. If Western culture offers an interesting matrix for discussing the theory-praxis split, surely it is Jonah.

Let me remind you of the story, which comprises only forty-eight verses in the Masoretic text used by most Jews and Christians—less than three pages in most editions. A plot summary goes as follows: rejecting God's command to preach in Nineveh, Jonah flees by boat toward Tarshish. God sends a violent storm, and the sailors reluctantly toss Jonah into the sea to pacify God, thus calming the storm. A "great fish" (usually thought of as a whale) swallows Jonah, who remains in the whale's belly for three days, after which he is vomited onto dry land. Jonah goes to Nineveh, prophesies destruction in forty days, and the Ninevites repent. God forgives the Ninevites, and Jonah complains bitterly because the Ninevites, whom Jonah dislikes, are not destroyed. God sends Jonah a bush for shade, then sends a worm to kill the bush, and then explains his rationale to a still-pouting Jonah. Simple enough. Most of us can imagine Jonah, like Pinocchio and Gepetto, languishing in the digestive tract of a Monstro-like fish. But, as with all things, the devil is not in the details; the devil is in the theories that reveal the details *as* details.

At least since the Protestant Reformation, and probably long before that, Jonah has been read by some as literal history, a true story that (1) tests the faith of believers, who must believe that God can create a sea creature large enough to swallow a grown man whole and keep him inside for three days without seriously injuring him; (2) confirms the community identity of believers who can believe no. 1; and (3) shows how a fallible, rebellious human can be saved by grace, even if he is reluctant and sinful. The key for this interpretation lies in Matthew 12:38–41, where Jesus seems to say both that the Jonah story is literally true and that Jonah's three days in the belly of the whale prefigures his own three-day descent into hell after the crucifixion.

A clear theory governs this reading: all of the Bible is literally true; thus, the true believer must develop a reading praxis that allows the seemingly impossible (e.g., a man can spend three days in the digestive tract of a sea monster and survive) not only to seem possible but also to seem obvious. A majority of those who read or hear the story of Jonah these days must confront this theory of reading the Bible. While most probably end up rejecting this theory, they at least consider it long enough to decide to reject the theory. It would be naïve to underestimate the intensity of this theoretical battle. This battle will, during the year 2000, probably irrevocably divide the Southern Baptist Convention, the nation's largest Protestant denomination, into those who read the Bible literally and those who read at least some parts of the Bible figuratively. Millions of dollars, numerous colleges and seminaries, thousands of churches, and millions of Baptists will take one stand or the other. Denominational budgets for mission work, retirement annuities for retired pastors, salaries and tuition rates at colleges and seminaries, even national political clout are all at stake.

There are, of course, several other theories of reading that can inform the praxis of reading Jonah. Perhaps the most common theory—certainly the oldest, and probably the most historically reliable theory because it grows out of Judaism, the tradition in which Jonah occurred and to which, at least historically, it belongs—is the theory that sacred scripture can include didactic fiction, which, because it is self-announced *as* fiction, is not literal and thus is not to be accepted as a record of true events. Not surprisingly, this theory of reading broadens rather than narrows the boundaries of interpretation. Here are just a few of the ways one might read Jonah if one approaches it as didactic fiction. Number 1: God is a universal God who is present everywhere. One cannot run from God because wherever one runs God will already be there. Jonah literally cannot run from an omnipresent God. Number 2: God does not belong to one nation or to one ethnic group and thus cannot be appropriated for nationalistic purposes. God loves the heathen people of Nineveh just as much as he loves the people of Judah. Number 3: God's will is immutable. Humans cannot subvert it. Jonah will preach to Nineveh whether he wants to or not, and God will spare the Ninevites if he chooses to do so. Number 4: Jonah is an ethical treatise, demonstrating both negative behavior (in the disobedient, rebellious, and sullen character of Jonah) and positive behavior (in the pagan King of Nineveh who hears God's word and repents). Number 5: Jonah is *māšāl* in the Jewish tradition or parable in the Christian tradition. Read this way, one usually makes a choice. The first choice reveals Nineveh as a symbol of the pagan but receptive nations of the world that can hear God's word in spite of their sinfulness. By contrast, Judah (or, for Christians, Christianity) is a symbol of believers who obey God only reluctantly and under protest-filled duress. The irony of this reading is that the believing nation (Judah, or Christianity) is symbolized by the pouty, reluctant Jonah. The second choice in the *māšāl* or parable reading reveals Jonah as a symbol of justice (Jonah wants the Ninevites punished because they have been bad) and reveals God as a symbol of mercy

(God forgives the Ninevites even though they deserve destruction). Justice, in other words, is a human convention; mercy, by contrast, is a divine gift.

And these are just the more common ways to read Jonah as didactic fiction. Number 6: One can read it as either a Christian allegory prefiguring Christ's burial and resurrection, or as a Jewish allegory in which the soul is embodied (on the ship), buried (in the fish), and resurrected (vomited onto land). Number 7: Some Jews read Jonah as *midrash* (or commentary) on 2 Kings 14:25 rather than as a true free-standing book in its own right. If one broadens the notion of didactic fiction so that other humanistic modes of inquiry can inform the reading process, the interpretations continue to expand. Number 8: One can read Jonah as philosophy: as philosophy of how one deals with life when life does not cooperate with one's wishes, as deconstruction in that every reading of Jonah carries within itself its own undoing; and so on. Number 9: One can read Jonah as symbolic history similar to the reading sometimes given to Job. In this reading, one must confront the possibility that God is more generous to and more lenient with nonbelievers who behave terribly over many years than he is with believers who try hard to live according to his laws. Whereas God often punishes his followers immediately and harshly for an indiscretion (or, in the case of Job, for no apparent indiscretion), God is willing to forgive the heathen Ninevites all their sins the moment they repent. Number 10: One can even read Jonah as drama. It can be read as refined satire with the bigoted, narrow-minded, ethnocentric Jonah as the butt, just as Gulliver is the butt in *Gulliver's Travels*. Or it can be bedlam and clamor. Imagine a movie of Jonah with Charlie Chaplin or Jim Carrey as the star.

But Jonah need not be read didactically (or even religiously) at all. One can read it as a text of culture. A cultural anthropologist who is both a professional and a personal atheist could see Jonah as a way of understanding the processes whereby multiple, differently authored texts are woven together as one text of culture, a text that blends the folktale of a storm at sea with the fairy tale of a person swallowed by a fish, with a psalm of praise, with a narrative of salvation, with a holy-man story about a conversation between a holy man and God. A Jungian psychologist, by contrast, à la Oedipus, might read Jonah as a nervous breakdown followed by a period of recalcitrant bitterness followed by the beginnings of recovery. A formalist critic could approach Jonah as an ancient, highly artistic short story, and an infinite number of complex readings would follow from this theory of the text.

To see the multiple theories of reading that govern Jonah, one need do no more than follow the tale as it makes its way into the Jewish tradition (probably in the fourth century B.C.E.), then gets picked up and made a Christian text in the gospels and by the subsequent Christian interpreters, then gets picked up again in Surah 10 of the Koran, and then gets picked up again in the Book of Mormon. Each accretion utterly recasts the text by revealing it in the light of a new set of theoretical assumptions.

Let me make clear that these theories are mutually exclusive. A cultural anthropologist or a Jungian psychologist will see a text different from the one seen by a Muslim mullah, a Mormon elder, or a Southern Baptist deacon. Each theory of reading creates a different matrix in which the text of Jonah becomes recognizable as a text; each theory sets different boundaries for interpretation and reveals different rules of evidence. A Harvard Ph.D. who is tenured in the Department of Anthropology at the University of Wisconsin-Madison and who attends regular services at a liberal Reformed Jewish synagogue will not see the same text as a Southern Baptist minister with a degree from Bob Jones University and a church in a blue collar neighborhood in Spartanburg, South Carolina. The only way that these two can even discuss the text is to foreground the different theoretical matrices in which they read. If they cannot undertake such foregrounding, they have few choices other than contemptuous disregard or violent suppression.

Reclaiming Theory

Everyone who has taught composition for several years has at one time or another felt somewhat like the Makah: alone, trapped, humbled, discouraged, and abandoned. The Jonah analogy is equally apt. Every composition teacher has felt himself or herself called to preach to the Ninevites. Every composition teacher has tried to run away from the call and has felt hopeless and abandoned, cast into a raging sea by those who do not and cannot understand the mission. Even when things go right and a class responds perfectly, there is always the chastening realization that there will be other classes that will respond poorly and accomplish little.

Composition becomes mature, however, able to sustain itself, when it constantly scrutinizes its theoretical underpinnings. The least satisfactory reading of Jonah, after all, is the charismatic, reductive demand to believe it as literal history—just as the least satisfactory, most easily exhausted approach to the teaching of writing is the highly charismatic teacher who draws a theory of writing from Wordsworth and Coleridge without knowing the origin of that theory and then demands to be left alone in the intuitive, magical, angst-ridden writing questroom.

Pedagogy, like wealth, occurs in a context. Transport a middle-class person of today to the year 1800 and that person would be wealthy; transported to 1600, that person would be extravagantly wealthy; yet such a person does not feel wealthy today. Rhetoric and composition as a field exists in the North American university. The North American university is perhaps the most theory driven, theory conscious situation in human history. It would be naïve to retreat from theory, and it would be exceedingly selfish, because the only faculty who truly have the option of doing so already have tenure and have already passed through the process of finding a voice with which to speak.

In large part, rhetoric and composition has undergone a process parallel to that of the Makah. By 1950, we had lost our theory of being, and then we lost both our cultural justification and our reason for being. Like the Makah, we can continue to abandon theory, and wait for the composition equivalent of cable television, McDonald's, and interstate highways across the tundra. Then we will be able to enjoy occasional moments of nostalgia as our discipline gradually evaporates. Or like the Makah we can try to reclaim our theoretical heritage, remaking it for a new time. The Makah may well hunt whales with sonar, motorboats, harpoon canons, disabling chemicals, and modern line and hooks. They may even sell whale meat in Asia. If they do, they will be assailed by a host of social activists. And maybe in some absolute ethical sense the social activists are right. Then again, maybe the social activists, who don't seem to mind all the beef, chicken, catfish, and pork killed and served across North America each day, are asking the Makah to cease to exist because the Makah are an easy, nearly defenseless enemy. It would, after all, be hard to oppose the beef industry in Iowa, the chicken industry in Arkansas, the catfish industry in Mississippi, and the pork industry in North Carolina, together with all those Americans who like eating these meats daily. Opposing the nearly invisible Makah and demonizing those bad-old-whale-eating Japanese makes for good TV footage on the high seas.

Just as Jonah remains invisible until some theory of reading brings it into relief, and just as the Makah become less visible with each passing whale-free day, rhetoric and composition can sacrifice itself on the alter of the Romantic ego. But before we do, we had better read Wordsworth and Coleridge carefully to make sure we are willing to sit in the center of the pedagogical ego supported only by those theories that we intentionally blind ourselves to.

In the "Preface to the Lyrical Ballads," Wordsworth revels in his own ignorance and sets his own perceptions and elevated responses to those perceptions as self-justifying precepts. At a time when all educated people had read Aristotle, Wordsworth makes clear that he himself has not. The problem with Wordsworth, as with all such high Romantics, is not, however, his monumental ignorance; rather, it is his conception of the writer. Wordsworth's poet is "a man . . . endowed with more lively sensibility, more enthusiasm and tenderness, who has a greater knowledge of human nature, and a more comprehensive soul, than are supposed to be common among mankind." Wordsworth goes on in this vein for several sentences, arrogating to the poet, and hence to himself, more joy, more delight, a finer sense of response, a better imagination, and a greater ability at self-expression than most people have.

The best thing a writing teacher can do with a Wordsworth is to stay out of his way. No theory is required other than the self-justifying belief that writers themselves will write themselves into whatever the moment requires. When one couples Wordsworth's notion of the superiority of the poet with Coleridge's notion of organic wholeness—the idea that each text grows from its own imperative and develops according to its own teleological destiny as that destiny emerges during the process of creation—then the writing teacher becomes little more than an occasion.

Theory, of course, calls all this into question—and, indeed, actually gives the writing teacher both something to do and a visible reason for doing that something. Theory forces one to interrogate one's position. Ignorance of theory usually permits one to remain unaware that one holds a position, one of many possible positions, a position that can change. Ignorance of theory blinds one to the knowledge that changing one's position changes what one sees and how one sees it.

2

Rhetoric and Composition as a Coherent Intellectual Discipline: A Meditation

C. JAN SWEARINGEN

A T SEVERAL MEMORIALS for Jim Kinneavy during 1999, students and scholars revisited the decade 1975–1985, when the first graduate programs in rhetoric and composition were created, drawing on a wide range of disciplinary sources. Kinneavy's *A Theory of Discourse* was published while he was still not allowed to teach graduate courses in the English department. Many of us were fortunate to work with him as teaching assistants when he served as Director of First-Year Composition in the same English department that refused him graduate courses. A year-long NEH seminar headed by Richard Young in 1978, then on his way from Michigan to Carnegie Mellon (with Richard Enos soon to follow), brought together what now looks like a proto-Olympian cast: Victor Vitanza, Lisa Ede, Eugene Garver, and more than a few members of what would become the Society for Critical Exchange. Young, Becker, and Pike's *Rhetoric, Discovery and Change* joined Linda Flower's work on problem-solving writing, which, like Janice Lauer's, emphasized heuristics and cognitive and compositional processes. *PRE/TEXT* was inaugurated only slightly later, focusing on publishing scholarly work in progress. *Rhetoric Society Quarterly* began to cast its net wider, as RSA meetings attracted not only historians and philosophers of rhetoric from fields other than English but also postmodern theorists challenging traditional historiography and conventional pedagogies. MLA discussion groups related to composition, the teaching of writing, literacy studies, and the history and theory of rhetoric and composition ascended to MLA Division status. *Written Communication* marked the presence of "discourse studies" as a growing field within rhetoric and composition. The *Journal of Advanced Composition* (later simply *JAC*) cultivated dialogues among literary theory, critical theory, and political debates circling around English departments in general, and curriculum—at all levels—in particular. *Rhetoric Review* published articles and bibliographical resources for scholarship in the fields now feeding into rhetoric and composition; many such works had until recently not been thought scholarly at all. It is impossible to estimate how crucial these developments have been to the redefinition of graduate programs and to reforms of rhetoric and composition courses in the undergraduate curriculum. The definition of what a Ph.D. candidate in English should have mastered has been forever changed—but not without continuing, energetic revision and debate.

A Developing Discipline

In our end we sometimes rediscover our beginnings; and in the present, our past. The current scene bears an uncanny resemblance to the scenes, acts, agencies, and ratios that started conversations twenty-something years ago. Exchanges among faculty and with graduate student colleagues include familiar questions. What does rhetoric have to do with composition? Why should anyone want a degree in rhetoric? Do you have a degree in rhetoric? Why do you study and teach literature? Is critical theory the same as rhetoric? How are linguistics or discourse studies (variously defined) related to rhetoric, or composition, or both? Now, as at the beginning, some faculty and students openly scorn and discourage graduate courses and degrees in rhetoric and composition unless rhetoric is strongly aligned with critical theory and composition returns to the undergraduate writing program, where it has belonged all along. At the very beginning, precisely the same anxieties of status and self-definition presented a common topic for discussions and research in the field.

One theme that marked the earlier years of doctoral studies in rhetoric and composition was a preoccupation with anxious self-definition and redefinition, sometimes at the expense of focusing on theoretical and critical issues. Similar discussions are now amply available in a host of not-so-new journals, caucuses, coalitions, and resolutions. From Maxine Hairston's 1982 "Winds of Change" article to numerous, more recent "Redefining . . ." appraisals, the discipline as a whole seems never to have quite settled down.

Rather like the flight of the loon, it plunges energetically forward, again and again, loudly attempting to become airborne. While some celebrate the eternal and frequent return to fecund chaos, others tire of any further discussion of theorizing or problematizing, of anti-foundationalism, of interrogating or subverting dominant paradigms. Some compositionists have begun to repudiate theory quite loudly and propose returning to an untheorized, and even antitheoretical, pedagogy of "care" untainted by lofty and arrogant vocabularies that will never be understood by most students.

I recall only yesterday, twenty-something years ago, discussing with Louise Phelps drafts of what would become *Composition in a New Key,* an early attempt to define the conceptual, philosophical, and aesthetic bases for new composition theories. Numerous sessions appeared on the programs of the MLA and CCCC conventions on the future of doctoral studies in English, including the burgeoning new growth—real and proposed—of doctoral studies in rhetoric, or rhetoric and composition. At Michigan, Carnegie Mellon, Syracuse, Texas, TCU, Arizona, Purdue, Ohio State, the University of Southern California, the University of South Florida, and a growing number of other Ph.D.-granting institutions, rhetoric and composition studies, variously defined, became bona fide graduate programs. Some eventually separated from the Ph.D. in English for various reasons; some remained within English Ph.D. degree programs as tracks or concentrations. Figures we had known first through their work in *College English, JAC, Rhetoric Society Quarterly, Research in the Teaching of English, College Composition and Communication, Written Communication, PRE/TEXT, Rhetoric Review,* and related journals emerged as leaders within the new doctoral programs. Scholars whose work had begun within composition programs, theoretical and historical studies in rhetoric, sociolinguistics, and discourse theory began, with their students, to define areas of scholarly inquiry and research that remain with us. Various intellectual streams merged. Literary theory and scholarship dealing with particular authors and groups of authors joined rhetoric and composition scholarship to formulate solid new areas of research. Studies of the composing process were joined to studies of minority cultures and marginalized voices. Historiographical debates about recuperating figures and genres versus redefining historical studies burgeoned; essentialist versus social-constructionist models of self, voice, and meaning informed ever more detailed outlines of the nature and purposes of rhetorical theory, composition theory, their relationships to one another, and their relationships to curriculum and pedagogy.

New themes developing in theory affected scholarship and curriculum but were influenced as well by institutional changes that shaped Ph.D. programs: new directions in hiring patterns, job descriptions, and job placements. Critical theory employed in rhetoric and composition scholarship began simultaneously to critique and be critiqued by institutional and employment patterns. The production of Ph.D.'s in English specializing in rhetoric and composition, alongside or apart from training in literature and theory, coincided with increased employment of part-time and adjunct faculty as teachers of writing courses. At many schools, part-time and adjunct ranks grew from 15 percent to over 35 percent between the early 1980s and the early 1990s. Inquiring minds began to ask whether Ph.D. programs in rhetoric and composition, wittingly or unwittingly, were churning out faculty who would never attain tenure-track or even full-time faculty status unless they were willing to enter academia untenured as writing program directors.

Recent MLA and CCCC meetings have seen renewed discussions of these issues. At MLA panels and Delegate Assembly meetings, the MLA Graduate Student Caucus has become increasingly active in lobbying English departments to self-regulate their use of English Ph.D.'s as non-tenure-track teaching faculty, part-time and full-time. Sometimes at odds with the Two-Year College Association and with various groups representing part-time and adjunct faculty, the MLA Graduate Student Caucus has been aligned at times with the MLA Radical Caucus in advancing resolutions critical of English departments' treatments of adjuncts and part-time faculty. At other times, the Graduate Student Caucus has been more closely aligned with part-time and adjunct unions defending their right to choose part-time employment but demanding equal pay and benefits. With a few new interesting wrinkles, an old rift punctuates debates about the relationship between Ph.D. courses and programs in rhetoric and composition and those in other concentrations within the English Ph.D.

Although not always named as such, literature has remained the Other of rhetoric, of composition, and of rhetoric and composition. Literature's little brother, as Other, is critical theory. Over the past decade-plus, for both literature and rhetoric and composition, variously defined, critical theory has become something like Greek citizenship as defined by Isocrates: simultaneously a common ground newly shared by former dissidents, and a site of disputes over identity politics. The longer history of rhetoric and literature in relation to one another reminds us that claiming older brother status has long been a topos of language studies. Well before Cicero's time, early enough to allow him to compile its history, the dispute had begun between skill-oriented craftsmen of language, and culture buffs who wanted the curriculum to focus on literature and rhetoric as edifying vehicles of individual and collective values. Rhetoric, always variously defined, has hovered in between, sometimes a bridge and sometimes a barrier at the border between craft and value, skill and content, art and science, knowing how and knowing that. The shorter recent history of the hegemony of critical theory marks a point of attempted, or wished-for, conjunction, with both rhetoric and literature claiming a closer, earlier tie to high theory. The more theory is agreed upon, however tacitly, as the lingua franca of citizenship, the more composition feels defined out; many compositionists once again feel themselves strangers in the land they have helped create—or in many cases emigrants, by choice. The future direction of scholarship in composition, within rhetoric and composition, much like the futures of important stocks, invites special watching. It is ironic that in defending itself against repudiation by literature twenty-something years ago, rhetoric and composition adopted postmodern theory as a welcome ally. Today, in some contexts, and according to some versions of the story, theory has become the instrument of rhetoric's repudiation of composition. How did this reversal of fortunes, and of meanings, come about?

Paradoxes of Postmodernism

Deconstructionist daddies and their feminist children were among the first to theorize and colonize rhetorical studies in the new scholarship and graduate programs of the late 1970s. Asserting equal footing, and some shared ancestry, with literary scholars and their favorite theorists, rhetoric and composition scholars turned to several tasks. Invoking Derrida, Foucault, and de Man, rhetorical scholars observed linguistic and rhetorical elements in much critical theory, and they adapted critical theory to the study of linguistic and rhetorical legacies. Ancestry and self-definition were among the first projects. Deconstructing "straight" historical studies in rhetoric, and hierarchical models of writing pedagogy, postmodern theories were adapted by rhetoric and composition scholars and graduate program designers to define several new sites for scholarship and pedagogy.

Postmodern theorists' uses of tropological models provided direct contact with literary critical theory in its own terms, and such models were readily adapted by rhetoric and composition theorists to challenge literature on its own grounds in departmental curricular debates. Alongside the requisite invocations of Foucault and Derrida, Hayden White's, Paul de Man's, Kenneth Burke's, and other established theorists' uses of rhetorical tropes as models for literary, psychological, epistemological, historical, and cultural analysis proved a mother lode for rhetoricians, a basis for propounding the rhetorical turn as direct heir to the linguistic turn in critical theory. Its spin was developed by adapting a number of theories familiar to literary scholars, building upon the rhetorical tropes utilized by critical theorists, and deploying a tropics of discourse to deconstruct the epistemologies and identities of earlier rhetorical systems and curricula. We are still working out the challenges that postmodern rhetorical theory introduced into rhetorical theories and practices of knowledge, identity, language, community, curriculum, invention, discovery, and change.

Rhetorical theorists working with deconstructionist and tropological methods defined several new master tropes. Supplementing Derrida's deconstruction of Plato as an idealist and foundational figure, rhetorical theorists rescued the sophists from the Gulag to which Plato banished them. The sophists debuted as exemplary models for contemporary rhetorical theory and pedagogy. It was out with Truth and in with contingency, incommensurability, situatedness, and local and not global constructions of identity. As the 1980s ground to an end, deconstruction ran out of steam. Ludic reconstructionism emerged as a rhetorical practice of self-invention. Feminists, compositionists, and proponents of ethnic diversity in language practices developed variants of ludic reconstructionism; since everything is already written—a memory, dream, or recollection—playing with the "always already there" became the model for both writing pedagogy and scholarship. Within the first-year writing classroom, doctrines of ludic reconstructionism and local identity politics proved amiable companions to the shift to "personal" essays as the predominant writing task of the first-year course. Student writing was reconceived, realigned with all writing as interrogation of self and identity, as questioning relentlessly the already constructed in order to reinvent a more self-aware self and writing voice.

The psychoanalytic bases of Derrida, Lacan, and de Man were never far away from the deconstructionist writing pedagogies that merged with personal essay assignments. Many current studies of identity politics (and curricula based upon them) can be traced at some point to the knowledge-identity topos in postmodern rhetorical and composition theory. Computer classrooms in which collective e-discussions deliberately fragmented tradi- tional discourses in designer moos assisted the institutionalization of notions of identity and discourse as interrelated, ever changing, never completed, always situated. In some practical curricular applications, writing courses, particularly those centered on the personal essay, began to resemble thera- peutic practices; some invoked direct ties with twelve-step programs. Para- doxically, a point of division threatening to resegregate composition from rhetoric is an as yet to be interrogated similarity between the psychoanalytic bases of recent high theory and the therapeutic atmosphere that pervades many personal essay, self-investigating, and empowerment-based college writing courses. Many compositionists have developed allergic reactions to Baudrillard, for example, yet continue to define the goals of writing courses in terms of liberatory and therapeutic psychologies that Baudrillard along- side Freire can help define.

The Prospects of Foundationless Critique

Seemingly at odds with its deconstructionist fragmentarianism and neo- sophistic doctrines of contingency and situatedness, the historical project of reclaiming the sophists has over the past fifteen-plus years contributed to a second major topos within rhetoric and composition studies: reconstructions of communitarian and social models for defining the nature, sites, and goals of rhetoric. Earlier twentieth-century rhetorical figures such as Burke, Rich- ards, Habermas, Perelman, and Olbrechts-Tyteca have been rehabilitated and debated as guides for different social- and community-based definitions of rhetorical theory, practice, and pedagogy. Bakhtin and Vygotsky make an appearance from the Russian front not only as linguists but also as students of collective oral and written speech genres, an alternate term for trope in the lexicon of many language-based theorists. In community-centered rhetorical and composition theory, the "civic discourse" goal of writing courses has been exhaustively interrogated and redefined. Contributing to various versions of rhetoric as training the citizen and as developing politi- cal consciousness, the critical pedagogies of Freire and other Marxist-based pedagogies have been theorized as instrumental in fostering empowering constructions of the individual and community alike.

Unlike personal essay and other self-interrogating pedagogies, and the psychoanalytic theories behind them, social-constructionist rhetorical theories and civic discourse curricula have promoted several, not always compatible, objectives. One civic discourse model embraces the goal of training "the good citizen," a pedagogical model that can be traced initially, in recent history, back to Edward Corbett's *Classical Rhetoric for the Modern Student,* and ultimately to Cicero and Isocrates. A second civic or communitarian model emphasizes the pedagogical goal of training students to perform cultural critique in order to challenge and reform society. In asserting this goal, rhetorical models of the individual "against" society join psychoanalytic rhetorical models for interrogating the inner self in their focus on questioning the always already given, and in propounding the need for ongoing epistemological and political consciousness raising. The basis and purpose for such an emphasis on critique has not always been defined, perhaps because it has been developed within a theoretical lexicon that repudiates foundations.

In repudiating the Truth of Plato's *logos,* neo-sophistic deconstructionists and social constructionists alike have installed *mythos* in its place, celebrating the doctrine that "everything is story." Everything from an individual identity to a city's history is "just a story" according to this view; the role of theory and classroom alike is to teach people how to invent good stories; meaningful—or at least beautiful—fictions. Here, a potential point of reconciliation with literature may be emerging. Operating under the rule of narrative, that everything is story, a language that seems to have been borrowed from westward expansion is often used to define the purposes and themes of individual, always local, discourses. "Staking a claim" and "exploring a site" are used to mark topics of discourse and structures of argument. To forgive any hegemonic appearances of a land rush, such stories are presented as temporary ephemera, to be replaced tomorrow by another claimant and another site. In contrast to Gadamer's metaphor of an infinitely cumulative hermeneutic horizon, each layer building on its antecedents, land-rush metaphors employed by social constructionists create a landscape in which all traces of former inhabitants are erased, leaving a clean and vacant site for the next claimant. The purpose of such discourses is not entirely clear; attempts to define political value for the agency of local and temporary identities has not yet succeeded. In the land of always-already constructedness, agency is hard to come by.

The uses of Freire among social-constructionist theorists developing new liberatory pedagogies provide an instructive example of how difficult it is to sustain political and social critique without foundations and without agency. Adapting Freire's work to fit rural, inner city, and other marginalized U.S.

student populations, most liberatory and empowerment pedagogies have borrowed Freire's Marxism, but not his religious concerns for the soul. Without the latter, and lacking any model of interior selfhood that can be inspired to agency, Freire-based liberatory pedagogies can lead to poorly focused critique and to teachers who insist that their students imitate the language and stance of critical consciousness without having a clear sense of where such resistance can or should go. On a similar point, language and society scholars versed in Russian linguistics can observe that the earlier Bakhtin of *Dostoevsky's Poetics,* who emphasized "inner speech" and "inner voices" and "dialogue," has been replaced in *Speech Genres and Other Late Essays* by a determinist describing case after case of the always already written, a closed linguistic loop in which agency, invention, and change barely exist.

The Return to the (Socio)Linguistic Turn

The agency crisis is especially troubled among rhetorical and language theorists who make it their primary purpose to denounce normative standard language hierarchies at all levels: lexicon, syntax, discourse, and genre. Joining affirmations of students' rights to their own languages and dialects, and value-neutral writing process composition pedagogies, such theorists have adapted anti-foundationalist theories to fit social constructionist models in order to assist in the formulation of a critical language pedagogy. The student's role as a scholar-writer is defined as it is in cultural critique theory and pedagogy; the teacher's role continues to be defined as a peer-critic and guerrilla coach, encouraging the student to look outward at a culture in need of analysis and political/ethical critique. What language-critical pedagogy adds to social-critique pedagogy is the zeroing in on language itself as the instrument of individual and social oppression, specifically "standard English," variously defined, most recently as "the language of wider communication" (see Keith Gilyard's chapter in this volume). In its singular focus on language as the object of analysis and source of consciousness, critical language theory and pedagogy come very close to returning to the linguistic turn, if not to orthodox deconstruction.

The development of current language-critical pedagogy may be regarded not only as a direct descendant of 1970s sociolinguistics but also as a subset of social critique and civic discourse models. Some may want to flip the script, in Keith Gilyard's phrase, and see language-critical pedagogy as perhaps the most important or prior development, the big brother as it were of other critical pedagogies. Historians and theorists of rhetoric and composition are now reexamining the relationship between the current uses of descriptive sociolinguistics and discourse theory in the newly revised CCCC Language Policy and Students' Right to Their Own Language documents. And yet, critical language pedagogy may place the student even further outside the practices of standard language and culture, even when the languages encouraged by critical pedagogy are themselves consonant with academic discourse. The agency taught in such pedagogies is agency against, from the outside, and not from within.

The immediate tasks of equalizing the status among English language variants, and of affirming linguistic diversity in the United States, may provide surprisingly common ground for dialogue with the culture wars and theory wars within rhetoric and composition. The practical difficulties that have emerged out of anti-foundationalist social critique models affect the implementation of tolerance- and diversity-based language pedagogies. It is nothing new to ask, If everything is equal, what is it equal to? Tolerance can be a low-level goal, akin to tolerating a food or drug that is not particularly agreeable. Linguists' recent responses to the Oakland Ebonics incident are revisiting many of the sites that were examined in the wake of the Ann Arbor "Black English" trial of 1978: the King Decision. Theory and pedagogy have yet to define methods by which we can accomplish the goal of pluralism alongside the goal of empowering students to succeed individually and socially in the language of wider communication: standard edited English. NCTE has never affirmed the CCCC Students' Right to Their Own Language document. Will the renewed close partnership between CCCC and NCTE foster collaborative efforts to join forces and define clearer goals in these areas? It is too early to tell.

It is not too early to observe an institutional consequence of strained relations between rhetorical theory and composition practice. *L'affaire* Brodkey at the University of Texas at Austin brought to the surface tensions between the practicalities of running and maintaining a writing program and the theories that have so richly informed the improvement and diversification of writing curriculum during the past twenty-something years. As institutions, and institutional practices, rhetoric and composition seem poised for segregation, or divorce. Many rhetorical theorists now want nothing to do with writing programs and have joined the theory elite within English departments generally. Writing program administration, with its own national organization and graduate courses, functions increasingly as a distinct professional venue for compositionists. Many universities have resisted the pressure to develop remedial courses staffed by English departments and other units internal to the university. However, most universities are moving toward a model in which a writing center, sometimes along with the writing program, are moved to a unit almost entirely separate from the English department. At Austin, post-Brodkey, this has become the Division of Rhetoric and Composition, a semi-independent unit with its own faculty and a large number of adjuncts, both full- and part-time, teaching writing courses and working in the writing center alongside TAs. Similar structures are developing in other universities, with variations.

The cultural history of recent writing programs within institutions as therapeutic and nurturing collectives has yet to be written; and it should include the hospice role that such collectives have begun to play for otherwise abandoned or marginalized Ph.D.'s: part time and adjunct faculty. This history should observe yet another renewed focus upon community: the notion of collectivity has itself become a topos, with variant definitions and practices, not all of them benign. It will be very ironic indeed if twenty-something years after the founding of graduate courses and programs in rhetoric and composition, the Ph.D.'s produced by those programs have no professional prospects outside largely nontenure track ghettos—the "projects" from which rhetoric and composition emerged in the first place.

3

The Death of Composition as
an Intellectual Discipline

GARY A. OLSON

N EARLY A DECADE AGO, in 1991, I was invited to present a plenary speech
to the relatively new Research Network Forum at the Conference on
College Composition and Communication Convention. This was at the time
in our disciplinary formation that we now refer to as "the theory wars." Led
by a past chair of CCCC, Maxine Hairston, a small but vocal group of compositionists decried the rise of theoretical scholarship in the field and the
move away from an expressivist orientation. One commentator characterized
theoretical scholarship as "nothing but the voices of vested academic interests and a kind of political-professional careerism" that takes "almost per-
verse pleasure" in avoiding "the problems of the classroom" and in burying
"reality in clouds of words" (Kogan 474). Hairston wrote "with increasing
irritation" about "unreadable, fashionably radical articles" that "have little to
do with the concerns of most college English teachers" (695). Another past
chair of CCCC complained that the "dizzying display of specialized vocabulary" in a collection of theoretical articles about writing nearly gave her a
"splintering headache" (Lunsford 267). What distressed some compositionists at that time was that the field of composition was no longer defined
simply as self-reflection about the teaching of writing or about one's own (or
one's students') writing practices; while it included these concerns, composition had become much more expansive, encompassing broad and diverse
investigations of how written discourse works.

The reason that the Research Network organizers invited me to address

This essay was presented as a plenary speech to the Research Network Forum at the Conference on College Composition and Communication Convention in Minneapolis in 2000 and
published in *Composition Studies* 28.2 (2000): 33–41, reprinted here by permission.

the forum back then was that they wanted someone to present an *apologia* for theory, a strong statement as to why composition should be defined in these broader, more inclusive ways. As someone who had (and has) devoted his entire professional life to helping develop rhetoric and composition as an intellectual discipline, I was delighted to accept. In that speech, I argued that if postmodern discourse has taught us anything, it is that "rhetoric" is at the center of all knowledge making, even in the sciences. As a field devoted to how discourse works, composition, then, is perfectly situated to participate in the exciting cross-disciplinary investigations of the interrelations between epistemology and discourse. That is, I argued that while we all desire to learn more about the teaching of writing or about our own writing processes, these are not the *only* intellectual concerns we should have as a discipline. Constituting rhetoric and composition as a discipline whose raison d'être is the teaching of writing—that is, all research, all theory, all scholarship exists for the sole purpose of furthering and refining the *teaching* of composition—is dangerously and unacceptably narrow and even, in some people's eyes, anti-intellectual (Olson "Role"). Louise Wetherbee Phelps expressed a belief that many of us held at the time:

> Deep in the disciplinary unconscious runs a strong undertow of anti-intellectual feeling that resists the dominance of theory in every institutional context of the field—journals, conferences, writing classrooms, textbooks, teacher education—and even in some forms of theory itself. (206)

Since that speech, I had thought that as a discipline, we had come to terms with our intellectual diversity. I watched the field grow in sophistication as it addressed scores of important questions about the workings of discourse. I read with great pleasure and pride a number of smart, insightful works by a variety of established scholars—people like Jim Berlin, Pat Bizzell, Linda Brodkey, Marilyn Cooper, Sharon Crowley, Lester Faigley, Susan Jarratt, Susan Miller, Jasper Neel, and John Trimbur. And I was especially impressed with the whole new generation of scholars who brought to the field an intellectual rigor and sophistication that bodes well for the future of rhetoric and composition as an intellectual discipline—people like Michelle Ballif, Diane Davis, Julie Drew, Christy Friend, Xin Liu Gale, Min-Zhan Lu, Arabella Lyon, Krista Ratcliffe, Eileen Schell, Todd Taylor, and Lynn Worsham. It seemed to me that as a field, we had finally learned to value theoretical investigation of a wide range of subjects related to how discourse works.

But, clearly, I was mistaken. Just as we are experiencing a renewed back-lash against feminism — as Beth Flynn so poignantly describes — composi-tion is also witnessing a revitalized backlash against theoretical scholarship, especially that associated with efforts to draw connections between the work we do in composition and the critical work done in other disciplines. For example, one might read the recent special issue of *College Composition and Communication* on "teaching writing creatively" (51.1, 1999) as an opening salvo in what undoubtedly will come to be known as "the new theory wars." Led by yet another chair of CCCC, this backlash threatens to undermine a two-decade-long tradition of substantive theoretical scholarship. I'd like to respond to this attack by examining the lead article in that special issue of *CCC*, a piece written by Wendy Bishop. It's not that I consider this essay to be especially cogent or influential; it's that I find it representative of a trend I see developing in the field, and it carries special weight by virtue of its being authored by the elected chair of our major professional organization.

Where Have All the Writers Gone?

Most of what Wendy argues in her article has been recycled from the debates of a decade ago. She claims that she no longer recognizes the field that she had entered ten years before, that good teaching has fallen prey to "career-ists," that "good writing" is devalued at the expense of a kind of convoluted prose from which she can derive no "joy," and that the field has rudely mar-ginalized "expressivists" such as herself. (Can someone who serves as chair of our major professional organization — a position of power, prestige, and privilege — really claim to be "marginalized"?)

While I have no doubt that Wendy sincerely feels the injustices she is com-plaining about, I can't help but think that what we really have here is a "straw man" conveniently set up to be knocked down. For instance, she asserts that the idea of "the writer-teacher and/or teacher-writer" — that is, "one who advocates that teachers write with and for their writing students as well as with and for their colleagues" — is under attack (9). She claims that we no longer value the Donald Murray types (those who see themselves first as "writers" and who then try to teach their craft) or the Peter Elbow types (those who see themselves as "teachers" and who then write about teaching). No one seems to care about good writing and teaching, she claims; the teacher-writer is dismissed or used for target practice. She echoes com-plaints that there is "no room" in composition for classrooms, students, or teaching (20). Nor do these people write or, she suspects, read. But does any-one really believe all this? Who *are* these people who don't value good writ-ing? Who *are* these people who don't value good teaching? Who *are* these people who don't write and read? I would like to meet one—just one person in the field who fits that description. The fact is, that person simply does not exist.

What Wendy is really saying is that a substantial portion of the field does not share her own values and priorities. It's not that few of us write anymore; it's that we don't write the kinds of prose that *she* wants to read. It's not that we don't read anymore; it's that we read different kinds of texts from the ones *she* enjoys reading. It's not that we don't value teaching; it's that we don't value teaching to the exclusion of every other intellectual concern. To suggest that those of us who are interested in theoretical scholarship are somehow contemptuous of good writing is like saying, "Unlike you, I read and write the good stuff. When will you, too, finally see the light?"

We all have written and perhaps published poetry; we all, I suspect, have written and perhaps published short stories; and I'm willing to bet that a good many of us, myself included, have written novels—probably unpub-lished, probably resting peacefully at the bottom of some drawer somewhere, but nonetheless attempted. And there are undoubtedly a good many of us who enjoy crafting and reading critical scholarship. We all went into English studies because we had a deep and abiding love of language—of its cadences, its power, its beauty. Whether we happen to be theorists or writer-teachers or teacher-writers, each of us has a love of good writing—that's not something that any one person can claim to have a monopoly on.

A Place to Stand?

In her diatribe against the language of theory, Wendy cites a sentence from an article I published as an example of the kind of theory talk she despises. Here's the sentence that she finds so objectionable:

> While Pratt's notion of contact zone has been useful in interrogating how teachers exercise power and authority, especially in the multicul-tural classroom, some compositionists have tended to deploy it in such a way as to defend a kind of liberal pluralism, thereby subverting attempts to come to terms with the truly colonizing effects of the ped-agogical scenario. ("Encountering" 47)

Certainly, this is no example of high theory; nor is it particularly difficult to understand. Presumably the vocabulary—*interrogate, deploy, subvert*—is foreign, not part of the vocabulary of the type of prose she reads and writes. Here's her comment on that sentence: "For me, the sentence, I realized, had no clothes, and no heart (no organs at all, no human substance) no place for the interested writer/reader/teacher in me to stand" (26). Let me bracket the question of whether when composing "scholarly" writing the most important organ is the heart and instead ask, Aren't there different understandings of what it means to "have a heart"? For Wendy, it's a neat turn of phrase or a colorful metaphor; for me, it's a passionate concern for, as the sentence suggests, how the pedagogical scene is often one in which power is used and abused, where students suffer in the name of being "taught," where well-intentioned teachers can reinscribe sexism and racism. Why doesn't *that* count as having "a heart"? Why doesn't *that* count as being "human"? And why, I ask, is someone who repeatedly proclaims that she is ardently concerned with good teaching—why is she not "standing" right there beside me in my effort to help us all improve our teaching? Clearly, what we have here are two completely opposed ways of seeing the world, of defining "heart," of defining what it means to be "a compositionist," and of constructing the field that we both inhabit.

Wendy goes on to say that I am "intentionally *not* interested" in "inviting eighteen-year-olds to enter the sentence." Now here is a statement that genuinely mystifies me. I certainly did *not* intend that prose for eighteen-year-olds. For a quarter of a century, I've been teaching that good writing is all about addressing a particular audience for a particular reason. Why in the world would I want an undergraduate to "enter" a piece that is explicitly about composition "scholarship"? The audience is the undergraduate's teacher. Yet, this is a theme of her critique. She cites Toby Fulwiler, who similarly complains that the "exclusionary use of language" by the discourse community of composition scholars "makes it difficult for eighteen-year-olds to enter and participate" (Fulwiler 220). Since when is scholarship in any field written with undergraduates in mind? Do we now have to certify that nuclear physicists write in such a way that sophomores can "enter and participate" in their scholarly discussions? Surely, there is serious confusion here between the goals of and audiences for *scholarly* writing and the goals of and audiences for other types of writing.

The language of a discipline becomes "specialized" (what we so often call, usually pejoratively, "jargon") for good reason: a shared vocabulary makes communication more efficient. When I say the word *prewriting,* everyone in the field understands what I am referring to, even while an outsider to the discourse would not. If I couldn't use this word of jargon, then I would necessarily need a great many words to capture all that we have come to associate with that term. Being able, within our particular discourse community, to employ this term and therefore evoke a whole array of associations that attach to it, allows me to communicate efficiently *to my intended audience.* What's more, because a disciplinary word does evoke an array of associations, because it "resonates," it allows me to communicate more effectively as well. That is, far from being a detriment to communication, critical jargon, when used well, is a valuable tool to make communication more effective and efficient.

The real point, I think, is not that Wendy or Toby or Maxine despise jargon. Presumably they have no problem with *prewriting* or *freewriting* or *audience invoked,* but they do with *interrogate, deploy,* and *subvert.* What they detest is the particular *type* of jargon that is evolving in the field. Why? Because they hate how the field itself is evolving. Quite clearly, what we're seeing here is ideological difference, ideological struggle, masquerading as a love of "good writing," a love of "good teaching."

A Sense of History

It's unfortunate that in these so-called theory wars, some commentators stoop to attacks that border on the ad hominem — only that a "homme" is never expressly named. Ten years ago it was Maxine Hairston and Steve Kogan; today it's a new generation of commentators. For example, Wendy blames what she sees as the sad state of affairs in composition on "careerism." Apparently, she believes that so-called Current-Market-Forces drive compositionists into "rapid professionalism" by creating the "need to appear ever-more scholarly, historical, and theoretical" (12). She claims that "professionalism" compels certain people to write "a certain type of professional text." To suggest that those who engage in scholarly work are somehow selfishly careerist not only is an insult to a good many colleagues but also couldn't be further from the truth — at least for the scholars that I mentioned earlier. Far from being selfish, most "scholars" make enormous sacrifices to produce their work, gladly devoting huge spans of time to their projects — not simply to further their careers but because they love the subject and are devoted to the discipline itself. Does anyone really believe that Susan Miller, whose three books have all won national awards, is a careerist driven by market forces? Or Jasper Neel? Or Lester Faigley? Or any one of the scholars I mentioned? Accusing colleagues who do a particular kind of work of being careerist (or bad writers or bad teachers) simply because they do a different kind of work from what you do is not a productive way to further the debate over disciplinary identity. Wendy adds that not only is professionalism "blunting" her "fervor" for composition but it is "dismantling" much of what she "had come to care for—composition as [a] community that writes also" (20). Of course, composition *is* a community—or, more accurately, communities—that writes; it just doesn't always write in the way that Wendy does, and *that* is what she simply cannot abide.

My own sense of the field's history is much different from Wendy's, perhaps because I've been around to see a lot more of it. Wendy thinks that a bunch of careerist social constructionists (her characterization) suddenly and without provocation began cruelly "marginalizing" the expressivists. But this is not an entirely accurate description. In every discipline, there is hegemonic struggle over the identity of that discipline. That is, one group of like-minded individuals attempts to further *its* vision of the field, while other groups do the same. For example, throughout the 1970s, the people that we have come to call "cognitivists" and those we have come to call "expressivists" battled between themselves over how the field should be defined, and in doing so, they both maintained tight control over the means of dissemination of scholarship: the few journals available to publish work in composition. Those of us who were interested in philosophical, critical, theoretical scholarship (and in broadening the disciplinary borders of composition to include such interests) were effectively excluded from the conversations. *Research in the Teaching of English* published only empirical work; under Dick Larsen, *College Composition and Communication* had a decidedly cognitivist bent; *College English,* while it was a venue for some "expressivist" work, was less a "composition" journal than it is today. And, of course, few presses in those days would take a chance on publishing a scholarly book on composition. Consequently, the only compositionists who had a reasonable chance to get published, to be heard, were those doing cognitivist or expressivist work; the rest of us were muted.

This imbalance dramatically changed in 1980, when, out of frustration with being silenced, several scholars created "alternative" venues for publishing composition scholarship. During that year, *PRE/TEXT* and *JAC* were born, followed closely thereafter by *Rhetoric Review,* and then by a whole range of other, specialized journals. (Subsequently, editorial changes in the NCTE journals reflected these same changes in orientation.) Finally, for the first time, scholarship other than the cognitivist/expressivist types could be heard; finally, those of us who thought that rhetoric and composition could be a much broader, more inclusive, more theoretically informed discipline could be heard. And lo and behold, many in the field were receptive.

Hegemonic Struggle and the Future of Composition

What I am describing are the workings of hegemonic struggle. Since the beginnings of composition as a field, we all have been struggling over how to define it, over its heart and soul. Certain people—with good intentions and pure motives—labored to make it a social science, drawing heavily on developmental psychology and related fields. Others—with equally pure motives—disagreed, insisting that composition should be a more humanistic discipline that draws on the work of "creative" writers and on our own self-reflection about the writing process. Interestingly, the challenge to the two dominant groups in composition coincided with the opening up of new and alternative publishing venues. Those who wanted to define the field as one devoted not just to the teaching of writing but to all aspects of how discourse works turned to critical theory from a wide variety of disciplines, including anthropology, feminist theory, philosophy, and sociology. Clearly, this latter group has made substantial progress. For twenty years, composition scholarship has developed as an interdisciplinary, "intellectual" enterprise—and we are much the richer because of it.

Hegemonic struggle is not a bad thing; in fact, a democracy cannot function without it. Yet, such struggle can be collegial and congenial or malevolent and mean spirited. In her discussions of the intricacies of how hegemonic struggle works, Chantal Mouffe distinguishes between "enemies" and "adversaries." Enemies attempt to destroy each other, while adversaries "respect the right of the opponent to defend his or her point of view" (qtd. in Worsham and Olson 166). That is, between adversaries, "respect for difference is put into practice as the principle of action in a democratic political community" (Worsham and Olson 166). We all wish to convince others that our way of seeing the world is best; that's the basis of hegemonic struggle, of democracy, and of rhetoric itself. My own sense of how rhetoric best works, how one can best persuade one's colleagues that a certain way of defining the world is superior, is not through straw-man attacks, not through mischaracterizations, not through ad hominem assaults, but through dialogue, through persuasion, and, finally, through mutual respect. Wendy says that, for her, being a teacher-writer is "an ever-evolving process of finding places to stand and be counted" (20). And this is exactly the point: we *all* want to find such places. Wendy wants creative writers to "matter," and I want composition studies to matter as an intellectual discipline. I don't begrudge Wendy's attempt to swing the discipline in a certain direction, and she shouldn't begrudge me the same.

Let me make something very clear: this exchange is not about Wendy, and it's not about me; it's about the future of composition as a discipline, and it's about whether we as individuals will position ourselves as "enemies" or as "adversaries" in this struggle. And the stakes are high: for me, it's the potential death of composition as an intellectual discipline.

Works Cited

Bishop, Wendy. "Places to Stand: The Reflective Writer-Teacher-Writer in Composition." *College Composition and Communication* 51 (1999): 9–31.

Flynn, Elizabeth. "Strategic, Counter-Strategic, and Reactive Resistance in the Feminist Classroom." *Insurrection: Approaches to Resistance in Composition Studies.* Ed. Andrea Greenbaum. Albany: State U of New York P, 2001. 19–47.

Fulwiler, Toby. "Looking and Listening for My Voice." *College Composition and Communication* 41 (1990): 214–20.

Hairston, Maxine. "Comment and Response." *College English* 52 (1990): 694–96.

Kogan, Steve. "A Comment on College English." *College English* 52 (1990): 473–74.

Lunsford, Andrea A. Afterword. *(Inter)views: Cross-Disciplinary Perspectives on Rhetoric and Literacy.* Ed. Gary A. Olson and Irene Gale. Carbondale: Southern Illinois UP, 1991. 267–69.

Olson, Gary A. "Encountering the Other: Postcolonial Theory and Composition Scholarship." *JAC* 18 (1998): 45–55.

———. "The Role of Theory in Composition Scholarship." *Freshman English News* 19 (1991): 4–5.

Phelps, Louise Wetherbee. *Composition as a Human Science: Contributions to the Self-Understanding of a Discipline.* New York: Oxford UP, 1988.

Worsham, Lynn, and Gary A. Olson. "Rethinking Political Community: Chantal Mouffe's Liberal Socialism." *Race, Rhetoric, and the Postcolonial.* Albany: State U of New York P, 1999. 165–201.

4

The Case for Writing Studies
as a Major Discipline

CHARLES BAZERMAN

L ITERATE ACTIVITY, directly and indirectly, occupies much of the day of
people in modern society. Literacy—in its basic and in its more elaborated, specialized forms—is the cornerstone in the education of the young.
Literacy and symbolic artifacts underlay the information age and its information economy. Literacy—with its enabling technologies and consequent
forms of social, political, and economic organization—has long supported
ways of life that distinguish us from humans of five thousand years ago. Literate engagement is also associated with forms of belief, commitment, and
consciousness that shape modern personality. Yet, the study of writing—its
production, its circulation, its uses, its role in the development of individuals
and societies, and its learning by individuals, social collectives, and historically emergent cultures—remains a dispersed enterprise. Inquiry into the
skills, practices, objects, and consequences of reading and writing is the concern of only a few scholars fragmented across university disciplines; such
inquiry has no serious home of its own.

How is it that a subject of such enormity is the interest of a few linguistic
anthropologists, a very few psychologists, an occasional sociologist, scattered
cultural historians and scholars, some applied linguists, some education
researchers, and an increasing but still limited number of people in the
teaching of writing in higher education? It is as if, for example, universities
had no departments of psychology—denying that cognition and affect were
significant and worth organized energetic inquiry—or no departments of
sociology—denying that society had any significant and regular impact on

our lives worth studying—or no departments of economics, mathematics, physics, or biology. These disciplines address fundamental issues in the constitution of our physical and social worlds. Yet, writing is also a fundamental matter of the constitution of our world—but the organization of research and of the university itself remains consistently blind to this fact.

The historical particulars of disciplinary formation determined that in the field of linguistics, spoken language became more primary than written; in English departments, literature gained dominance over literacy; in education, literacy came to mean reading (particularly in its beginning stages) more than writing. Only the relatively young field of composition has paid primary attention to writing, but our core attention has tended to be narrow: on students and classes in a few courses in universities in the United States over the last several decades, with particular attention to the underprepared student. However, we have had glimpses of how big our subject could be. Writing across the curriculum and writing in the disciplines have shown us that the first-year course hardly represents all the writing or learning of writing that goes on in universities. Areas such as technical writing, business writing, writing in the professions, writing in the workplace, and rhetorical studies of writing in the agora have reminded us that writing in universities is only a small slice of the writing that goes on elsewhere in the world. The national writing project and other forms of school/university cooperation have reminded us that students have writing lives before they get to the university, and that far from all students get to the university. Outreach programs have given us glimpses into the role writing can have for those who are elderly or those with disabilities, and other marginalized or transitional populations. Work in such areas as applied linguistics has helped us to notice the range of writing practices, pedagogies, and uses around the world. And historical studies of literacy, of writing instruction, of printing, and of the development of the book have helped us to appreciate the particularity of our set of literate conditions, the many forces and events that our literate practices respond to, and the monumentality of the literate accomplishment.

Of all disciplines, composition is best positioned to begin to put together the large, important, and multidimensional story of writing. We are the only profession that makes writing its central concern. What's more, the university—as central to contemporary society's knowledge, ambitions, and professions; as the heir to many of the literate movements of history; and as an international meeting place of global projects—is as good a standpoint as any from which to view writing at this juncture in history. Yet, we as a field must be willing to lift up our eyes to this larger charge. It is time for us to rise above the accidents of disciplinary history that have kept our truly significant subject only minimally visible and that have blinded us to the enormity of the material we have taken to instruct our students in. It is time to recognize that writing provides some of the fundamental mechanisms that make our world work, and it is time to assert that writing needs to be taken seriously along with the other major matters of inquiry supported by institutional structures.

Adopting a "Life-Span" Perspective

So what would be parts of such an inquiry? Fortunately, we do not need to make this up out of whole cloth. Fragmented but numerous publications dispersed across such disciplines as anthropology, linguistics, history, classics, cultural studies, psychology, sociology, science studies, education, and composition suggest major outlines of the inquiry. "Writing" as the subject of scholarly investigation has such power that when people begin inquiring into it, they immediately are drawn into stories of great importance and their studies become motivated and extensive—even though they may not necessarily find continual institutional support for such work.

The greatest energy, both in the field of education and in rhetoric and composition, has gone into studies of learning to write, whether through anecdotal descriptions of individual students, ethnographies of classrooms, or quantitative studies of the efficacy of various pedagogies. Scholars have tried many pedagogies, have observed many students at all levels, have documented their observations through many methods, and have analyzed their data using many theoretical and disciplinary lenses. From such work, we have learned about the trajectories and success of various paths of learning, in various circumstances, with various students, for various purposes. Because learning to write will remain a major imperative in education and society for the foreseeable future (even though forms and occasions of writing may shift rapidly with the introduction of information technologies), such studies must remain a major concern. Since writing is developed and supported throughout one's life span in every new occasion of writing for every new purpose—as any writer, no matter how experienced, is constantly reminded—we need to go further in extending our full range of studies from the earliest years onward, in school and out, as part of the continuum of learning that for only a transient period alights in the university but that then moves out into the workplace and agora and continues into the retirement years of reflection and renewed social engagement. There are now studies in all of these areas, but they would benefit from greater dialogue and from an entire life-span perspective. The scholars who study emergent literacy in pre-school years have much to say to those who teach eighteen-year-olds, as do those who study the writing of the socially powerful and those who study the writing of the powerless. Also, since our life spans of writing are now being supported through technology, we need to understand more fully the ways in which technologies are reshaping these writing experiences, how the technologies may provide new kinds of support, and how people move through various supportive literate technologies throughout their lives.

The life-span perspective on writing development also leads us to take even more seriously the great variety of writing engagements that individuals address in schools and outside of academia, for it is through the socially distributed and socially organized forms of writing that people develop as writers and form their literate consciousness. Understanding that writing is deeply integrated with our development as individuals and as social collectives necessitates that the study of writing be deeply embedded in psychology, sociology, political science, and history—just as those fields need to attend to writing as deeply constitutive of their subjects of inquiry.

Examining writing within the complex of our unfolding lives also suggests that research in writing across the curriculum, writing in the professions, writing in the workplace, and writing in the public sphere are far more than studies of instrumental exercises in the conventions of getting things done. They are studies in how people come to take on the thought, practice, perspective, and orientation of various ways of life; how they integrate or keep distinct those perspectives in which they are practiced; and how we organize our modern way of life economically, intellectually, socially, interpersonally, managerially, and politically through the medium of texts.

The particularity of our current literate arrangements is highlighted by comparative international, cultural, and historical studies that indicate how literate practices and their consequences vary. Historical studies reveal the emergence of our current practices, and the underlying assumptions and choices embedded in our current forms, distribution, and uses of writing. Historical and comparative studies also reveal how the introduction of literacy or a change in literate practices reshapes the various spheres of human endeavor.

In short, the study of writing is a major subset of the study of the history of human consciousness, institutions, practice, and development over the last five millennia; and composition—the learning and teaching of writing—is in the middle of all that. It appears, then, that composition is a *serious intellectual endeavor.*

Three Syntheses

To give a bit of concrete substance to this broad intellectual charge for the study of writing, and to suggest how I came to see the field in such sweeping terms, let me outline my own work. In teaching writing to underprepared first-year college students so that they could address the demands of their undergraduate career, I found myself focusing on how students could use, respond to, and criticize the materials they were reading in their classes. This issue of intertextuality led me to examine those intertextual fields of disciplines that undergraduates were engaging in, the ways in which they could engage with those fields, and what happened to them as they developed particular forms of engagement. Pedagogically, these concerns led me to write about reading and writing across the curriculum. In research, they led me to study the discourses of the disciplines, in particular the sciences, focusing on the emergence of forms of experimental reporting. Theoretically, I turned to theories of genre as a social construct, intertextuality, and activity. But underneath these were a wider range of theoretical sources in language, sociology, and psychology that treat human language, personality, activity, and interrelations as historically emergent through the purposive actions of individuals within social fields.

Several kinds of related syntheses have continually guided my work. The first is an emergent historical picture of writing practices, genres, systems of circulation, and related institutions and social systems. That is, in the same way as I saw the emergence of science related to its emergent forms and systems of written communication, so I began to see all aspects of the modern world in relation to the emergent infrastructure of written communications that shaped, regulated, and provided ongoing matters of attention. Although my studies seem to spread all over literate history—from early letters in the Near East to political Web sites in recent elections to the rhetoric of political activism in the last half of the twentieth century—I see them simply as elaborating different spots on the same four dimensional map. My recent book, *The Languages of Edison's Light,* although overtly concerned with just the literate actions of a small group of individuals over a few years of the late-nineteenth century in the New York area, places those written communications in the multiple worlds of unfolding literacy in this country and worldwide over that century. This project gives a bit of the flavor of the larger historical synthesis I have striven for.

A second synthesis is a theoretical one that has attempted to re-see rhetoric from the perspective of writing and to place writing within some of the major strains of twentieth-century social theory and social science. I have tried to integrate, from the point of view of writing, the following: Vygotskian and neo-Vygotskian theories built on a Marxist-Hegelian history of consciousness; utterance-based linguistics of a Bakhtinian sort; phenomenological sociology emerging from Schutz; the American pragmatist tradition leading to symbolic interactionist, structural, and structurational sociologies; linguistic anthropology; and interpersonal psychiatry. All these theories point to an historically emergent sense of the human in social settings, mediated by communications. While theoretical issues inform a number of my earlier studies, and especially *Shaping Written Knowledge,* I more explicitly foreground theoretical issues in several essays in *Constructing Experience,* including "Whose Moment? The *Kairotics* of Intersubjectivity" and a long introduction, "Sketches Toward a Rhetorical Theory of Literacy." Several essays on genre theory and activity theory have further helped articulate this synthesis. I am currently working on a multivolumed rhetorical theory of literacy.

The last kind of synthesis has been from the perspective of the individual—both as a writer and as a learner of writing. While this synthesis has been informed by my studies of the practices and development of several historically prominent scientists and rhetoricians—A. H. Compton, Isaac Newton, Otto von Guericke, Joseph Priestley, Adam Smith—it has been tied most closely to my own reflection on my students, on my pedagogical practices, and on myself as a constantly (I hope) developing writer. While this work is very much about the craft and technical choices facing writers, it is deeply tied to writers' socialization into communal activities; the forms of engagement, positioning, and goals within those communal endeavors; and their emergent identities, commitments, and accomplishments as literate social beings. This synthesis guides my daily struggles with writing, and my daily practice as teacher and friend working with students or teachers of students from early childhood through graduate students and working professionals. The most public and practical expression of this synthesis is in my textbooks, such as *The Informed Writer*, *The Informed Reader*, and, most recently, *Involved: Writing for College, Writing for Your Self*.

To me, these three syntheses—the historical, the theoretical, and the practical—tell the same story, for the theory is an attempt to understand how we live our lives at the unfolding edge of history, using literacy in the ways that make most sense for us in our lives, to continually make a future from our own skills and choices as writers. While I have been pursuing these visions— trying to ground myself within the realities of historical evidence, the best wisdom of contemporary social science, my own experience, and the learning of my students—others interested in writing have been engaged in their own inquiries. Writing is powerful along many dimensions, various in its manifestations, and composed of many elements and processes. There is much that we can and ought to know, and I can hardly delude myself that the subject is exhausted by the work that is close to mine. We need a thousand flowers to bloom, but it would help if these plants got a bit more regular support, if the harvesting were a bit more coordinated, and if the various cultivations were institutionally recognized as part of a significant cooperative endeavor.

Perhaps to some the study of writing is just too interesting and too much fun to be called a serious endeavor, but I certainly believe that composition is a serious intellectual endeavor and that it is time for our own field and for the university to take it more seriously.

Works Cited

Bazerman, Charles. *Constructing Experience*. Carbondale: Southern Illinois UP, 1994.

———. *The Informed Reader: Contemporary Issues in the Disciplines*. Boston: Houghton, 1989.

———. *The Informed Writer: Using Sources in the Disciplines*. 5th ed. Boston: Houghton, 1995.

———. *Involved: Writing for College, Writing for Your Self*. Boston: Houghton, 1997.

———. *The Languages of Edison's Light*. Cambridge: MIT Press, 1999.

———. *Shaping Written Knowledge: The Genre and Activity of the Experimental Article in Science*. Madison: U of Wisconsin P, 1988.

Part Two

Historical Inquiry

5

Writing Studies as a Mode of Inquiry

SUSAN MILLER

COMPOSITION STUDIES contains such various forms of intellectual work that we choose one title for the field, even the familiar "composition studies," only with difficulty. Nor is it easy to assume that "writing practices" are in fact the objects of study that unite the field's currently favored questions. Given this multiplicity on both counts—both words *and* things—we easily enough call our intellectual work "rhetoric and composition" or "composition theory," and we call its topics "cognitive/learning processes," "pedagogical theory and history," "situated discourse analyses," or, lately, "culture." Given that over the last twenty years much of our collective energy was spent arguing that pairing "intellectual work" and "composition" did not constitute an oxymoron, such internal competitions may appear trivial.

But as a still emerging field matures, its particular methods and goals need a strategically calculated descriptor that can assure its future development, as well as general agreement over the particular set of intellectual questions that such a descriptor entails. For reasons that I think go beyond my own history and admittedly situated (but not entirely biased) perspectives, I want to argue for "writing studies" as both the content and a name that can create the greatest success and shared integrity for our field. Writing studies places a nonevaluative spin on the more traditional label "composition studies," offering a way to describe the cultural work undertaken in any act of writing. By defining that work as the conjunction of a specific composing process and a resulting text, "writing studies" thus decisively promotes attention to the production of texts over their interpretation. Its theoretical bibliography, which I will outline, is perhaps unfamiliar among those who divorce their interest in writing processes from currently approved regard for theorizing reading and meaning. But writing studies—again as both title and topic—identifies the professional expertise that first delineated our intellectual work, and it can continue to justify support and prominence for that work among competing inquiries.

Adopting "Writing Studies"

This label, "writing studies," can gather, if certainly not unite, questions and methods in any inquiry that takes up texts *as* texts—as shaped graphic utterances that can be disassociated from human sources. Those texts may be historical, to take the case I will stress here. But they are not examples in writing studies if they are analyzed apart from the personal and social/material circumstances in which they are produced, as only a collection of formal characteristics and statements. Writing studies, engaging both historical and contemporary concerns, addresses acts of writing and their products as evidence of a particularly crucial cultural work in which a whole text offers an intellectual/expressive act that intersects circulating discursive practices. This inquiry does not detach "popular" from "high" texts, nor does it separate "ordinary" from "creative" writers on the basis of relative visionary talent or levels of access to the ethical and economic status requisite to authorship. But it does define *culture* as a conjunction of specific acts of composition and their resulting texts. That is, it asserts that what we know and ask about historical and current lives, like what we know and ask about circulating strands of textuality, is asked and known only through the inevitably partial documentation of framed language. Insofar as our only evidence of events is shaped discourse, acts of composing and their results comprise the cultures, which we can mis-recognize as different from a document's "content." Composing collapses what we term "experience" into what we also can only *term* "reality" and "representation." But writing also constitutes specific discursive cultures, which we bracket as the patterns and differences of conversations among texts.

   In this view, literate acts enable the always abstract language that is indistinguishable from the contexts it evokes. "Writing studies" gathers many varieties of intellectual work around the discrete questions about relations between writers and texts that first formed composition as a field. This rubric implies concern with formations of textuality as a new center for contemporary rhetoric, writing pedagogy, studies of writing processes, analyses and history of literature, critical discourse analysis, and other forms of applied linguistics—all with knowledge of material forces around these projects. The title names our work as a discrete academic undertaking in which teaching, specifically teaching composing, is a cultural action that embodies hegemony, not a demeaned labor around which a field sprang up opportunistically. This undertaking never addresses *either* a process *or* a product. It is itself an enduring socialized site where discursive traditions saturate any instance of composing. *It is a study*

I favor this framework not only because it authorizes my favorite historical research into relations between extant texts and the writing processes that produced them. The discrete learning produced by investigating relations between a writer and a text is also as robust as its counterparts; it is especially as visible as the projection of individual perspicacity that is practiced as hermeneutic interpretation, and as visible as the evaluation of texts performed by cognitive sciences. Both of those methods have certainly elevated the status of composition-as-teaching, as they by turns compete to dominate methods of writing research. Lately in this competition, literary and other forms of systematic interpretation are replacing discussions of writing processes as cognitive events, exchanges that increasingly appear to trace nineteenth-century beliefs in mental "faculties" and evaluative phrenology. But in "writing studies," we can ally interest in the motives, skills, and extended development of single writers with knowledge of regulated social expectations. Writing studies views as crucial a discursive history available not only to discretely educated classes but also to particular writers. The title implies that acts of writing and the social legibility of the texts that result from them always combine to show how a writer or a new genre may be more and less deeply embedded in or ignorant of specific textual contexts.

Of course, the familial stake in a child's language learning always places a writer-plus-text in the discourse of status and acceptance. This ethical stake is traced in the obviously evaluative perspective from which "composition" begins its teaching and its scholarship. Were we to shift to "writing studies," we would be making more than a convenient decision to connect composing to specific texts. We would, that is, be foregoing the sort of detachment that still classifies writers as "expert" versus "novice" and that equates the normal Western habit of composing one proposition at a time with the wretched nominalizations of bad prose style. Composition studies still praises *or* blames, elevates *or* demeans, in order to set marginal writing against often unmarked ideals that offer emotional satisfaction only as "important" and "effective" work(s). The field's maintenance of a literary, judgmental, aesthetic perspective has required "attitude" to appraise writers and acts of writing. The contemporary field never entirely escapes its distant but still powerful Master Texts, an ancient and repeated use of varieties of usage and speech to assign human or inhuman status to those more and less like us. The field traces class-maintaining ancient rhetorical tutors and schools, their modern revitalization by class-critiquing Scottish rhetoric, and the class shifting that warranted a re-formation as nineteenth-century American Harvard composition. All doom it to its almost inescapably dour righteousness, which is now complemented by surety of gaining intellectual status by borrowing literary hermeneutics to "read" culture. Nonetheless, writing studies might tell a less evaluative story. As intellectual work undertaken to extend justifiable curiosity about textual production, not to judge curious locutions, writing studies can at least assert that composition's evaluations must fit a world where everyone belongs, by right and by self-identification, to a middle class.

My claims for writing studies suggest that the modern discipline of English works under mistaken assumptions about historical examples of literary and other schooled writing. That proposition is clearly demonstrated in recent archival scholarship, which inevitably rewrites disciplinary stories in which the field has direct access to propriety. Archivists, that is, regularly switch off the electrified canonical fences that separate "standard" from "ordinary" texts. Even in first-wave evaluative feminism, which argued that women are "equal" to men, feminist archivists acknowledge the absurdity of assuming that only racially and economically *unmarked* men would have been schooled, become rhetorical virtuosos, or left substantial numbers of traditional compositions. In the name of this equality, Cheryl Glenn's *Rhetoric Retold: Regendering the Tradition from Antiquity Through the Renaissance* and Jacqueline Jones Royster's display of Ida May Wells's writings against lynching both exemplify this awareness, despite their desires to reevaluate the archive. But these recoveries, as Linda Ferreira-Buckley notes, do not simply add to the kinds of texts that were or should have been preserved. This work involves "a revolutionary shift in who counts" and who must be counted by sophisticated scholarship (578). That shift similarly characterizes prize-winning investigations like Thomas Miller's *The Formation of College English: Rhetoric and Belles Lettres in the British Cultural Provinces* and

Sharon Crowley's *Composition in the University: Historical and Polemical Essays.*

But apart from admirable wishes to promote equity, evaluative "attitude" begs a number of questions. Concern about "what should be in our archive, [and] how access can be broadened," is set aside by the different mood of writing studies, which assumes interest in *all* available writers and *all* available writings, even forgeries, for their own sake (Brereton 574). It undertakes to gloss available texts with their precedents and counter-voices, speculating about the identity of relevant textual ghosts haunting an archived writer's allusions, even at a remove. If necessary, it sets aside "authorship," biography, and direct citations to point out a conduct book or widely circulated model text that may be a plausible template for the document at hand. That is, it reads *around* a historical text, in contemporaneous history and analogous collections, often to discover positive value in what is *not* evident. Writing studies leads archivists to look for evidence of writing practices, of pedagogy, and of individual modes of composing, for the sake of identifying the plausible cultural work a text may have accomplished. Formal generic and linguistic qualities are measured not against "good" or "bad" style and "educated" or "lower class" content but as signs of how a text "got this way" through the complex *energeia* of a rhetorical performance.

Writing and Commonplace Books

These issues require, of course, that a researcher reveal his or her motives, even as further research shows their insufficiency. I, for instance, began *Assuming the Positions,* an analysis of the Virginia Historical Society's commonplace books, with strongly held liberal views derived from partial information. My vaguely warranted beliefs held (despite ample evidence to the contrary) that females in the eighteenth and nineteenth centuries did not write and that well-schooled writers of either sex usually adhered to the conventions of the edited texts we read now. I assumed that commonplace books would usually be copy-books like those prescribed since Aristotle, not the owned discursive property that John Locke's *A New Method of Making Common-Place Books* recommends. My experience of transcribing the three hundred volumes in this collection was thus a series of "What?!" and "Oh!?" realizations, punctuated by an occasional whispered "What?!" and "Oh!?" traded among other archivists. I abstracted from those surprises a new set of descriptive questions: What genres, purposes, information, or exchanges were written in a specifically demarcated time, place, and political/economic context? Who wrote them? (That is, how is this writer, identifiable or not, situated in relation to prior reading experience, writing lessons, and contemporaneous expectations for class, gender, and racial discourses?) What evidence is there that a writer took form, content, and, even, specific language from already empowered models that create textual authority?

My selection of commonplace books, historically a simultaneous writing practice and pedagogy, also complicated my initial theory of writing as a culturally constitutive action. If I had instead selected all the failing, or passing, written examinations, all the long poems from one place and time, all the published textbooks, or all the documents representing one or another political and/or social position, I assuredly would have limited an intriguing *corpus*. But these generic categories do not contain writing practices as they turn out to be — decisively irrelevant to the accepted hierarchies set by institutional interests. Full investigation of *all* the writing undertaken in a more generally defined context uncovers uneven, casual, peripheral, subsidiary, and egalitarian practices. They represent people and informed conventions that institutions necessarily flatten into invisibility. To take but one example, neither the representative content of all the textbooks published over a particular time nor slight variations in that content that can be traced by Great Textbook Authors make a great deal of cultural *sense* apart from economic and status attitudes that textbooks purvey in particular exigencies. Here, as Nina Baym argues in "Early Histories of American Literature: A Chapter in the Institution of New England," considering status and economics shows that Houghton Mifflin's nineteenth-century textbooks entrench a New England bias in even current American literary studies. Their content and editorial judgments still allow "America" to be imagined without reference to its founding Southern politics; to Midwestern German immigrants who imported its high cultural opera, museums, and symphonies; to terrains of Native Americans and Spanish settlement. Long after subsequent textbooks normalize diversity and multiculturalism, they do so in relation to the partiality of early New England Puritanism that Houghton Mifflin made an unmarked ideal for its own economic sake.

To move closer to our professional homes, in writing studies a student theme is not interesting as a historical instance of ability, of assigned topics, or of teachers' comments, unless we account for its archival locale. If found in a school's records, we read it in relation to other writings by the same student or that student's classmates, other writing assignments, available instruction and materials, and the place, mission, and stature of the school itself. But if found in a family's papers, the preservation itself portrays the text differently, as an instance of a particular kind of family communication. The many letters I transcribed from eighteenth- and nineteenth-century American fathers to their sons away at "school" (at Eton, an apprenticeship, Yale College, Hampton-Sydney College) provide much more than family biographies and historical information about commerce and courses of study, despite their rich contributions to those inquiries. In writing studies, however, it is the frequency of these letters, the paternal advice they contain, and especially stringent comments on the sons' writing that together reveal how attitudes toward written language were circulated among educated men. Here, the language of the fathers, not the always passive comments of private tutors and academy faculty, presages the strident voices of teachers in mass public schooling. These fathers directly assert that writing and speaking like other propertied men will crucially demarcate a son's entitlements. Their often challenging critiques vividly show how communications among men are identical to boundaries around "manhood."

Such evidence of "counter-history" does not always appear, so my examples are not meant to set Draconian laws of significance for inquiry into historical writing practices. But from the perspective of a textual ethnography, other research will uncover how writer-plus-text constitutes a cultural act that "history" may ignore, for familiar hegemonic reasons. The situated writing subject is the focus of writing studies, not authorial biographies, glimpses of exquisite skill, texts construed as more and less formally "effective." Its texts are not evidence for historical accounts that can exist without them. They are primary sources, whole compositions whose analysis always begins in their writers' purposes and situations and in the assumption that preserved writing is itself, in the face of easy losses, a history.

Many examples of this intellectual work are undertaken outside historical projects. For instance, Linda Brodkey's "The Literacy Letters," which analyzes an institutionally prescribed correspondence among English teachers and students, achieves the descriptive results I am sketching. It focuses on what the letters *say*, in order to emphasize how learning and acts of writing crucially depend on access to family stability, on transportation to classes, on peace of mind, and, unfortunately, on having teachers without the biased professional detachment of Brodkey's correspondents. Anne Ruggles Gere's "Kitchen Tables and Rented Rooms: The Extracurriculum of Composition" portrays writing practices without reference to the strains of cultural studies that stratify them against literary production.[1] Gere demonstrates that making any text is an activist politics of social growth, a source of entitled cultural activism, no matter where it occurs. Similarly, Marcia Farr regularly connects writing practices and social action without stratifying textual categories, as in her "Essayist Literacy and Other Verbal Performances" and research about Chicago and Mexican literacy practices (for example, "Literacy and Religion: Reading, Writing, and Gender among Mexican Women in Chicago").[2]

Historical Writing Practices

At least as I write, however, writing studies most often addresses historical writing practices. To assert that these texts remain visibly *composed*, scholars like Jean Ferguson Carr situate nineteenth-century domestic scrapbooks as homemade volumes whose female "keepers" write themselves into a particular cultural fiction: domestic bliss. These early multimedia compositions show how ordinary textual making appropriates while resisting the virtues attributed to domesticity. Like scrapbooks, both almanacs and pre-indexed commonplace books (like contemporary Day-Timers and Palm Pilots) insert a mobile writing subject into what are later imagined as exclusively "public" discourses. That mobility also appears in the writings of the nineteenth-century club women analyzed by Anne Ruggles Gere in *Intimate Practices* and by Theodora Penny Martin in *The Sound of Our Own Voices*. Both studies show how club women intuitively interpret and debate literary analyses, editorials, and other documents, composing responses for comment and correction by their peers. As Gere says, these social texts represent a textuality from which later genre categories — schooled and unschooled, high and low — emerge in the general nineteenth-century process of categorization. For Gere, the club women set the terms for the professional study of literature by borrowing from already established modes of religious interpretation.

Gere's inference represents the counterintuitive analysis of historical writing practices that writing studies allows. By identifying one of many practices that merged into newly categorized discourses, she avoids the common error in that genealogical attention to traditions: mistaking a recirculated practice

What does that mean?.

for ex nihilo creation. This inference underlies much of the work in Catherine Hobbs's collection, *Nineteenth-Century Women Learn to Write*, which analyzes activist writing by college women (Ricks, Harmon) and uses of writing to further African American women's causes (Logan), both within established literate practices that encourage textual gender equality. Suggesting that we need to trace circulations of discourses earlier than those of Gere's club women, Hobbs says that we need a broader account of history to "begin to *provide a sample of the various cultures and practices* that informed women's literacy" (4; emphasis added). Similarly, Heidi Maria Schultz's "Southern Women Learn to Write: 1830–1860" portrays seventy-nine upper-class Southern women writing in seventy-six postsecondary institutions. They write from mixed stimuli: domestic demands set against equally powerful political beliefs, the need to develop scientific knowledge, and participation in legal and religious discourses. Such analyses or historical practices repudiate serviceable patriarchal parables based on later categories. But even here, few highlight how specific writers and texts merge localism or personalism into continuously circulating discourses from which they take identity and authority without necessarily imagining their writing as "public."

What is that?

Historical writing studies, at least as practiced in these ways, suggests many unsanctioned inferences. There is, for example, compelling evidence that we need information about the status of a document's signatories before we characterize as illiterate a notation like "signed with his mark" from supposed illiterates. This mark sometimes shows that people forget how to write, or that closely affiliated groups rely on "illiterate" inscriptions in times of stress (Ames 66). In the late-seventeenth century, Virginia's Governor Richard Bennett and his son, who attended Harvard in 1655–56, both "signed" with an *X* a remonstrance supporting a later governor. Another instance of how explicit data can re-form usual patterns of inference is Lynne Templeton Brickley's "'Female Academies Are Everywhere Establishing': The Beginnings of Secondary Education for Women in the United States, 1790–1830: A Review of the Literature." Brickley critiques the proposition that hard-won public schooling created *new* access for the disenfranchised in statistical research that shows that "a *far greater proportion of young women attended academies in the 1790 to 1830 period* than the proportion of young men who attended academies and college" (56; emphasis added).[3]

Such inferences in writing studies are not without a theoretical basis. As Paolo Valesio says, textual surfaces and their production are complex enough, and informative enough, to warrant devoted attention within a rhetorical, not philosophical, theory that is grounded in the visible, not hidden, implications of texts (61). Yet, emphasizing writing over reading, production over consumption, and description over always tacitly evaluative interpretation is not accomplished by retrieving the categories and legitimacy of formal systems of rhetoric. My claim that writers necessarily precede readers instead follows from work that tacitly reevaluates patriarchal histories of rhetoric as manly influences and Great Performances. To take a few prominent examples, Raymond Williams's germinal *Writing in Society* enables the study of composing precisely *written* texts as a "means of production" of cultures (3). Roger Chartier's many studies of the history of the book, especially his introductory *The Order of Books,* articulate intellectual conditions in which writing studies may provide a sociology of texts that is knowledgeable about writing and rhetorical *processes* so as to "reconnect the text with its author; the work with the intentions or the positions of its producer." As Chartier says, this inquiry uncovers "the categories and the experiences that are the very matrices of writing" (28, 29). These views of writing are themselves historicized in Frederick Kittler's *Discourse Networks 1800/1900.* As David Wellbery says, Kittler undertakes to specify the genealogy of hermeneutics "as an observer of the system and not as its interpreter" (x). He works from an "outside" to show the radically historicized nature of any textual practice, not its "truth" or its inadequacies. Kittler materializes Derridian and Lacanian poststructuralism, analyzing not *écriture* or signifiers in general but "historically specific machineries . . . the linkages of power, technologies, signifying marks, and bodies that have orchestrated European culture" (xii–xiii).

Inquiry into the material circumstances around writing practices is equally, if differently, materialized by Robert Darnton. His *The Great Cat Massacre* and *The Business of Enlightenment* describe printing and publishing practices whose thick descriptors include not just archival records but the folklore, mythology, religious politics, and labor relations of eighteenth-century France. Darnton's work takes up a middle period and place among similar studies: William V. Harris's *Ancient Literacy,* Stephen Justice's *Writing and Rebellion: England in 1381,* Mary Carruthers, *The Book of Memory,* David Vincent's *Literacy and Popular Culture: England, 1750–1914,* Rajeswari Sunder Rajan's *The Lie of the Land: English Literary Studies in India,* and Susan Stewart's *Crimes of Writing.* In each study, "literacy" is not a measure of cognition, civilization, or economic status, nor is it only an "ideological" formation that Brian Street's *Literacy in Theory and Practice* describes. This scholarship, more productive than both old and new approaches to "literacy" as an ability instead of a culture, connects the *fact of* a writing event to *both* its content and its signification among other texts.

With few exceptions, these studies are not commonly included in the composition theory or the literacy studies canons. But they access specific writing practices across class, regional, and personal boundaries, and they demonstrate variable composing processes and multiple purposes for composing. These works assume that writing is an activity. They cannot match our expertise in composing, rhetoric, discourse analysis, and language. Yet, these studies do re-frame our work and its ties to educated elites to whom we now assign a defunct high literacy. They demonstrate how the academy has produced a mythological disenfranchised populous with no access to a civilizing pen. They show that writers are much more various and much less rigidly enclosed, now and historically, than judgmental inquiry can reveal.

Without such open-handed attention to practice, it is too easy to hide the regulatory purposes of bourgeois instruction in writing. But in that blind spot, we also conceal how that instruction promotes the privileged social/ intellectual inadequacy that so definitively marks middle-class sensibilities. Persuaded that it is entitled, even ethically required, to judge—but that it never interprets as acutely as its always absent Masters—this class's scholars, teachers, and students all categorize their own texts as never quite good enough to "count," but as nonetheless intuitively "individual" and protected by that uniqueness. Writing thus remains an ethical practice outside history. It is too "mental" to result from material circumstances or to demonstrate uneven access to schooling. Institutional boundaries enclose its significance, not the families, communities, civic horizons, and activism that texts actually comprise.

Professional Benefits

Already overburdened teachers of writing may object that my pleas for writing studies, like many earlier impositions on their intellectual work, do not get papers read or comfort the tentative beginnings of their students. I want to close, therefore, by elaborating the professional benefits I first claimed for the intellectual inquiry promoted under this new title. Most important, the distinct focus in writing studies on writing itself as our object of study is much more likely than many alternatives to undo the ancillary status of writing instruction and to graciously invite students into discourses new to them. Those who witnessed the response of literary critics to Mina Shaughnessy's explanations of Basic Writing can attest that it is knowledge of how texts "got this way" that justifiably defines our recognized expertise. That is, our own archive readily shows how the twentieth-century formation of composition as a discipline first depended on our knowing more about composing than others do. We find identity there, in taking up what, who, to what ends, and, especially, *how* people have written and do write. Answers to these questions distinguish our unique place in the reproduction and delineation of cultures. There, we know reproductive forces at their linguistic heart a great deal better than most. And we can critique these forces more authoritatively than other versions of our field allow.

As the recent archive also shows, if we claim expertise about relations between specific writers, their processes and their texts, we easily grow and successfully divert out-worn attempts to marginalize our teaching and research. This is the greatest benefit of writing studies to all: the provision of well-formed, vividly engaging information about how and to what far-reaching ends people write and have written.

Notes

1. See, for example, Easthope; Turner.
2. See the Feminism(s) and Rhetoric(s) Conference Homepage at http://femrhet.cla.umn.edu/. See also Susan Miller, *Assuming*.
3. Brickley also presents evidence that the pattern of women going South to teach—for instance, in the twelve Virginia female academies operating before 1830—was well established by the early 1800s.

Works Cited

Ames, Susie M. *Reading, Writing and Arithmetic in Virginia, 1607–1699: Other Cultural Topics.* Williamsburg, VA: Virginia 350th Anniversary Celebration Corporation, 1964.

Baym, Nina. "Early Histories of American Literature: A Chapter in the Institution of New England." *American Literary History* 1 (1989): 459–88.

Brereton, John C. "Rethinking Our Archive: A Beginning." *College English* 61 (1999): 574–76.

Brickley, Lynne Templeton. "'Female Academies Are Every Where Establishing': The Beginnings of Secondary Education for Women in the United States, 1790–1830: A Review of the Literature." Diss. Harvard U, 1982.

Brodkey, Linda. "On the Subjects of Class and Gender in 'The Literacy Letters.'" *College English* 51 (1989): 125–41.

Carr, Jean Ferguson. "As Schooling Travels: Literacy Exchanges in Nineteenth-Century United States." MLA Convention. Toronto, 1997.

Carruthers, Mary J. *The Book of Memory: A Study of Memory in Medieval Culture.* Cambridge: Cambridge UP, 1992.

Chartier, Roger. *The Order of Books: Readers, Authors, and Libraries in Europe between the Fourteenth and Eighteenth Centuries.* Trans. Lydia G. Cochrane. Stanford, CA: Stanford UP, 1994.

Crowley, Sharon. *Composition in the University: Historical and Polemical Essays.* Pittsburgh: U of Pittsburgh P, 1998.

Darnton, Robert. *The Business of Enlightenment: A Publishing History of the* Encyclopédie, *1775–1800.* Cambridge, MA: Belknap, 1979.

———. *The Great Cat Massacre and Other Episodes in French Cultural History.* New York: Vintage, 1984.

Easthope, Anthony. *Literary Into Cultural Studies.* London: Routledge, 1991.

Farr, Marcia. "Essayist Literacy and Other Verbal Performances." *Written Communication* 10.1 (1993): 4–38.

———. "Literacy and Religion: Reading, Writing, and Gender among Mexican Women in Chicago." *Language in Action: New Studies of Language in Society: Essays in Honor of Roger W. Shuy.* Ed. Joy Kreeft Peyton et al. Cresskill, NJ: Hampton, 2000.

Feminism(s) and Rhetoric(s) Conference Homepage. 25 Oct. 2000. http://femrhet.cla.umn.edu/.

Ferreira-Buckley, Linda. "Rescuing the Archives from Foucault." *College English* 61 (1999): 577–83.

Gere, Anne Ruggles. *Intimate Practices: Literacy and Cultural Work in U.S. Women's Clubs, 1880–1920.* Urbana: U of Illinois P, 1997.

———. "Kitchen Tables and Rented Rooms: The Extracurriculum of Composition." *College Composition and Communication* 45 (1994): 75–92.

Glenn, Cheryl. *Rhetoric Retold: Regendering the Tradition from Antiquity Through the Renaissance.* Carbondale: Southern Illinois UP, 1997.

Harmon, Sandra D. "'The Voice, Pen, and Influence of Our Women Are Abroad in the Land': Women and the Illinois State Normal University, 1857–1899." Hobbs 84–102.

Harris, William V. *Ancient Literacy.* Cambridge: Harvard UP, 1989.

Hobbs, Catherine. "Cultures and Practices of U.S. Women's Literacy." Introduction. Hobbs 1–33.

———, ed. *Nineteenth-Century Women Learn to Write.* Charlottesville: UP of Virginia, 1995.

Justice, Steven. *Writing and Rebellion: England in 1381.* Berkeley: U California P, 1996.

Kittler, Friedrich A. *Discourse Networks 1800/1900.* Trans. Michael Metteer with Chris Cullens. Stanford, CA: Stanford UP, 1990.

Locke, John, et al. *A New Method of Making Common-Place Books.* Greenwood: London, 1706.

Logan, Shirley Wilson. "Literacy as a Tool for Social Action among Nineteenth-Century African American Women." Hobbs 179–96.

Martin, Theodora Penny. *The Sound of Our Own Voices: Women's Study Clubs 1860–1910*. Boston: Beacon, 1987.

Miller, Susan. *Assuming the Positions: Cultural Pedagogy and the Politics of Commonplace Writing*. Pittsburgh: U of Pittsburgh P, 1998.

Miller, Thomas P. *The Formation of College English: Rhetoric and Belles Lettres in the British Cultural Provinces*. Pittsburgh: U of Pittsburgh P, 1997.

Rajan, Rajeswari Sunder, ed. *The Lie of the Land: English Literary Studies in India*. Delhi: Oxford UP, 1993.

Ricks, Vickie. "'In an Atmosphere of Peril': College Women and Their Writing." Hobbs 59–83.

Royster, Jacqueline Jones. *Traces of a Stream: Literacy and Social Change among African American Women*. Pittsburgh: U of Pittsburgh P, 2000.

Schultz, Heidi Maria. "Southern Women Learn to Write: 1830–1860." Diss. U of North Carolina at Chapel Hill, 1996.

Stewart, Susan. *Crimes of Writing: Problems in the Containment of Representation*. Durham, NC: Duke UP, 1994.

Street, Brian V. *Literacy in Theory and Practice*. Cambridge: Cambridge UP, 1984.

Turner, Graeme. *British Cultural Studies: An Introduction*. 2nd ed. London: Routledge, 1996.

Valesio, Paolo. *Novantiqua: Rhetorics as a Contemporary Theory*. Bloomington: Indiana UP, 1980.

Vincent, David E. *Literacy and Popular Culture: England, 1750–1914*. Cambridge: Cambridge UP, 1989.

Wellbery, David. Foreword. Kittler v–xxxiii.

Williams, Raymond. *Writing in Society*. 1983. London: Verso, 1991.

6

Claiming the Archive for
Rhetoric and Composition

SUSAN WELLS

IT IS, AFTER ALL, another kind of reading—which is to say, another kind of writing. You sit at a table too high for your laptop; someone brings you a document; you pass your eyes, and often your hands, over the pages, finding what you knew (one way or another) was there. Then you draw breath and scan the pages again, seeing what you did not expect. The text can be faded and fragmentary; pages can be out of order. Or perhaps you receive a box of scraps—papers, cards, lists arranged by the year of their composition. Or the writing is full of echoes, so that you ask yourself whether you've seen this document before. Sometimes, you feel that you are writing the text as you read it, piecing together words and phrases. Many times, you yourself suture together the relation between one text and another.

This quite material labor has been, for some scholars in rhetoric and composition, deeply rewarding. For others, it may seem mindlessly antiquarian. But we need the gifts of the archive just as much as we need to ask why we, as rhetoricians, as compositionists, might want to do this work. If the archive is a treasury, what does it hold for us? My own first answer to that question is autobiographical.

The Three Gifts of Archival Work

Picture an overcrowded room full of women in various states of bad temper. It is 1977; the 1960s are over, but the women's movement is not. We are trying to figure out why that year's International Women's Day celebration had been such a monumental failure. (The event had been unbelievably contentious: walkouts in virtually every talk, interrupted performances, cascading fragmentation.) None of the organizers felt comfortable talking to the audience we had, least of all to women who had come out for their first feminist event. They were horrified; we, the organizers, were fairly horrified ourselves. We asked why things had gone so badly, and one answer was that we had relied on male logic. That answer was, in important ways, right. If "male logic" meant drawing inferences from explicit principles, bringing the singular under the domain of the general, or preferring objectivity to emotion, then "male logic" had been no help to us at all. After all, we were dealing with contending principles, with singularities that had not been worked up into generalizations, with the emotions that accompany all common work. But the condemnation of male logic was also dead wrong: if logic is male, then emotion is female, and such a categorization would cut us off from the world of reason and abstraction. In that room, we needed (among other things) reason. We were—and are—in trouble, and we could not afford to discard the tools of analysis that might have helped us.

I was shaken then, and shaken again years later when I heard very similar arguments in academic feminist circles: versions of Gilligan's theory about women's affinity for connected knowledge, rejections of agonistic argument as inherently masculine, and characterizations of scientific work as a kind of allegorical rape of nature. How would we learn abstraction, agonistic conflict, experiment—those indispensable tools for producing knowledge—if we decided that they were alien to us? How would we survive as rhetoricians and writing teachers if we continued to reenact the nightmare of particularity and care to which the academy had consigned us? How would our students, women and men, learn to reflect critically if we devalued essential tools of reflection? How would they write effectively if we saw persuasion as violence? I taught class after class of male technical writing students, watched the tiny trickle of women engineers and scientists slowly gather strength, and realized that I was seeing a momentous event: a generation of American women was achieving scientific literacy. I wanted a theory of scientific discourse that would not configure these students as aliens or outliers.

That political and pedagogical question became a historical inquiry. Was it in fact true that women's absence from the scientific record was not just a matter of historical erasure? Had women avoided science as an alien mode of thought? Aided by Sandra Harding's work, I could imagine a feminist "successor science." Could I help us all to remember one? There had, of course, been women scientists in the past, and recovery of their work has been one of the glories of feminist historical research. But they were singular figures, usually aristocratic, isolated in a male world. I wanted to find a community of women doing scientific work. Finally, a friend reminded me that I was living a half mile from the Medical College of Pennsylvania, formerly the Women's Medical College, which graduated its first class in 1850. Their archives held documents recording the scientific work of scores of women engaged in constant collaboration with one another; these women also wrote short stories, popular self-help books, bad memorial verse, manifestos, and defenses of their right to medical study. And these women physicians were normal nineteenth-century correspondents, which is to say that they were active, verbal, and given to tiny handwriting and interesting spellings.

These documents invoked for me a world of writers. I looked again and again at photographs of Women's Medical College graduates; they seemed to me to be the faces of my friends. I traced out documents — theses, minutes, official correspondence — that may never have been read in any serious sense, but simply acknowledged and filed away. I wondered over and over how it had been for these writers, what tools they had brought to bear on the problems they faced. When they talked of a "phlegmatic diathesis," did they mean to invoke humors theory? Was a nineteenth-century "orgasm" the same as a twentieth-century orgasm? I found evidence that a great many nineteenth-century women physicians did scientific work in much the same spirit as their male colleagues; I also found that, for women, the professional life of a physician was much more problematic than the scientific discipline of medicine. Women strongly disposed toward experimentation and investigation were hard put to find male physicians who would consult with them or admit them to the surgical amphitheater. The rhetorics women physicians invented to confront and transform this situation were complex: they used plenty of "male logic," to be sure, but also caustic irony, disguise, and parody.

Reading their texts, I confronted the issue Derrida poses at the opening of *Archive Fever:*

> It goes without saying . . . that wherever one could attempt . . . to rethink the place and the law according to which the archontic becomes instituted, wherever one could interrogate or contest, directly or indirectly, this archontic principle, its authority, its titles, and its genealogy, the right that it commands, the legality of legitimacy that

depends on it, wherever secrets and heterogeneity would seem to men-
ace even the possibility of *consignation,* this can only have grave consequences for a theory of the archive, as well as for its institutional
implementation. (4)

Directly or indirectly, archival work demands such rethinking, a project radically realized in Walter Benjamin's *The Arcades Project.* In the "Convolutes,"
or sections, of the Arcades, Benjamin assembles quotations from a variety of
sources, his own reflections, news items, oddments of fact, and turns of
phrase. Each Convolute is a confected archive, a way of forcing intimacy
between the legitimate, the hegemonic, and the everyday and subversive. In
the Convolute on Boredom, for example, lists of dusty streets adjoin historical quotations and literary references to dust. Benjamin observes that in
1757 there were "only three cafés in Paris," and then we learn in which of
them Marx, years later, explained historical materialism to Engels—but not
before we have read speculations about language, weather, the cosmos, ignorance of the cosmos, the erotics of weather, and dreaming (108). Benjamin's
is an archive that refuses institutionalization, that even refused publication
for a full half century. It is an impossible model for the rhetorician, but it
demonstrates three precious gifts (all of which Benjamin enjoyed) that we
can expect from the archive: resistance to our first thought, freedom from
resentment, and the possibility of reconfiguring our relation to history.

The archive resists knowledge in a number of ways. It refuses closure;
often, it simply refuses any answer at all. Indeed, many researchers have stories of loose ends they could not leave alone: I have spent many fruitless after-
noons tracking down the woman physician whose victory in an anonymous
competition was news in London, but completely unknown in the United
States. That resistance to closure, inscribed in Benjamin's text as a principle
of composition, is fruitful. It forbids totalization. It prompts us, as contending scholars, to resist early resolution of questions that should not be too
quickly answered. My work in the archive of women and medicine was
intended to show that women had been productive and original scientific
writers; to some extent, I was able to carry out that intention. But the archive
also resisted my own drive to demonstration, told me that I needed to do
more, and other, kinds of work to situate the experience of scientific research
within the institution of medicine. Jacqueline Jones Royster describes eloquently how the resistance of the archives broadened the context of her
research:

My basic vision as a researcher was deeply affected, changing rather significantly the paradigm through which, from that time forward, I would draw meaning from women's experience. Before the shift, I had understood that there was much to know about these women because they were people of African American descent. After the shift, I became conscious of how much *more* there was to know because these people were women and mostly poor, held certain cultural values, and can be placed at a particular point in time within a particular set of socioeconomic conditions. . . . I conclude all these years later that I was developing the habit of caring as a rhetorician (a researcher who centralizes the use of language), but I was constructing meaning with a transdisciplinary view in defiance of clearly rendered disciplinary boundaries. (258)

The resistance of the archive is also a counterweight to the headlong pace that the demands of pedagogy have trained us to keep. Pedagogical problems are always demanding, always exigent: the readiness with which we solve them serves us well in many contexts and coheres with the urgency of our work in a new discipline. But it is not the only possible tempo for intellectual work.

Archival work is not, of course, the only scholarly method that meets resistance. Ellen Barton has argued convincingly that we should value the resistance of data in broadly focused ethnographic studies; the classroom and the public sphere offer their own surprises. But the resistance of the archive is deeply linked to the particular status of the written text as a material object, disseminated in time and space and "consigned," in Derrida's term, to a particular collection. These resistances bring us very close to what is difficult, complicated, and worth knowing in any written document; they pose for us, again and again, the basic questions of our discipline.

The second gift of the archives is a loosening of resentment. Academic disciplines often consider themselves embattled or undervalued; ours is no exception. Nor are compositionists especially subjective or florid in their complaints about these difficulties — consider Jane Tompkins on the difficulty of teaching literature in elite institutions. Surely, our resentment is provoked by statements such as Wlad Godzich's characterization of writing programs as "lacking either tradition or legitimation"; the archival recovery of both the traditions of our discipline and the broad practices of writing corrects such ignorance (12). Archival study of other kinds of texts also broadens our own sense of how difficult it is to write in new and untried ways. By recovering the work of club women, of schoolchildren, of new trade unionists, we can understand the stakes of the broad struggle to define the terms of literacy with which we have associated ourselves. It is really nobody's work but our own to recover these texts; through our reconstruction and reading, their production of literacy speaks more loudly than the arrogance that neglects it.

The final gift of the archives is the possibility of reconfiguring our discipline. Both the work done by past rhetoricians and compositionists and the literacy practices of engaged speakers and writers help us to rethink our political and institutional situation, to find ways of teaching that are neither narrowly belletristic nor baldly vocational. Even a relatively specialized educational practice like that of training physicians required students to learn about public health, forensics, and hygiene, raising questions about professionalism and expert knowledge that are still significant. And broader historical investigations engage central contemporary questions of educational theory and policy: Mariolina Salvatori, for example, has written eloquently about the relevance of early nineteenth-century pedagogy:

> At the present, at a time when pedagogy is increasingly invoked as the means to foster a teacher's critical understanding of different cultures, at a moment, that is, when pedagogy is called upon again to perform the humanistic and sociopolitical function that early proponents of pedagogy had claimed was within its province, we are, I believe, ideally positioned to learn from the stories of both hopes and disappointments, of successes and defeats, of intellectual honesty and compromise that constitute pedagogy's richly textured past. (61)

Shaping Intellectual Projects

To demonstrate more concretely how these gifts of the archive can shape specific intellectual projects, let us consider three exemplary books: Susan Miller's *Assuming the Positions: Cultural Pedagogy and the Politics of Commonplace Writing;* Robert Connors's *Composition-Rhetoric: Backgrounds, Theory, and Pedagogy;* and Jacqueline Jones Royster's *Traces of a Stream: Literacy and Social Change among African American Women.*

Miller's *Assuming the Positions* demonstrates the power of the archive to resist premature closure. Her examination of literate practices in eighteenth-

and nineteenth-century Virginia society is framed as an investigation of the power of *doxa,* of assumed cultural common sense—the ideological horizon of possibilities that never needs to be argued. Miller argues that we are always in danger of missing the message that the archive can send us, that of the invisibility and ubiquity of *doxa:*

> The historical correspondence we might have received, and have already absorbed, never arrives, despite its visibility in the most obvious places. So to learn *how* enduring Western cultural arrangements are matters of active (if only semiofficial) rhetorical education, we must peruse places that recently constructed psychologies teach us to call *personal.* Renaming this personal as the domesticated discourse to which letters (like Poe's) always return, we can perhaps see the power of ordinary writing. (19)

And *Assuming the Positions* sorts through some amazing old mail, uncovering messages that are surprising because they resist our own common knowledge. Miller finds practices of literacy among women far more significant than those acknowledged in conventional scholarship on antebellum domestic education. She catches writers in the act of subject formation, so that the self no longer seems monolithic or imperial, but fragile and problematic. She treats seriously the common sense of the nineteenth century—dismissals of the right to public education, notions of familial "ownership" of children. These writers are read as forming a new national culture from the available materials. Methodologically, Miller avoids both hagiography and the pointless scolding of dead people. Elaborating Linda Brodkey's notion of "writing on the bias," Miller observes that

> [f]inding a true bias ... does not serve the same end as mapping a field by placing its elements on a preexisting grid. Fabric hanging on the bias has an oblique tension in its drape, just as the biases that determine a text's ambivalent "substance." ... Finding a true bias ... allows us to move across the straight lines of analytic categories that make material intelligible, while simultaneously rejecting them to design a path through their neatly arranged but often useless absolutes. (145–46)

Such an investigation, honoring the resistance of archival materials, fulfills the rhetorical responsibilities Steven Mailloux ascribes to archival work in "Reading Typos, Reading Archives"; it gives an account of its own status as a work of persuasion, an attempt to create a new community of readers.

Robert Connors's *Composition-Rhetoric: Backgrounds, Theory, and Pedagogy* demonstrates the power of archival work as a guard against resentment. *Composition-Rhetoric* demonstrates, by undoing it, the close link between contemporary rhetoric's dismissal of "current traditional rhetoric" and its need to distance itself from literary study—a need so pressing that it sometimes leads to demonization. It thereby dissolves our resentment against both friends and enemies. Connors understood quite well the mutually defining weaknesses of both literary study and rhetoric and composition, but there is no inlet of this backwater that he did not patiently explore. The quality of attention that Connors brought to his archival investigation allowed him to present the originators of the "current traditional paradigm" as our colleagues: they solved their intractable problems, made the best use they could of unpromising materials, and invented the intellectual tools that they needed. These early figures in the discipline emerge as individual, situated scholars and intellectuals, responding to broad social movements (like women's fight for coeducation) that were so successful that they have been virtually forgotten. At the same time, Connors delineates the institutional situation in which rhetoric and composition was consolidated as an anomalous discipline, one with a thin research record and no purchase on graduate programs. Here again, Connors does not mince words: he makes it clear that the development of the underclass responsible for teaching composition had everything to do with both the development of specialized literary study and the gendering of that study as male. But his account of these developments is completely without rancor: once again, we meet specific agents, charged with specific tasks, solving insoluble problems with limited means. Connors's account of the growth of English departments and writing programs does not reduce the story to one of the institutionalized exploitation of drudges by mandarins. Instead, we read of uncontainable forces to open and democratize education, to meet the needs of new women students, and to develop a hybrid university that sponsored both research and undergraduate education, forces that balance, almost inevitably, the writing classroom and the graduate seminar.

Archival work, Connors's "starting place and consistent control," creates the space for his powerfully distanced account in which our other—our disciplinary forbears, our institutional antagonists—is reconstructed (19). The past that his book offers us is thoroughly disenchanted, and therefore immensely useful. Connors described *Composition-Rhetoric* as a traditional rather than a subversive history; Linda Ferreira-Buckley concurred with this characterization, which accurately describes the book's use of textual resources. As a speech act, however, *Composition-Rhetoric* demonstrates how powerfully the archive supports strategies of containment and distancing that allow us to get even rather than to continue to stay mad.

Finally, Jacqueline Jones Royster's *Traces of a Stream: Literacy and Social Change Among African American Women* suggests some of the ways in which our discipline might be reconfigured, broadened, and grounded by archival work. *Traces of a Stream* investigates literacy practices within the context of the social structures and political aspirations that shaped them. This is a challenging task: archival materials, especially for antebellum African American women, are not easy to find, read, or interpret. Royster addresses these gaps in the record by drawing on a rich body of historical and linguistic scholarship; her reflections are informed by literary and rhetorical theory, and the whole treatment is animated by a deep imaginative and political commitment to the memory she reconstructs:

> Recognizing the limitation of our ability to substantiate with traditional documentation this type of ontological perspective, however, I have chosen . . . not to be constrained by just the facts, although certainly in this case there are many. I have chosen instead to use the community of discourse, invigorated by available documentation, to look imaginatively at the points at which women's lives, in all their variability, seem to have converged. . . . My specific intent is to extrapolate (from what at minimum are points of curiosity and at maximum are actual points of convergence) inferences that seem fruitful in positing an explanation for beliefs and actions from which African American women could form a sense of community and ethos. (100)

Within this context, the new canonic figures that Royster discusses (Maria Stewart, Alice Walker, Anna Julia Cooper) are deeply situated. For her, the genre of the essay is understood as a strategic intervention undertaken by situated writers and readers. And Royster's account is reflexive: *Traces of a Stream* is itself a series of essays: the reader is addressed directly; the texts combine disparate materials. The book works cumulatively toward an argument rather than mechanically coupling thesis to support.

Royster's book serves as a model of reconfiguration, finally, because like Miller's and Connors's books, it combines close attention to "the documentary record" with a deep engagement with the issues facing us as scholars and as writing teachers. All of these texts broaden our sense of the possibilities of writing instruction; all of them engage our deepest commitments as democratic intellectuals. We could see these books, and others like them, as texts propped up on our own outsized tables, waiting. They ask us for an inventive reading and patient, courageous rewriting.

Works Cited

Barton, Ellen. "More Methodological Matters: Against Negative Argumentation." *College Composition and Communication* 51 (2000) 399–416.

Benjamin, Walter. *The Arcades Project.* Trans. Howard Eiland and Kevin McLaughlin. Cambridge, MA: Belknap, 1999.

Brodkey, Linda. *Writing Permitted in Designated Areas Only.* Minneapolis: U of Minnesota P, 1996.

Connors, Robert J. *Composition-Rhetoric: Backgrounds, Theory, and Pedagogy.* Pittsburgh: U of Pittsburgh P, 1997.

Derrida, Jacques. *Archive Fever: A Freudian Impression.* Trans. Eric Prenowitz. Chicago: U of Chicago P, 1996.

Ferreira-Buckley, Linda. "Rescuing the Archives from Foucault." *College English* 61 (1999): 577–83.

Godzich, Wlad. *The Culture of Literacy.* Cambridge: Harvard UP, 1994.

Harding, Sandra G. *The Science Question in Feminism.* Ithaca: Cornell UP, 1986.

Mailloux, Steven. "Reading Typos, Reading Archives." *College English* 61 (1999): 584–90.

Miller, Susan. *Assuming the Positions: Cultural Pedagogy and the Politics of Commonplace Writing.* Pittsburgh: U of Pittsburgh P, 1998.

Royster, Jacqueline Jones. *Traces of a Stream: Literacy and Social Change among African American Women.* Pittsburgh: U of Pittsburgh P, 2000.

Salvatori, Mariolina Rizzi, ed. *Pedagogy: Disturbing History, 1819–1929.* Pittsburgh: U of Pittsburgh P, 1996.

Tompkins, Jane. *A Life in School: What the Teacher Learned.* Reading, MA: Perseus, 1996.

7

New Dispositions for
Historical Studies in Rhetoric

SUSAN C. JARRATT

Since Edward P. J. Corbett wrote *Classical Rhetoric for the Modern Student,* rhetoric and history have become subjects for the intellectual work of the newly constituted field of "rhetoric and composition."[1] Over the last two decades, debates have arisen about whether or not histories of rhetoric (particularly classical rhetoric) have anything to do with the contemporary teaching of writing in U.S. universities (Knoblauch and Brannon) and, for those who do allow histories of rhetoric into the field, about historiographical approaches (Vitanza). Rather than rehearse those debates, I will use the opportunity provided by this project to suggest a different direction that historical studies in rhetoric might take: a way that traditional rhetoric can use analytics of space to confront social differences.

Rhetoric

One distinguishing feature of this recently reinvented field is its instability, producing a continual need for definition. There is a tradition of historians limiting the object of study in rhetoric to treatises explicitly addressing "rhetoric" as a named theory and practice (for example, Kennedy; Schiappa), but numerous recent studies have been stepping outside those boundaries (Glenn; Mailloux; Walker; Wertheimer; and others). Like many of the scholars in the second group, I see "rhetoric" as a comprehensive analytic frame rather than as more narrowly instrumental or as a "metarhetorical" group of texts (duBois 167).

Changing practices in the future are underwritten by changed visions of the past. In *Rereading the Sophists,* I reinterpreted the genesis of classical rhetoric by exploring the significant contribution of the first sophists in fifth-century B.C.E. Athens. Although that study expanded the traditional canon of participants, it remained within the conventionally accepted spatial and political parameters of "classical rhetoric": the world of Athenian citizens (and their non-Athenian teachers) in assemblies, courts, and other scenes of public display oratory. A historian of ancient rhetoric might now take a more temporally and geographically expansive approach to ancient rhetorics—one that articulates a panoply of practices with contemporary critical theory—and in so doing, join forces with progressive studies in the humanities in dislodging a stifling view of tradition based in "classicism": the classics as "a fixed thing that supports one's own prior certitudes, fending off any ambiguity as 'extreme relativism'" (Wills; Mailloux; and Nussbaum).[2] Given the persistence and cultural prominence of such "classicizing" returns, it is still necessary to outline carefully the historiographical terms under which a project involving ancient sources might be launched.

My historiographical approach does not argue for the continuation of an unbroken tradition, but, rather, in the words of John Bender and David E. Wellbery, it "presupposes a discontinuity within tradition, and an alternation that renders . . . rhetoric . . . a new form of cultural practice and mode of analysis" (4).[3] Bender and Wellbery's narrative of and argument for the "end of rhetoric" offers stimulating material for reflections on historiography. "Rhetoric," in their terminology, signifies an ancient art of oratorical practice, affiliated closely with power and property, that became an organizing theory for premodern European educational curriculum, and that was decisively "ended" by Enlightenment science, modern social differentiation, and Romantic subjectivity (6–7).[4] These forces, they argue, "exploded the hegemony of classical tradition and created the historical gap following which a return or repetition of rhetoric—not its continuation—becomes possible" (5).

Their narrative of rhetoric's birth, flourishing, and demise—rich in detail and historically irreproachable—nonetheless runs the risk of reproducing a whig narrative of progress. DuBois points out the drawback of such developmental tales: "It has been easy to personify rhetoric, to see it developing almost anthropomorphically, emerging from infancy, stretching its limbs, blooming eventually into arthritic, formulaic atrophy" (167). To the extent that such a narrative might obscure differences within and among historical rhetorics, it could offer unwitting aid to a "classicism" that "pays too little attention to difference, diversity, and heterogeneity in the ancient world" (167). But Bender and Wellbery argue that such an "end" of "rhetoric" was necessary so as to enable a return. Drawn from psychoanalysis, languages of return and repetition allow the historian to put that anthropomorphized body of historical rhetoric on the couch, unearthing seemingly minor memories and distant events as sites of contestation whose resuscitation may have serious implications for changing contemporary understandings and uses of rhetorical power. To shift the metaphor slightly, Bender and Wellbery enable the historian to turn the insights of "rhetoricality" — their term for the "infinitely ramifying character of discourse in the modern world," along with the theories that seek to account for it — back onto pre-Enlightenment sites, salvaging from them scraps for use in modern reconstructions (25, 26).

The spatial domain of the academic project supporting such historical inquiries is best described as interdisciplinary: designating places, differently constructed in different institutions, on which ancient rhetoric, classics, critical theory, literary studies, pedagogy, and projects of public action actually meet and forge mutually comprehensible languages. In my view, this term serves better than "transdisciplinary" (suggesting motion across but leaving vague the terms of connection) or "multidisciplinary" (suggesting irreducible fragmentation, in Bender and Wellbery's view, such that "one cannot study rhetoric *tout court,* but only linguistic, sociological, psychoanalytic, cognitive, communication, medial, or literary rhetorics" [38]). If, in Bender and Wellbery's terms, ancient rhetoric was about *property,* and rhetoricality designates *impropriety,* then I would propose a return of the issue of power in the form of questions about *appropriation* (38–39). When groups of people have been excluded from public spaces, which rhetorical practices have they captured, borrowed, or reinvented, and how? What rhetorical materials can contemporary critics and theorists appropriate from the past without obscuring difference? And can such plunderings turn ancient tradition from an oppressive dead letter into productive memory? Posing such questions of the rhetorical tradition has led me to reimagine some of its materials.

Disposition

Classical rhetoric was taught as a set of five "canons," or stages, in the composition of a speech. They are often referred to in Latinate terms: invention (finding arguments), disposition (arranging arguments in a speech or written text), elocution (composing elegant, clear sentences and choosing appropriate words; style), memory (memorizing a whole speech, or the main points of argument), and delivery (using effective voice control and gestures). In Greek and Roman antiquity, and at other important moments in Western education up to the modern period, invention has been the most important of these canons. Aristotle's *Rhetoric,* for example, is more about how to marshall arguments than any other subject. Cicero's *De Inventione* was a vital text for medieval rhetorical education, and despite the Renaissance interest in style, invention remained vital to a humanistic education through the early modern era.

The scientific revolution of the seventeenth century, however, dealt a severe blow to classical invention, a transformation detailed by Sharon Crowley in *The Methodical Memory.* Crowley decries—rightly, I believe—the loss of rhetorical invention and the deadening influence of a modern focus on arrangement in composition from the inception of that institutional practice in U.S. universities during the late 1800s. In a historical narrative similar to Bender and Wellbery's, she tracks an epistemological shift to the "modern" that ultimately disabled classical rhetorical invention. Descartes's rationalism along with Locke's fusion of language and idea placed knowledge in the mind of the individual subject, not in the collected wisdom of a group. The development of empiricism and the scientific method (Bacon) disarmed rhetorical deliberation as a means of creating knowledge. Truth was in the sensible world, and method was used to apprehend it. The methodical mind could discover it, and the knowledge produced would be authoritative because of its form. Invention as the process of collecting relevant positions already known within the culture in response to a rhetorical situation gave way to the methodical arrangement of data read off of the orderly mind of the knower.

Other historians of nineteenth- and twentieth-century rhetoric in U.S. universities tell similar stories. James A. Berlin, for example, finds the invention of probable arguments around social, political, or moral issues (in other words, rhetoric in its classical practice) faltering in the face of the production of knowledge through the scientific method about the concrete problems of agriculture, commerce, and industry—the newly significant subjects of university study. As inventional rhetoric declined, he points out, the work of the rhetoric classroom devolved into arranging materials (disposition) and perfecting forms. For those teaching composition who even today are using one of the dozens of textbooks based in this current-traditional paradigm, "composition" can be experienced as mechanistic, contentless drudgery. Crowley makes the point that the persistence of such textbooks perpetuating modernist epistemological assumptions has more to do with institutional needs than with students learning to write (147).

Crowley makes a convincing case for the revival of a classically informed invention on the grounds that such a change would shift the source of knowledge from the mind of a knower to the communal act of producing situated knowledge:

> Because of its intimate ties with the ethics, politics, and epistemology of the culture it serves, invention is crucial to the maintenance of a complete and effective theory of rhetoric. Invention reminds rhetors of their location within a cultural milieu that determines what can and cannot be said or heard. The only effective arguments are those to which the community is prepared to respond, whether negatively or positively. (168)

And this revival of invention needs to put disposition or arrangement in its place:

> To teach writing as though the composing process begins with arrangement or style, then assumes that speakers and writers can deploy discourse in a cultural and ethical vacuum, and hence that what they say or write doesn't matter very much beyond its immediate scene of production. Composition becomes the manipulation of words for its own sake. (168)

Crowley's persuasive argument for invention follows in the tradition of work by Richard Young and Janice Lauer, who found in invention a rhetorical launching point for composition studies, connecting it with philosophy, cognitive science, physics, and process writing in composition.

Why, then, in the face of these persuasive and historically informed arguments for invention, would one want to resuscitate disposition? Certainly, not to return to a focus on the kinds of arrangement described in Crowley's book: prescribed orders like the five-paragraph theme that rigidly exclude context or situation, an orderly discourse arranged to reflect models of coherence along a universalized pattern of movement from generalization to specific, a disposition that serves the academy as what Crowley calls "a useful mud fence, guarding it from the unsupervised and uncontained sprawl of self-initiated analytical or critical student discourse" (153).

I'm proposing that we might see disposition in a somewhat different light. Crowley argues for a return to a classical invention in a postmodern era. By "postmodern," she means a time after those assumptions about knowledge discussed above (rationalism, language representing unproblematically an available world, authority inhering in the mind of the knower) had lost their force. I'm wondering, however, whether "invention," in some of its current applications, remains tainted by the epistemologies it tries to cast off. In the move from classical invention to composition's brainstorming, freewriting, and so on, there is a persistence of the assumption that knowledge is in the mind of the writer—we just have more "inventive" ways of getting it out. These techniques can create a slippage into expressive and vitalist theories of the subject: one can invent one's writing out of self, in relation to self. Lester Faigley has shown how persistent this version of the "subject" is in composition studies. Of course, Crowley would not call this "invention," but I'm suggesting that a reconsideration of disposition might more dramatically shift the terms of the discussion. In concentrating on disposition, I don't offer an argument against invention but rather a rumination on the potential within a historical term to be renewed—recreated within a particular historical/cultural/intellectual milieu. What is so interesting about Crowley's discussion of invention and disposition is the way the two oscillate around one another: discussions of classical invention almost always cast it in spatial terms. Invention is beneficial because it insists that writers be located in time and space (151). The most striking example of the spatiality of invention resides in the *topoi:* "places" where arguments are discovered. Crowley quotes a richly suggestive passage from Quintilian on topics as "the secret places where arguments reside, and from which they must be drawn forth" (5.10.21; qtd. on 3). She goes on to paraphrase Quintilian's comparison of places to "the haunts or localities frequented by certain species of birds and fish" (3). Contained within that metaphor is the sense of limited accessibility; there is an eerie resonance here with the modern idea of the mind as an internal space wherein ideas can hide. This spatial concept fits with the modernist scene of writing described by Linda Brodkey, which overlays the physical isolation in the actual act of inscription (in the garret) with the figurative isolation of a mind understood to be an interior space (159). By concentrating on spaces outside the mind, rather than on the invention of ideas, I hope to help us focus more directly on the production of discourse by people in actual material conditions.[5]

I propose using the term in an analogical and imaginative way to inquire into the arrangement not only of ideas and language in texts but also of people and images in public spaces—to work visually and geographically in the interest of more material histories of rhetoric. In the adaptation of rhetorical terms, Roman Jakobson stands as a venerable and highly influential exemplar, with his elevation of metaphor and metonymy from their role as lowly figures of speech within classical rhetoric to the twin pillars of a system dealing with "large-scale tendencies of semantic production" (Bender and Wellbery 30). Bender and Wellbery are worth quoting at length on an operation they call "displacement":

> What we find in Jakobson's inquiry, then, is a fundamental displacement that affects the traditional terminology of rhetoric, a generalization of certain items within that terminology and a wholesale abandonment of other items. Certain old rhetorical terms have come to designate general processes that are at work, in their juxtapositional interplay, across the entire field of discourse, that are anterior to any instrumental choices a writer might make, and that even govern such transindividual phenomena as the succession of period styles. Exactly this shift in the theoretical function and significance of concepts is what we are calling the move from rhetoric to rhetoricality. (30)

In its new "rhetoricality," disposition marks the connection between rhetorical practices and the postures or orientations connected with social positions. Unlike *ethos*, which refers to the status of the speaking subject in relation to an audience, disposition extends the inquiry beyond the immediate rhetorical situation to social relations more generally. It is a way to account for the presence or absence of difference within historical and geographical spaces, to build into our rhetorical terminology a reminder of the fact that history should attempt to investigate not only those who spoke but also those who were made silent.

Difference and Situation

One of the major problems with traditional rhetoric in almost every era is the very narrow group of people by, about, and for whom it was developed:

Western European males meeting various other qualifications of race, sexual practice, property ownership, age, and religion. In principle, rhetorical tools should be available to any member of a culture. But history tells different stories. Crowley's discussion places these questions under the heading of "situation" or rhetorical context. In her text, invention signaled the situatedness of students and their writing missing from the curricula and textbooks in current-traditional composition. "Rhetorical situation" becomes a way of explaining an exercise of power across an axis of institutional difference: teacher/student. Situatedness has been a powerful tool with which the disenfranchised challenge normalcy, making visible the particularities at work in the construction of discourses of power (Haraway, for example). As Crowley (and others) have explained, the convention of anonymous authority in the text shields the specificities of the speaker. Evoking "situation" is one way to break open that authority. Rhetorical situation has served Crowley and others working for politically progressive ends well, and my challenge to it should not be construed as an argument against those uses but rather an attempt to move into another set of words for similar purposes.

Lloyd Bitzer's germinal discussion of rhetorical situation is an interesting place to observe the way rhetoric can hold out the possibility of critical transformation and withhold it at the same time. Bitzer defines rhetorical situation as "a natural context of persons, events, objects, relations, and an exigence which strongly invites utterance; this invited utterance participates naturally in the situation" (5). An exigence is "an imperfection marked by urgency; it is a defect, an obstacle, something waiting to be done, a thing which is other than it should be" (6). Other features of the rhetorical situation in Bitzer's analysis are constraints and audience. Examples of rhetorical situations that Bitzer offers include the assassination of President Kennedy, Roosevelt's declaration of war, Lincoln's Gettysburg Address, and—strangely—an account of the words exchanged by Trobriand Island fishermen recorded in Bronislaw Malinowski's essay on meaning in primitive language (2–5).

Bitzer's essay has not gone unchallenged in the three decades since it inaugurated the journal *Philosophy and Rhetoric* in 1968. Richard E. Vatz takes issue with Bitzer's terms by inverting them: "I would not say 'rhetoric is situational,' but situations are rhetorical"; "not 'the situation controls the rhetorical response . . .' but the rhetoric controls the situational response" (159). Vatz views rhetoric as "a creation of reality or salience rather than a reflector of reality" (158). This position relies on meaning making or interpretation, but as Barbara Biesecker points out, it keeps in place an autonomous human subject as the initiator of the meaning. Biesecker's reconstruction of the rhetorical event in deconstructive terms dethrones both humanistic subject and audience, putting in their place the operations of *différance*: "A deconstruction of the subject gives rhetorical critics and theorists access to the radical possibilities entailed in rhetorical events" (112). The structuralist basis of deconstruction imagines both language and the speaking subject in spatial terms: "Only to the extent that we are able to differ, as in spatial distinction or relation to an other . . . are we able to produce anything" (117). On the side of reception, Biesecker points out that "audience" as a concept has received little critical attention in rhetoric and that most discussions of audience, even within epistemic rhetoric, presuppose a group of sovereign, rational individuals (122, 123). At this point in her argument, Biesecker offers a more detailed version of Derrida's critique of the humanistic subject, inviting us to think of the human being "not as an essence but as an effect of the subject's place in an economy of differences" (124). While I endorse the critique of the subject offered here, it is interesting that this very well-drawn picture doesn't offer us a way to distinguish between the persons in the producing and receiving positions of the rhetorical event. Biesecker's summary comments, articulating the shift from "rhetorical situation" to "rhetorical event," are compatible with the orientation I offer here: "The rhetorical event may be seen as an incident that produces and reproduces the identities of subjects and constructs and reconstructs linkages between them"; "it marks the articulation of provisional identities and the construction of contingent relations that obtain between them"; it is "an event that makes possible the production of identities and social relations" (126). I suggest, though, that we can take another turn, using disposition, space, and the public — public space — as a way of making material the sites on which such events occur without reinstating the humanist subject. In so doing, a historian might look more closely at the power relations involved using the heuristic provided by the public to understand the import of differences between and among producers (speakers, writers, representers) and receivers (listeners, readers, viewers).

Neither Bitzer's original article nor Biesecker's revision theorizes such power differentials explicitly. A deconstructive analysis of *différance* is decidedly more helpful in opening up questions of power than "rhetorical situation," which reveals only the already-fixed power positions scripted into naturally given "situations." And with the exception of the example of the Trobriand Islanders, it seems that Bitzer's idea of exigence is firmly lodged within the status quo: the world of great men and their deeds. What may seem a "natural" exigence to some (women's disenfranchisement, for example) would seem to others not to be "something other than it should be." And if those others are in positions of power, there is no "situation." Norms will be evoked, but there is no way of measuring their power or attaching it to particular groups of people. Who is present in an "audience"? Those not present would have no way of placing constraints on the rhetorical situation.

Only the example of the Trobriand Islanders opens a tiny, puzzling break in this very conventional rhetorical world. Bitzer's choice of it reveals an interesting paradox. While he reads the Trobriand Islanders' speech as exemplary of a rhetorical situation — that is, pragmatic and embedded in context — Malinowski himself uses the example to distinguish "primitive" speech: "It is a mode of action and not an instrument of reflection" (qtd. on 4). Reflection is not a category in Bitzer's formulation, nor is rhetorical situation of interest to Malinowski. There's no obvious way to account for the appearance of this non-Western, "primitive" example within the terms of the article; and, on my reading, Bitzer does not persuasively show how the dialogue quoted is particularly rhetorical — that is, persuasive, or aimed at establishing a group identity or deciding on a collective action. It seems more instrumental/technical or perhaps ritualized. Rather, the example could be read as an eruption of otherness or difference into the world of Western, civilized culture: a symptom, in psychoanalytic terms, of the other that is necessary and necessarily repressed in order to create the "same." But its disjunctiveness — its unremarked bad fit with the theory itself and with the rest of the completely conventional examples (Lincoln, Kennedy et al.) — seems only to throw more light on the way Bitzer's theory itself is solidly situated within a particular culture and history.

My effort here in this kind of "intellectual work" is to find rhetorical materials most useful for the project of challenging power hierarchies and for incorporating difference. While rhetorical tools have been created by those in positions of power, they are available to others. Which tools will be the most useful at a particular historical moment for those challenging domination and seeking the equitable distribution of power? A growing body of work in rhetoric seeks to answer this question—most of it in terms of the rhetoric of a particular group. Keith Gilyard, Shirley Wilson Logan, Jacqueline Jones Royster, and others have begun the project of sketching an African American rhetoric, both historical and contemporary. Scholars like Cheryl Glenn, Krista Ratcliffe, Joy Ritchie, and Kate Ronald are writing women's histories of rhetoric and analyzing feminist rhetoric. New projects in American Indian rhetoric are appearing (Lyons). When work from literary criticism and theory is included, the bibliography on writing and difference is extensive. While endorsing those projects, I'm suggesting a slightly different direction: using disposition rather than a particular identity category to call attention to the uses of rhetoric in public spaces, foregrounding questions of power, participation, and representation.

Shifting the perspective to space, as I do with disposition, raises questions of access and social context obscured or assumed under a "rhetorical situation" model. Instead of asking, How did great men handle momentous rhetorical situations? the historian would ask, Who is present in a space of rhetorical performance? Who is allowed to speak or write? How is speaking ordered differently in different spaces and to what effect? Theorists of difference studies (a term comprising the work of feminists, queer theorists, scholars of antiracism, postcolonial studies, and ethnic studies) incorporate such questions into their work. Rhetoric needs to link up to such studies, finding out where its materials might enable and be enabled by them.

New directions in rhetorical study lead outward, not around and around in a closed circle. Thinking in terms of dispositions makes us aware of where we are—whom we include within and exclude from our circles of intellectual exchange—and it helps us imagine whom we might reach by turning outward from narrow constructions of the field of rhetoric and composition.

Notes

1. This essay is drawn from the introduction of a book-in-progress titled *Dispositions: Rhetoric, Difference, and Public Space.*

2. The shift in disciplinary terminology from "classics" to "studies of the ancient Mediterranean"—informed by structural anthropology, feminist history, and studies in sexuality—signals the move away from "classicism." See, for example, duBois; Rabinowitz and Richlin; and Winkler. Ancient studies of non-Western rhetorics—including

Egyptian, Chinese, and Japanese practices—broaden the field even further (see, for example, Mao).

3. There has been a flood of work in the historiography of rhetoric over the past two decades. See, for example, Berlin, et al.; Poulakos; and Vitanza.

4. C. H. Knoblauch and Lil Brannon offer a similar narrative, using it as support for their argument that the study of classical rhetoric is irrelevant to the field of composition.

5. Nedra Reynolds has made a persuasive case for a similar practice under the rubric of a "geographic study of composition," inviting us to "explore how spaces and places are socially produced through discourse and how these constructed spaces can then deny their connections to material reality or mask material conditions" (13).

Works Cited

Aristotle. *On Rhetoric: A Theory of Civic Discourse.* Trans. George A. Kennedy. New York: Oxford UP, 1991.

Bender, John, and David E. Wellbery. "Rhetoricality: On the Modernist Return of Rhetoric." *The Ends of Rhetoric: History, Theory, Practice.* Ed. John Bender and David E. Wellbery. Stanford: Stanford UP, 1990. 3–39.

Berlin, James A. *Rhetorics, Poetics, and Culture: Refiguring College English Studies.* Urbana: NCTE, 1996.

Berlin, James A., et al. "Octalogue: The Politics of Historiography." *Rhetoric Review* 7 (1988): 5–49.

Biesecker, Barbara A. "Rethinking the Rhetorical Situation from Within the Thematic of *Différance.*" *Philosophy and Rhetoric* 22 (1989): 110–30.

Bitzer, Lloyd F. "The Rhetorical Situation." *Philosophy and Rhetoric* 1 (1968): 1–14.

Brodkey, Linda. "Modernism and the Scene(s) of Writing." *College English* 49 (1987): 396–418.

Cicero. *De Inventione.* Trans. H. M. Hubbell. Loeb Classical Library. Cambridge: Harvard UP, 1949.

Corbett, Edward P. J. *Classical Rhetoric for the Modern Student.* New York: Oxford UP, 1965.

Crowley, Sharon. *The Methodical Memory: Invention in Current-Traditional Rhetoric.* Carbondale: Southern Illinois UP, 1990.

DuBois, Page. *Sappho Is Burning.* Chicago: U of Chicago P, 1995.

Faigley, Lester. *Fragments of Rationality: Postmodernity and the Subject of Composition.* Pittsburgh: U of Pittsburgh P, 1992.

Gilyard, Keith. "African American Contributions to Composition Studies." *College Composition and Communication* 50 (1999): 626–44.

———. *Voices of the Self: A Study of Language Competence.* Detroit: Wayne State UP, 1991.

Glenn, Cheryl. *Rhetoric Retold. Regendering the Tradition from Antiquity Through the Renaissance.* Carbondale: Southern Illinois UP, 1997.

Haraway, Donna. "Situated Knowledges: The Science Question in Feminism and the Privilege of Partial Perspective." *Feminist Studies* 14 (Fall 1988): 575–99.

Jarratt, Susan C. *Rereading the Sophists: Classical Rhetoric Refigured.* Carbondale: Southern Illinois UP, 1991.

Kennedy, George A. *Classical Rhetoric and Its Christian and Secular Tradition from Ancient to Modern Times.* Chapel Hill: U of North Carolina P, 1980.

Knoblauch, C. H., and Lil Brannon. *Rhetorical Traditions and the Teaching of Writing.* Upper Montclair: Boynton, 1984.

Lauer, Janice M. "Issues in Rhetorical Invention." *Essays on Classical Rhetoric and Modern Discourse.* Ed. Robert J. Connors, Lisa S. Ede, and Andrea A. Lunsford. Carbondale: Southern Illinois UP, 1984. 127–39.

Logan, Shirley Wilson. *"We Are Coming": The Persuasive Discourse of Nineteenth-Century Black Women.* Carbondale: Southern Illinois UP, 1999.

Lyons, Scott Richard. "Rhetorical Sovereignty: What Do American Indians Want from Writing?" *College Composition and Communication* 51 (2000): 447–68.

Mailloux, Steven. *Reception Histories: Rhetoric, Pragmatism, and American Cultural Politics.* Ithaca: Cornell UP, 1998.

Mao, LuMing R. "Invitational Discourse and Chinese Identity." *Journal of Asian Pacific Communication* 3.1 (1992): 79–96.

Nussbaum, Martha C. *Cultivating Humanity: A Classical Defense of Reform in Liberal Education.* Cambridge: Harvard UP, 1997.

Poulakos, Takis, ed. *Rethinking the History of Rhetoric: Multidisciplinary Essays on the Rhetorical Tradition.* Boulder: Westview P, 1993.

Quintilian. *Institutio Oratoria.* 4 vols. Trans. H. E. Butler. Loeb Classical Library. Cambridge: Harvard UP, 1920.

Rabinowitz, Nancy Sorkin, and Amy Richlin, eds. *Feminist Theory and the Classics.* New York: Routledge, 1993.

Ratcliffe, Krista. *Anglo-American Feminist Challenges to the Rhetorical Traditions: Virginia Woolf, Mary Daly, Adrienne Rich.* Carbondale: Southern Illinois UP, 1996.

Reynolds, Nedra. "Composition's Imagined Geographies: The Politics of Space in the Frontier, City, and Cyberspace." *College Composition and Communication* 50 (1998): 12–35.

Ritchie, Joy, and Kate Ronald, eds. *Available Means: Women in the Rhetorical Tradition.* U of Pittsburgh P, forthcoming.

Royster, Jacqueline Jones. *Traces of a Stream: Literacy and Social Change among African American Women.* Pittsburgh: U of Pittsburgh P, 2000.

Schiappa, Edward. "*Rhêtorikê:* What's in a Name? Toward a Revised History of Early Greek Rhetorical Theory." *Quarterly Journal of Speech* 78 (1992): 1–15.

Vatz, Richard E. "The Myth of the Rhetorical Situation." *Philosophy and Rhetoric* 6 (1973): 154–61.

Vitanza, Victor J., ed. *Writing Histories of Rhetoric.* Carbondale: Southern Illinois UP, 1994.

Walker, Jeffrey. *Rhetoric and Poetics in Antiquity.* New York: Oxford UP, 2000.

Wertheimer, Molly Meijer, ed. *Listening to Their Voices: The Rhetorical Activities of Historical Women.* Columbia: U of South Carolina P, 1997.

Wills, Gary. "Hanging Out with Greeks." *New York Review of Books* 13 May 1993: 10–14.
Winkler, John J. *The Constraints of Desire: The Anthropology of Sex and Gender in Ancient Greece.* New York: Routledge, 1990.
Young, Richard E. "Paradigms and Problems: Needed Research in Rhetorical Invention." *Research on Composing: Points of Departure.* Ed. Charles R. Cooper and Lee Odell. Urbana: NCTE, 1978. 29–47.

Part Three

Ideological Inquiry

8

Ideological Critique in Rhetoric and Composition

GARY A. OLSON

Y OU MAY HAVE NOTICED the recent controversy over the release of *Goblet of Fire*, the fourth in the series of children's books about a young "wizard" named Harry Potter. This book series has been so stunningly successful that over thirty-five million copies are in print in thirty-three languages, and it has been credited with enticing countless millions of children to switch off their video games and to discover the pleasures of old-fashioned reading. Despite its role in generating this unprecedented surge in new readers, the Harry Potter series has been the subject of sustained and vociferous attack. Groups such as Focus on the Family have tried to mobilize thousands of parents to urge schools and school boards to ban the books because they fear that the books are creating a generation of children "desensitized to the occult" (Murray). The American Family Association is convinced that the books "promote witchcraft and wizardry" (Kjos). One Internet Web site even argues that the books promote drug use (magic potions) among the young ("Potter Takes"). Another group circulated a mass letter urging grassroots action against the books for "teaching sorcery and satanism" (Chew). (You might be amused to hear that at one point the letter writer comments, "If children and adults are excited about a book, it must be suspect.") And even more mainstream sources have weighed in: an editorial in *USA Today* refers to the books' "cross-pollination of paganism and Christianity" ("Something").

These efforts have been partially successful. Since their release in the United States, the Potter books were challenged twenty-five times in seventeen states (McCuen). One school board in Canada required parents to sign a consent form before allowing the books to be read in the classroom, although this rule was eventually overturned ("Potter Wins"). Besides the more obvious issue of censorship, what this story is about is the power of representation and the struggle over who gets to control the creation and dissemination of representations in this culture. The presidential impeachment trial, the Florida election controversy in 2000, and even the controversies over certain of George W. Bush's cabinet nominees are all in many ways similar struggles over the right and power to represent through language. It seems to me that such struggle is exactly what all of us in rhetoric and composition are concerned with—that in one way or another we are all united in our work with representations, in the production and reception of meaning. That's why I believe that the work we do in rhetoric and composition is exceptionally important. The students we train will help determine the future shape of our culture. We offer students the languages and critical faculties to engage in the struggle over representation and thereby empower them to shape the society they will live in. This is why I so passionately believe that rhetoric and composition is much more than teaching students to "express themselves"; it is also about helping them learn to engage in ideological critique so that the language skills they acquire are relevant not only to their lives but also to their material existence—students can employ these skills to effect real change in their lives.

The Tradition of Ideological Critique

The tradition of ideological critique derives from a leftist orientation that has always been part of our field. While it's true, as Lester Faigley suggests in *Fragments of Rationality*, that rhetoric and composition has generally remained a conservative discipline, it has also enjoyed a long tradition of progressivist, often Marxist-inspired, scholarship. As early as Paulo Freire's *Pedagogy of the Oppressed*, compositionists began to introduce into our scholarship substantive discussions of critical pedagogy, liberatory learning, teacher authority, and ideological critique. Richard Ohmann—beginning with his recently republished *English in America* and extending through and beyond his editorship of *College English*—did much to expose compositionists' complicity in furthering the objectives of the military-industrial complex, for serving, in a sense, as linguistic drill sergeants for the Ideological State Apparatus of education. It's interesting to observe how this three-decade-long tradition of progressivist criticism has evolved and even become central to much of the intellectual work we do today. Many of the notions of such theorists as Freire, Ohmann, Donaldo Macedo, Ira Shor, and others—notions that seemed so shockingly revolutionary in the 1970s—now regularly inform composition scholarship, and even official NCTE and CCCC resolutions.

The move toward a more progressivist agenda in the intellectual work of composition has accompanied the move toward more theoretical types of scholarly inquiry and the concomitant focus on the interrelatedness of discourse and ideology. Fueling this shift has been a rich body of scholarship from other disciplines that those of us in rhetoric and composition have been able to draw on productively, including work in feminist theory, critical literacy studies, neo-Marxism, and various postmodern discourses. Work in these and other areas has contributed substantially to a complex and constructive critical discourse in composition theory.

Ohmann, Shor, Macedo, Henry Giroux, and other early importers of Freirean theory paved the way for a number of progressive critical theorists by opening for discussion a whole range of investigations into how power, ideology, and discourse intersect. At the forefront of more recent scholarship has been James Berlin. In fact, Berlin is largely responsible for introducing the concept of ideology into composition studies in his now canonical "Rhetoric and Ideology in the Writing Class." His posthumously published *Rhetorics, Poetics, and Cultures,* however, is likely to exert the most lasting influence on such intellectual work in composition. He begins this book with the assumption that English studies is in a state of crisis, and he interrogates the political and intellectual concerns central to English studies with an eye toward how the discipline might be "refigured" as a potent force in fostering the kind of critical education that strengthens democracy. He argues forcefully that English studies plays a special role in the mission of democratic education, and he articulates how we might position the discipline at the forefront of educational and social reform. And his critique is optimistic, positive, hopeful; it moves beyond constructive critique to productive change.

While Ohmann and others have argued that traditional composition instruction serves the state and the military-industrial complex, Berlin contends that it is the institutional bifurcation of rhetoric and poetic, of writing and reading, that has positioned English studies to serve the "privileged managerial class" and to discriminate against those who are not members of that class. That is, the traditional political and intellectual arrangement of English departments and the curricula deriving from that arrangement conspire to turn us all into servants of the state and the dominant class—obedient and unwitting workers in the Ideological State Apparatus of education. Berlin believes that ideological critique can help us challenge the traditional assumptions upon which English studies is based and to rearrange the political and intellectual formations of the discipline so as to better meet the challenges of postmodern democratic society.

Some progressive compositionists have argued that the field should simply reject the notion that its job is to help students successfully enter the workforce, but Berlin believes that we should not abandon this goal. The real problem is that the current arrangement prepares students to become successful workers in a postmodern economy but fails to prepare them to meet the intellectual challenges of postmodern culture. Drawing on the work of Freire, Giroux, and other theorists of critical pedagogy, Berlin insists that the main task of English studies is to prepare students to become critically literate citizens so that they can participate fully in the democratic process. To achieve this end, we must reconceptualize the work of English studies. The bifurcation of rhetoric and poetic must end; we must come to understand the discipline's main objective to be the examination of discursive practices in both the production and consumption of text. That is, if we understand our task to be that of helping students acquire the ability to analyze and produce signifying practices, we can help them position themselves intellectually to acquire agency in their worlds. Consequently (and not surprisingly), English studies moves closer to cultural studies and ideological critique.

Wedding Foucauldian analysis with Freirean critique, Berlin in effect puts a postmodernist spin on Freirean theory. The result is a critical pedagogy featuring a more elaborated analysis of signifying practices and cultural formations. While language has the power to oppress and dominate, it also has the power to liberate. What's more, helping students acquire sophisticated critical abilities not only leads to individual growth but also enables a radically participatory democracy where all voices can at least be heard, where everyone at least has the opportunity to engage in the struggle over representation.

Significantly, the kind of pedagogy that Berlin and many of us envision is thoroughly rhetorical: it is deeply concerned with context, audience, and how signifying practices are employed to further particular ideological interests. It is, in short, especially concerned with ideological critique. Such a pedagogy is especially well articulated by Judith Goleman in *Working Theory*, an engaging attempt to theorize a counter-hegemonic praxis that bypasses the theoretical difficulties inherent in traditional critical pedagogy. While a number of progressive scholars address ideological critique in the classroom, Goleman's is the most thoroughly elaborated, sustained treatment of the subject.

Like Berlin, Goleman insists that because writing and reading, rhetoric, and poetic are always already ideologically determined, effective writing pedagogy must derive from rigorous ideological critique. If reading and writing are thoroughly inscribed by ideology, and if both knowledge and individuals as subjects are also constructed through discursive practices, then ideological analysis carries with it the necessary pedagogical function of helping us to identify ideology in our representations, to read ideology as a specific way of understanding reality, and to alter that reality for the good. Thus, critical pedagogy entails helping students both to read the forms of their own historically situated individuality and to learn the mechanisms of such reading.

Many scholars concerned with ideological critique draw heavily on Michel Foucault's demonstration of how power relations are materialized in discourse, in systems of representation. Once authoritative discourses are formed, the power relations they support and the interests they further are often invisible. The very naturalness of authoritative discourses serves to discourage interrogation, analysis, problem posing. This is why it becomes so easy for those of us in rhetoric and composition to remain complicitous in the reproduction of dominant ideology, to further the interests of the managerial class or the military-industrial complex. A truly critical pedagogy would engage in constant ideological critique; it would help students examine not only how authoritative discourses constitute their experience and understanding of the world but also why such discourses are privileged over others.

I want to point out, however, that the kind of pedagogy espoused by Goleman and others like her is not simply a "new and improved" mode of "critical thinking" or close analysis. Central to the process is constant self-reflexivity. Students (and teachers) must consciously examine their own reading and writing processes and their own cultural and intellectual contexts, since these factor significantly into the meaning-making process. Only by situating oneself in the interpretive process can one move toward a fuller understanding of a text and the ideological framework it supports. Thus, Goleman's critical pedagogy encourages students to make a double move: to fully interrogate a text (both Goleman and Berlin use the word *text* in its larger, postmodern sense) so that one explores historical context, ideological assumptions, and power relations; and simultaneously to interrogate one's own position and context in relation to the text.

Both Goleman and Berlin believe that the ability to engage in ideological critique, to interrogate systems of representation, can lead to the kind of heightened awareness that opens the way to political action. That is, if a pedagogy is to be truly critical, truly liberatory, it must help students gain subject position, a place of agency in their worlds. Such agency has profound implications for the future of democracy in the postmodern age. It is important, however, that such pedagogy not be presented as a panacea for either classroom difficulties or world problems. Goleman, for example, takes pains to caution that encouraging students to engage in ideological critique brings with it no guarantees; one can just as easily substitute one authoritative discourse for another, and only continual critique, and self-critique, can help prevent that from occurring.

Ideological Critique and the Role of Emotion

Perhaps the most original and substantive contribution to the intellectual work on ideological critique has come from Lynn Worsham, especially her sophisticated tour de force "Going Postal: Pedagogic Violence and the Schooling of Emotion." Most scholars, at least tacitly, treat ideology as simply a cognitive phenomenon—as a web of ideas, assumptions, values, ways of seeing the world, and so on; few include the role of emotions or the affective dimension in the workings of ideology. Worsham, however, demonstrates that a central operation of the reproduction of ideology is the "schooling of emotion," a kind of pedagogic violence. Extending the work of Louis Althusser, Michel Foucault, and Pierre Bourdieu and Jean-Claude Passeron, she examines how society disciplines individuals by "educating" their emotions and inculcating in them specific affective relations to the world. In this view, ideology's roots run much deeper than many of us have assumed; the work of decolonization is not a simple matter of changing someone's "ideas"; one's entire affective universe must be altered. Thus, for Worsham, the fundamental task of ideological critique is to reeducate emotion.

Worsham begins with Althusser's contention that the family and the educational system, working in tandem, constitute the primary (in the sense of
"first" and "central") pedagogy that interpellates us into dominant ideology,
but she adds that it is this very same duo that is most responsible for schooling our early emotions — for creating a strong affective attachment to the
ideas, assumptions, and values of dominant ideology, but also for instruct-
ing us on *what* and *how* to feel. That is, the process of interpellation not only
tells us what *to think;* it also tells us what, when, and even whether *to feel.*
Because such pedagogical lessons are imposed on us from the outside (they
are "imposed" in that society disciplines and punishes those of us who are
not "socialized" well), they constitute a form of violence — hence her term
"pedagogical violence."

Of course, Worsham is using the term *pedagogy* in its broadest sense —
that is, pedagogy is not just the formal kind of teaching that occurs in a classroom; it is education in general. She identifies two principal forms of
pedagogical violence: the violence implicit in education itself, in which the
"legitimate" mode of conception and perception is imposed on, inculcated
in, individuals; and the violence implicit in the early childhood organization
of one's emotional life — the violent psychic separation from the mother that
forms the basis of individuation and subject formation, for example. It is the
former type of pedagogical violence, however, that is especially fruitful for
the creation of a more developed, richer form of ideological critique. Drawing on the work of Bourdieu and Passeron, she writes:

> *Pedagogy* refers to the power to impose meanings that maintain and
> reinforce the reigning social, economic, and political arrangements as
> legitimate when in fact they are entirely arbitrary. The dominant ped-
> agogy in a disciplinary society consists of the ruling ideas of the ruling
> class or group — or, the framework of meanings that most thoroughly,
> though most indirectly and inconspicuously, expresses and safeguards
> the material and symbolic interests of the dominant group or groups.
> (221)

This imposition, however, is not a simple matter of "forcing" someone to
think a certain way. The pedagogical system works to sway individuals to
cathect to the very ideas and structures that they are being taught, to inter-
nalize them not only intellectually but emotionally, thereby causing individuals to embrace the authoritative, dominant world view as their own and to

believe that adopting such a world view was a matter of their own "choice," their own free will.

Thus, for Worsham, pedagogy is more than the simple imposition of ideas on individuals:

> Its primary work is to organize an emotional world, to inculcate patterns of feeling that support the legitimacy of dominant interests, patterns that are especially appropriate to gender, race, and class locations. Pedagogy locates individuals objectively in a hierarchy of power relations; but also, and more importantly, it organizes their affective relations to that location, to their own condition of subordination, and to others in that hierarchical structure. Pedagogy binds each individual to the social world through a complex and often contradictory affective life that remains, for the most part, just beyond the horizon of semantic availability, and its success depends on a mystification or misrecognition of this primary work. (223)

One example of the organization of one's emotional world (and what Worsham calls the "principal work of the family") is the family's role in teaching children a proper affective relation to authority—instruction that not only teaches individuals to receive the "authoritative" pronouncements of dominant ideology docilely but that also helps create a structure of exploitation that "organizes the unequal exchange of emotion-work between men and woman" so that woman are required by society to dispense more nurturance and emotional support then they receive (225). One might say, then, that the very roots of sexism itself lie in ideology's efforts to interpellate us into our "proper" roles in society.

For Worsham, ideological critique—as well as the struggle for social change—must necessarily take place first on the level of emotion. If the kind of ideological critique proposed by Berlin, Goleman, Giroux, Ohmann, and the others is to be successful, and if we are really to have a chance to help students position themselves to participate productively in democratic processes, to struggle effectively for the right and ability to "represent," then we must engage in more than analysis of representations on the cognitive level, the level of intellection; we must, following Worsham, also begin to analyze (and help our students to analyze) our emotional investments in particular ideas, assumptions, theories, and worldviews. And, what's more, we must analyze how dominant ideology "teaches" us to feel certain ways (or not) in certain situations. The most effective ideological critique, then, combines cognitive and affective analysis.

A Final Word

Ohmann, Giroux, Macedo, Shor, and other early Freireans did much to expose how discursive, pedagogical, and institutional practices further social injustice; Berlin, Goleman, and other more recent scholars have interrogated how power, discourse, and ideology support systems of domination; and Worsham adds an important missing ingredient of effective ideological critique in her analysis of the role of emotion in the interpellative process. Berlin's, Goleman's, and Worsham's works are particularly useful because they suggest avenues of resistance through ideological critique, ways to change our pedagogical and institutional practices so as to better achieve the very goals we often espouse; and they illustrate intellectual work in composition at its finest.

This kind of work in critical pedagogy and ideological critique serves as a perfect example of why theoretical inquiry is so important to composition scholarship. Drawing on work from numerous disciplines, scholars such as those I've mentioned have been able to identify and articulate many of the problems arising from our institutional arrangements and pedagogical practices and to elaborate effective avenues of change. Such theoretical work has led to powerful new pedagogical practices and has the potential to reshape English studies itself. Far from being detached from the real-world exigencies of the classroom, far from being the preoccupation of a self-serving elite (as those who disparage theory have argued), the kind of critical pedagogical theory discussed here can revitalize composition theory and teaching at a time that we're in dire need of it—as the academy and even the teaching of composition come under attack by powerfully persuasive conservative critics, and as the university drifts ever more deeply into the control of corporate forces. Perhaps, in the end, ideological critique will be our only salvation.

Works Cited

Berlin, James A. "Rhetoric and Ideology in the Writing Class." *College English* 50 (1988): 477–94.
———. *Rhetorics, Poetics, and Cultures: Refiguring College English Studies.* Urbana: NCTE, 1996.

Chew, Kathleen. "Warning Against Harry Potter's Books and Pray Against Its Satanic Influences!" (25 July 2000). <http://www.antioch.com.sg/cgi-bin/HN_Open/get/prayer/364.html> (14 Feb. 2000).

Faigley, Lester. *Fragments of Rationality: Postmodernity and the Subject of Composition.* Pittsburgh: U of Pittsburgh P, 1992.

Freire, Paulo. *Pedagogy of the Oppressed.* 1970. Trans. Myra Bergman Ramos. New York: Continuum, 1986.

Goleman, Judith. *Working Theory: Critical Composition Studies for Students and Teachers.* Westport, CT: Bergin, 1995.

"Harry Potter Takes Drugs." (2000). <http://www.fflibraries.org/FFL_Index/w68_.htm>.

"Harry Potter Wins Round Against Canadian 'Muggles.'" (20 Sept. 2000). <Wysiwyg://5/http://www/cnn/com/2000...ews/09/20/life.bookban.potter.reut/> (14 Feb. 2000).

Kjos, Berit. "Bewitched by Harry Potter." (2000). <http://www.crossroad.to/text/articles/Harry9-99.html> (14 Feb. 2000).

McCuen, Barbara. "Should Schools Ban Harry Potter for Promoting Witchcraft?" (2000). SpeakOut.com. <http://www.speakout.com/issues/Briefs/1319/> (14 Feb. 2000).

Murray, John Andrew. "The Trouble with Harry." (2000). <http://www.family.org/pplace/schoolkid/a0009678.cfm> (14 Feb. 2000).

Ohmann, Richard. *English in America: A Radical View of the Profession.* 1976. Hanover: Wesleyan UP, 1996.

"Something about Harry." *USA Today* 7 July 2000: 14.A.

Worsham, Lynn. "Going Postal: Pedagogic Violence and the Schooling of Emotion." *JAC* 18 (1998): 213–45.

9

Working Against the State: Composition's Intellectual Work for Change

TOM FOX

W<span></span>E NO LONGER need to argue about whether rhetoric and composition is a discipline, although our status is still low. We sponsor journals, doctoral programs, conventions, and scholarship, as well as some newer departments and programs that are independent of literature departments. Still, rhetoric and composition is not like other disciplines; while much of its intellectual work resembles that of other academic disciplines, some of it does not. One of the most distinctive features of intellectual work in composition is a focus on the relationship of the discipline of composition to the academic institutions in which it is housed.

Composition's difficult history—well told by James Berlin, Sharon Crowley, Susan Miller, Charles Paine, and others—accounts for much of the strangeness of composition's work. We are a discipline that began as a remedial enterprise designed to repair the poor language of students and to compensate for the poor job that high school teachers were doing. We wear these elitist albatrosses everywhere we go because the majority of people outside of composition studies still believes that remediation justifies our existence. We both love and hate our first-year composition programs: we labor to redefine their purposes so that they are not remedial, and we still work within a first-year screening structure that is defined not by our wishes or practices but by our institutions as a site for "winnowing and indoctrination" (S. Miller 63).

Institutional Critique

Historical work in composition has argued that we need to understand academic institutions not as separate from the culture surrounding them—as their "ivory tower" image would suggest—but as intimate with that culture. Because most educational institutions typically reproduce social hierarchies, one of composition's achievements in the last decade has been the critique of the ways that the institution uses literacy instruction and assessment to reinscribe cultural hierarchies of race, gender, sexuality, and class (for recent examples, see Gilyard; Jarratt and Worsham; Malinowitz; and Sheppard, McMillan, and Tate). The embeddedness of our discipline within the overall purposes of the institution has been central to my day-to-day life as a professor of rhetoric and composition.

These critiques of the academy have made me more aware of the ways that we—professors and students—are defined by our institutions. When I assert that I am defined by the institutions, I mean that more than abstractly. As a writing program administrator, I know that my provost, the bureaucratic committee that governs general education, and my colleagues in the English department all have the expectation that first-year composition will repair the "broken" language of students so that they will either fail or will go on to use the language of their particular discipline. Last year, a colleague in a discussion group of upper-division writing bitterly complained to me that first-year composition passes students who "can't write a simple sentence." Others complain that our curriculum doesn't meet their needs in history, nursing, or biology. When I field these complaints, I enter into a set of ideas about literacy and education that I don't share. The depth of the conflict between my institution's definition of me and the view of composition that I share with my colleagues in the field is sometimes astonishing.

So in quite concrete terms, I seek—through the intellectual work of composition studies—to find ways both to function ethically and politically within institutions and to find ways to change them. The intellectual work that describes my experience tends to be versions of cultural studies. My struggle with identity could be defined as a conflict between Althusserian interpellation (the institution calls "Hey you there!" and "I" answer) and the assertions of agency and resistance that characterize cultural studies.

Marxists, following Louis Althusser, classify academic institutions as Ideological State Apparatuses, as part of a larger network of ideological and repressive institutions. But Marxists can be abstract. I find it nearly impossible to be abstract when speaking of "the state." I work for a more clearly defined "state": the state of California. What has surprised me—and disheartened me—is how easily the state of California can be substituted for the oppressive State of Marxist theory. (That's less of a case for the relevance of Marxist theory than a claim about the behavior of the state of California.) In quite direct ways, I am governed by two state agencies. In my role as coordinator of first-year composition, I am governed by the policies of the trustees of the California State University. In my role as director of the Northern California Writing Project, I am governed by the legislature and the California Board of Education. For me, "the state" has become quite concrete.

My own work in *Defending Access: A Critique of Standards in Higher Education* explores the difficulties of resisting undemocratic institutional demands and the difficulty of making substantive changes in policies and practices. In the example of the mainstreaming of basic writing, a move led by my colleague Judith Rodby, state definitions of both students and writing instruction motivated a significant program change (see Rodby). The narratives of change in *Defending Access,* punctuated by frequent administrative resistance, were motivated in part by my sense that few such narratives existed. A broad range of research supports this political and practical action. In this particular case, practical and theoretical work supported and enriched our efforts. For instance, David Bartholomae's "The Tidy House," which critiques basic writing for contributing to the institution's desire to erase difference, enriched our understanding of how basic writing segregates students (a point extended by Ira Shor's "Our Apartheid"). Peter Dow Adams's "Basic Writing Reconsidered," which tracks the success of test-identified "basic writers" in regular composition classes, gave us a study that showed the promise of our mainstreaming experiment.

These articles, and indeed the bulk of composition's scholarship on institutional work, focus on institutional critique rather than institutional change. A recent article by James Porter and his coauthors, "Institutional Critique: A Rhetorical Methodology for Change," sees critique as part of the action of change. The authors describe varieties of institutional critiques in our field, categorizing the work into three areas: administrative critiques, classroom critiques, and disciplinary critiques. While the authors view all of these efforts as useful, they stop short of the work of changing institutions. They argue for three strategies of critique: (1) examining institutional

structures from "a spatial, visual, and organizational perspective"; (2) looking for "gaps or fissures, places where resistance and change are possible";
and (3) undermining "the binary between theory and empirical research by
engaging in situated theorizing and relating that theorizing through stories
of change and attempted change" (630–31). This article usefully organizes
past research and calls for new research. But once we understand the critique, once we understand the various ways that the social order is repro-
duced, then what? Porter and his colleagues are right: composition has
written fewer narratives of change, especially those narratives that help us
understand institutional change.

The work of institutional critique, as we found out in practice, is difficult.
It is difficult to know where to compromise, where to hold the line, when to
shout, and when to nod quietly. Richard Miller, in his contribution to Diana
George's *Kitchen Cooks, Plate Twirlers, and Troubadours: Writing Program
Administrators Tell Their Stories,* announces with his title that "Critique's the
Easy Part." Miller argues that institutional *change* is never free or easy; it's
always embedded in circumstance, in what's possible in a given place and
time. He concludes, "One is, in effect, compelled by circumstance to inno-
vate, negotiate, collaborate" (9). Understanding the complexities, the com-
plications, and the situatedness of institutional change, to my mind, is among
the most important work being done in composition studies today. As Porter
and his coauthors write:

> Dramatic and far-reaching social and institutional change cannot
> occur through innovative classroom practices alone or through curric-
> ular or departmental adjustments or through unsituated theorizing.
> The classroom certainly is one significant site for change, but some
> changes need to happen in order to influence how the classroom is
> constituted. (632)

Working Against the State

The question that focuses my research these days, is how to work against the
State: how to work against state-defined policies and procedures that reduce
the complexity and liberatory potential of literacy, thereby excluding students of color and non-native speakers of English, and ignoring the needs of
gay, lesbian, and transgendered people. To illustrate the challenges of insti-

tutional change and to show the intellectual work required by institutional change, I will briefly discuss the following three challenges to democracy from the "State" (of California):

1. The state required a junior-level writing test. This test was a ninety-minute, one-shot essay exam meant to screen students from entering their upper-division writing-intensive course. In practice, the test failed non-native speakers of English and returning women.

2. The state rewrote legislation, asking the California Writing Project to shape its work toward state standards instead of focusing on issues of diversity.

3. The state created a series of initiatives designed both to retain basic writing as a category and to harass students within that category, culminating in Executive Order 665, which prevents students from enrolling in the California State University system if they do not complete "remediation" within one year.

The Real Thing: Changing the Policies of the Institution

In the case of the junior-level test, the egregious practice of the institution has to be directly faced and changed. There seemed to be no way around the test, so the only option was to eliminate it. This kind of institutional change, which permanently alters policies and practices is, obviously, the most difficult. In this case, the test, called the Writing Effectiveness Screen Test (WEST), was broadly supported by nearly everyone except the three or four of us who studied rhetoric and composition. It was popular with the administration, who saw holistic scoring as faculty development; it was popular with many instructors across campus because they believed that the test screened out unbearably terrible writers from their upper-division courses. The main complaint was that the test didn't fail enough students.

The story of the test's elimination is complicated—and the topic for another essay. The means of its elimination are important, though. It took nearly eight years of constant pressure from the composition faculty on the administration, the faculty senate, the testing office, and others. Victor Villanueva, following Antonio Gramsci, characterizes modern political change as a war of position, a rhetorical war. This was certainly the case here, for the war against the WEST was fought in conversations, memos, and proposals. Finally, it was as if everyone in the university had heard our

argument countless times. In the end, it felt less that we had successfully persuaded our opponents than that they had become more tired than we. They
acquiesced. This was a major policy change for the university. The means
were collaborative. Colleagues Judith Rodby, Thia Wolf, and I continually
pressured faculty and administration to abandon the test. We offered alternatives; we countered arguments; we proposed and proposed. In the end, the
test was eliminated without a replacement of any kind.

La Perruque

In his classic *The Practice of Everyday Life*, Michel de Certeau makes a distinction between tactical and strategic resistance that I have relied on to
understand ways that people resist institutions. It is the tactical strategies of
everyday life that interest de Certeau. His most memorable example is *la per-
ruque*, which is the practice of "stealing time." This kind of resistance is when
workers use the time and space of the institution for their own purposes—
for instance, reading a book for pleasure on the employer's time. This practice can be used any time that one's employer does not have sufficient means
for constant surveillance.

  I have directed a site of the California Writing Project for over ten years
now, and I consider it to be among the most rewarding activities of my professional life. I have appreciated both the National Writing Project's and California's emphasis on diversity and have found the writing project's structure
to be well suited for progressive political action. In the early 1990s, under the
leadership of Republican governor Pete Wilson, the California Board of Education began a political witch-hunt for proponents of "whole language" and
other progressive pedagogies. The California Writing Project was temporarily included in this reactionary move, and its funding was eliminated. After
a difficult but successful fight for restoration of funding, the legislation governing the project was changed. With remarkable consistency, every reference to diversity in the old legislation was eliminated. Replacing the old focus
on helping students of color (in a state where whites are now a statistical
minority) was the demand that the project focus on calibrating teachers to
the new state standards (written by the same board of education).

  If our project were to follow this legislation to a T, it would be politically
regressive. However, the surveillance system of the California Board of Education is far less efficient than Foucault's prison. Our summer institute is vis-

ited two times per year by members of our advisory board, some of whom resist the legislation as well. So, while the annual report reads somewhat differently from what it used to, the project's activities proceed as they used to — only now on time stolen from the legislature. This kind of "change" is easier than that in the previous example, but also riskier. Our funding could be eliminated, or I could be asked to step down as director for not addressing state standards enough in our activities. Still, this type of action is widespread in institutions.

Mixed Practice

The last example is probably the most common type of institutional change. We have mainstreamed our basic writing program because we believed that the program did not make sense in terms of literacy practices and that it was regressive politically. We believed that it inhibited entrance of students of color to the academy instead of facilitating it. Judith Rodby and I have written about the process of change elsewhere (Rodby; Fox; Rodby and Fox). Our new model, unfortunately, retains the distinction between those who pass and those who fail the professionally indefensible placement test, but it significantly reduces the punitive response to the failure. In other words, while students are still required to take the bogus test, and are still required to do "time" in adjunct workshops, their time is spent doing the work of first-year composition, not some preparatory or purgatorial sequence of basic writing courses. This is both real change (for we no longer offer those non-baccalaureate basic writing courses) and "stealing" from the institution. We continue to accept money from the institution earmarked for "remediation."

The most recent outrage from the trustees, the most recent challenge to our efforts to resist the gatekeeping structure of first-year composition, is Executive Order 665. This new policy is part of an overall effort on the part of the California State University system to reduce the need for remediation in English and math. In January of 1996, the trustees were appalled to learn that 40 percent of entering students needed remedial English (and a higher percentage needed remedial math). They were appalled despite the fact that this percentage has been fairly stable for the last twenty years, and despite the fact that the test that measures writing ability does not meet any of the criteria set out in the CCCC document on writing assessment (which they no doubt have never read). As Mike Rose has written many times, students will always come to college with varying levels of ability in various situations. That is both the nature of literacy and the nature of students. Yet, "remediation" has been discussed as if it were a temporary situation, despite the fact that we've been remediating for the last 150 years. Nevertheless, the trustees issued EO 665 to

> require campuses to ensure that students needing remediation receive it beginning with the first time of enrollment, establish and enforce limits on remedial activity, and advise students who are not making adequate progress in developing foundational skills to consider enrolling in other educational institutions.

For those of us who hope that writing instruction can assist in the democratization of higher education, this memo was a bitter disappointment. You can hear the excluding voice: "Why don't you consider enrolling in another educational institution?" This new policy has to be resisted by high-intensity teaching and careful tracking of students. If students fail our course twice and are excluded from our university, in as many cases as possible, we need to make sure that it is not because of our pedagogy or curriculum. Our way of resisting this executive order is to work hard to make sure that very few students are in the category to be excluded.

The Value of Institutional Work

Eliminating the test mentioned above was one of the most demanding and difficult things I have done in my career. It was much more difficult (and maybe more time consuming) than writing a book. It required scholarship in the nature of literacy, writing assessment, writing across the disciplines, and other areas of our field. More than many actions, it also directly improved the academic life of students who were hassled and harassed by the test. Politically, without a doubt, it was a helpful action. Aside from my own inner satisfaction, there is not much recognition for such work in the field. That may explain why institutional change is not often taken on by untenured professors, myself included. *or because of uncertainty?*

Since institutional change is not valued by official retention, tenure, and promotion processes (and no wonder, since the "official" and usual way of doing things is under critique), that leaves institutional change to be done by those who have succeeded in the institution and who are thus less likely to want to change it. The lack of support for institutional change maintains the status quo. I doubt whether many other disciplines have much scholarship on their own complicity in maintaining undemocratic institutions. This move toward self-criticism, which one could say animates much of our scholarship, is one of the reasons I value the scholarship in rhetoric and composition. As we continue to become more entrenched in universities and colleges, we need to continue to support this kind of intellectual and political work.

Works Cited

Adams, Peter Dow. "Basic Writing Reconsidered." *Journal of Basic Writing* 12 (1993): 22–36.

Althusser, Louis. *For Marx.* Trans. Ben Brewster. New York: Verso, 1996.

Bartholomae, David. "The Tidy House: Basic Writing in the American Curriculum." *Journal of Basic Writing* 12 (1993): 4–21.

Berlin, James A. *Writing Instruction in Nineteenth-Century American Colleges.* Carbondale: Southern Illinois UP, 1984.

Crowley, Sharon. *Composition in the University: Historical and Polemical Essays.* Pittsburgh: U of Pittsburgh P, 1998.

de Certeau, Michel. *The Practice of Everyday Life.* Trans. Steven F. Rendall. Berkeley: U of California P, 1984.

Foucault, Michel. *Discipline and Punish: The Birth of the Prison.* 1977. Trans. Alan Sheridan. New York: Vintage, 1979.

Fox, Tom. *Defending Access: A Critique of Standards in Higher Education.* Portsmouth, NH: Boynton/Cook, 1999.

Gilyard, Keith, ed. *Race, Rhetoric, and Composition.* Portsmouth, NH: Boynton/Cook, 1999.

Gramsci, Antonio. *Selections from the Prison Notebooks of Antonio Gramsci.* Ed. and Trans. Quintin Hoare and Geoffrey Nowell Smith. New York: International, 1971.

Jarratt, Susan C., and Lynn Worsham, eds. *Feminism and Composition Studies: In Other Words.* New York: MLA, 1998.

Malinowitz, Harriet. *Textual Orientations: Lesbian and Gay Students and the Making of Discourse Communities.* Portsmouth, NH: Boynton/Cook, 1995.

Miller, Richard. "Critique's the Easy Part." *Kitchen Cooks, Plate Twirlers, and Troubadours: Writing Program Administrators Tell Their Stories.* Ed. Diana George. Portsmouth, NH: Boynton/Cook, 1999. 3–13.

Miller, Susan. *Textual Carnivals: The Politics of Composition.* Carbondale: Southern Illinois UP, 1991.

Paine, Charles. *The Resistant Writer: Rhetoric as Immunity, 1850 to the Present.* Albany: State U of New York P, 1998.

Porter, James E., Patricia Sullivan, Stuart Blythe, Jeffrey T. Graybill, and Libby Miles. "Institutional Critique: A Rhetorical Methodology for Change." *College Composition and Communication* 51 (2000): 610–42.

Rodby, Judith. "What It's For and What It's Worth: Revisions to Basic Writing Revisited." *College Composition and Communication* 47 (1996): 107–11.

Rodby, Judith, and Tom Fox. "Basic Work and Material Acts: The Ironies, Discrepancies, and Disjunctures of Basic Writing and Mainstreaming." *Journal of Basic Writing* 19 (2000): 84–99.

Rose, Mike. *Lives on the Boundary: A Moving Account of the Struggles and Achievements of America's Educational Underclass.* New York: Penguin, 1989.

Shepard, Alan, John McMillan, and Gary Tate, eds. *Coming to Class: Pedagogy and the Social Class of Teachers.* Portsmouth, NH: Boynton/Cook, 1998.

Shor, Ira. "Our Apartheid: Writing Instruction and Inequality." *Journal of Basic Writing* 16 (1997): 91–104.

Villanueva, Victor Jr. *Bootstraps: From an American Academic of Color.* Urbana, IL, NCTE, 1993.

10

Coming to Terms: Theory, Writing, Politics

LYNN WORSHAM

> I come back to the deadly seriousness of intellectual work. It is a deadly serious matter. I come back to the critical distinction between intellectual work and academic work: they overlap, they abut with one another, they feed off one another, the one provides you with the means to do the other. But they are not the same thing.
>
> —Stuart Hall, "Cultural Studies and Its Theoretical Legacies"

> Really free working, e.g., composing, is at the same time precisely the most damned seriousness, the most intense exertion.
>
> —Karl Marx, *Grundrisse*

THE DISTINCTION between intellectual work and academic work is an important one for understanding the recent history of composition studies and for steering its course in the future. Simply stated, the distinction is this: academic work is inherently conservative inasmuch as it seeks, first, to fulfill the relatively narrow and policed goals and interests of a given discipline or profession and, second, to fulfill the increasingly corporatized mission of higher education; intellectual work, in contrast, is relentlessly critical, self-critical, and potentially revolutionary, for it aims to critique, change, and even destroy institutions, disciplines, and professions that rationalize exploitation, inequality, and injustice. Both academic work and intellectual work are political, though differently so. Certainly, academic work can become intellectual in the strong sense I have given it here, while intellectual work can lose its political vision and become merely academic.[1]

Jim Merod comes very close to making precisely this distinction when he writes that literary studies is

> a grossly academic enterprise that has no real vision of its relationship to and responsibilities within the corporate structure of North American (for that matter, international) life. It is simply a way of doing business with texts. It is in fact a series of ways, a multiplicity of methods that vie for attention and prestige within the semipublic, semiprivate professional critical domain. (9)

The same should be said of composition studies today. For the last thirty years, composition studies has labored tirelessly to claim a place in the university as a legitimate academic discipline. We have been focused, in other words, on defining and legitimizing our work, on professionalizing ourselves in the context of university culture and conventions. With single-minded purpose, we have sought to stand alongside literary studies, as one scholarly profession among others, with our own ways of doing business with texts, with our own expertise. We have marked success in the usual ways: by the proliferation of graduate programs; the increase in the number of tenure-earning faculty positions held by composition "specialists"; the creation of a modest number of distinguished chairs for our own coterie of academic "stars"; and the increase in the number of scholarly journals and book series devoted to writing. Most significantly, perhaps, we have succeeded in wresting control of the administration of an increasing number of undergraduate writing programs, our authority secured by a professional organization whose purpose is to formulate policy for the accreditation and the efficient administration of such programs.

In short, composition, like literary studies, has become an institution, one that is more rather than less closed off from the larger social world in which it is situated by its own insular and professional disputes—the most consequential being the ongoing battle over the nature of "our" work. This dispute—often abbreviated as the "theory-practice split"—involves those who maintain that the field's proper work must remain strictly limited to the teaching of writing and the research required for that project, and those who insist that the scope of composition includes anything that bears on literacy, broadly conceived, and the workings of written discourse. A kind of dramaturgy ensues in which each charges the other with retarding the "progress" of the field—on the one side, by failing to answer the field's governing pedagogical imperative and its obligation to undergraduate (especially first-year) students; on the other, by remaining blind to the forms of instrumental rationality shaping the field and by failing to meet the minimal obligations of "scholarly" work in the humanities. The fact remains, however, that this dispute is entirely academic: no matter which side prevails (however momentarily or finally), the technical and professional authority of composition has already been established and, in my view, is not now in jeopardy. Furthermore, I suggest that if we persist in allowing the "theory-practice split" to govern the social relations of the field—and ultimately the way we articulate our role in the university and its relation to society—then we do so because we prefer to misperceive the nature of the task at hand: we must make the academic work of composition studies more vigorously, more resolutely intellectual.

The sine qua non of intellectual work is theory; thus, the primary way to make the work of composition more seriously intellectual is to make it more seriously theoretical. The way to do this, however, is not to engage in "theoreticism," which is a pursuit of theory over against practice or a pursuit of theory for theory's sake, as if it were an end (or a good) in itself (see Giroux 67). What we must do, instead, is to understand, and to make explicit, the profoundly rhetorical (and political) nature of theory. To be sure, theory can be written and read in any number of ways, but, in my view, it should be engaged as a rhetorical (and political) event that emerges out of and responds to the world, to social and political situations that are available to understanding through interpretation. As John Donatich says of intellectual work in general, theory claims the right "to worry the world and to believe that there is a symbiotic relationship between the private world of the thinker and the public world he or she wishes to address" (qtd. in "Future" 26). What Kenneth Burke says about literature could also be said of theory: theoretical texts are strategies for coping with concrete, material situations; they are equipment for living, for naming and changing, as Merod puts it, "the tangible conditions of the real world's unsatisfactory options" (3). Coming to terms with the real world, theory bridges the chasm between the actual and the possible; it provides an articulation between bitter truth and a vision of what might be.

The passion that drives the work of theory is a passion for questions, for a questioning attitude, rather than the "bottom line" comfort of easy answers and hasty conclusions. Theory is driven by a desire to entertain many hypotheses, a desire for alternate points of view, other stories. It is also driven by a respect for difficulty and complexity, not because difficulty and complexity are to be valued in and of themselves but because the real world from which theory arises and to which it speaks is itself complex—an almost incomprehensible network of discourses, practices, and forces. Most important, theory is driven by a passionate political consciousness that, in seeking to come to terms with the real world, seeks the conceptual tools, the explanatory frameworks, to engineer social change. In Merod's words, "Intellectual passion is not a style. It is a form of warfare (in Nietzsche's sense), free of gloom, that converts aggression to self-conscious energy" (3). It is a deadly serious matter.

In composition studies, the form that this kind of work takes is writing—both the writing that scholars in composition studies must do and the writing that we must teach. Writing certainly can be merely a school subject and a means to acquire tenure, promotion, and professional recognition. Indeed, it has been the exemplary school subject through which individuals are most effectively disciplined and normalized and through which the educational apparatus sorts individuals according to the "capacities" that that very apparatus has deemed "measurable," "useful," and therefore "valuable" (see Foucault; Watkins). As such, writing is an academic enterprise—and composition studies is a service profession—that seeks to meet the needs of the university and corporate capitalism for minimally literate and maximally docile and useful subjects. Understood in the broadest sense possible, however, writing can become the never-ending work of making "really free" places, lives, and identities.[2]

The most consequential aspect of the work of writing—of this utopian struggle to make "really free" places, lives, and identities—involves an understanding of the way that ideology works most efficiently and effectively through emotion to bind us to particular ways of life and to place us in the world in ways that make the workings of ideology virtually invisible to us. To loosen the ties that bind us—to undo this ideological work and intervene in the process of subjectification—writing must expose the ways that ideology works on and through emotion and in so doing create the kind of critical distance that, as a consequence, may serve to reposition us affectively and in ways that make political action possible. As Gilles Deleuze says, "The point of critique is not justification but a different way of feeling, another sensibility" (94). In other words, the purpose of the intellectual work of writing is not to justify what we already believe or to rationalize a framework of meaning; the point is to alter the affective relations that position us in a world that wants us to go quietly, silently into the good night that ideology has already prepared for us.

Emotion and the Pathos of Subordination

In the view I develop here, *emotion* refers to the tight braid of affect and judgment that is socially and historically constructed and bodily lived. This view opposes the Western philosophical tradition that regards emotion as reason's other, consigns it to the private sphere, genders it "feminine," racializes it "dark," and tolerates it only as part of the body's contrary magic. It also opposes the contemporary rehabilitation of rhetoric, which has focused much attention on logos in an attempt to show that reason is rhetorical and that knowledge is politically interested, while it has ignored pathos, or emotion and emotional appeal, altogether—a fact that should cause us to question the rationalist tradition that appears to shape contemporary rhetorical studies. Likewise, it opposes writing theory and pedagogy that address the topic of emotion simplistically by yoking it to an expressivist theory of the subject and an unreconstructed notion of "the personal."

More than a decade ago, Sandra Bartky called for a political phenomenology of emotion, an examination of the role that emotion plays "in the constitution of subjectivity and in the perpetuation of subjection" (98). She effectively identified emotion as a key political category; in my view, it is perhaps *the* key political and rhetorical category. Stated differently, ideologies of gender, race, class, and sexuality are properly understood, at least in large part, as ideologies of emotion; they provide the conditions in which a primary affective mapping of the individual psyche occurs, one that sets the stage for all subsequent socialization. Misogyny, for example, is not, first of all, a cognitive condition of individuals amenable to correction through an alteration in the content of thought or thought patterns. It is primarily a state-sanctioned disorder of affect, a learned disposition of fear and hatred that is the foundation of a pervasive affective attunement to the world. Likewise, racism is not only the result of "incorrect" thinking that can be remedied through, say, multicultural education; rather, racism is first and foremost a profound fear and loathing of the racialized other. It is an affective relation between self and other that runs much deeper than a cognitive understanding, and it signifies the absence of the kind of reciprocity that originates in empathy as a disposition (both affective and ethical) to "feel along with" and "live alongside" the other. Through a focus on emotion, we can begin to see that the strongest and subtlest appeal of any given ideology is through emotion, that ideology works most effectively through emotion to interpellate us as particular kinds of subjects who ideally are not disposed—that is to say, who ideally do have the affective disposition—to question or to sustain resistance to the structures of subordination through which we are constituted as subjects.[3] As Jessica Benjamin succinctly puts it, we must seek to understand "how domination is anchored in the hearts of the dominated" (5).

What I am suggesting, then, is that the primary work of ideology is more fundamental than the imposition of a dominant framework of meanings. Its primary work is to organize an emotional world, to inculcate patterns of feeling that support the legitimacy of dominant interests, patterns that are deemed especially appropriate to reigning gender, race, and class relations. Ideology locates individuals objectively in a hierarchy of power relations; but also, and more importantly, it organizes their affective relations to those locations, to their own condition of subordination, and to others in that hierarchical structure. Ideology binds each individual to the social world through a complex and often contradictory affective life that too often remains, for the most part, just beyond the horizon of semantic availability, and its success depends on a mystification or misrecognition of this primary work. In particular, dominant ideology provides a limited vocabulary of emotion and thereby seeks to ensure an inability to adequately apprehend, name, and interpret the social dimension of our affective lives. Ideology works to mystify emotion as purely a personal and private matter; it actively conceals the fact that emotions are prevailing forms of social life, that so-called personal life always takes shape in social and cultural terms.[4]

The way in which ideology organizes emotion may be understood in terms of Ann Ferguson's notion of systems of sex/affective production. Ferguson argues that historically there are diverse ways to organize, structure, and reproduce what she calls sex/affective energy (or emotion) as a social energy that is bodily lived (77–99). The main task of any society is to create the social desire to cooperate and unite with others and to organize this social energy by identifying the appropriate objects, aims, and persons for emotional attachments and by prohibiting others as legitimate loci of interest. The overall task of the dominant ideology of a given society is to coordinate and maintain a system of sex/affective production with a regime of meaning and with an economic system of production. Ideology provides a complex system for the production of "goods"—that is, forms of recognized and legitimate affect, meaning, and value. Furthermore, legitimate and illegitimate (or appropriate and inappropriate) objects of affective attachment are structurally or systemically related, and, in prohibiting particular objects or persons as legitimate attachments, a society automatically invests them with great value and interest—if only for their disciplinary value in reproducing or policing authorized distinctions.

The United States is a highly stratified, deeply bureaucratized, capitalist social and economic order in which white supremacy, patriarchy, and heteronormativity operate in what is in effect a war of the very few against the vast majority. As such, it is a system for producing and reproducing in individuals an array of so-called negative emotions and affective states, ranging, for example, from envy, embarrassment, apathy, and sorrow to shame, anger, rage, hatred, and bitterness. These may be passing or transient emotional responses, or they may be pervasive affective conditions that regulate every aspect of a person's life. While these emotions may be socially produced, the smooth and efficient functioning of the social order is ensured only if these emotions are depoliticized. This important work is accomplished, in large part, through therapeutic culture, which in the last thirty-five years has triumphed by installing itself at the center of the sex/affective production system of advanced capitalism. Together with popular cultural forms, therapeutic culture works to mystify emotions by making them purely a matter of personal psychology and private psychopathology. Therapeutic culture celebrates a self, as Jean Bethke Elshtain suggests, that "views the world solely through the prism of the self. . . . It's a quivering sentimental self that gets uncomfortable very quickly, because this self has to feel good about itself all the time" (qtd. in "Future" 28). Rather than claiming the right to worry the world, this self worries about itself, focusing entirely (and narcissistically) on self-validation, especially the validation of its personal experience and unique "feelings."[5] As Peter Lyman points out about the field of psychology, therapeutic culture serves the interests of capitalist patriarchal and racist hegemony "when it strips human experience of its collective and active character" (59). It effectively conceals structures of subordination and oppression by transforming the political into the personal and ultimately by treating the symptom rather than clarifying the cause of human suffering. A political phenomenology of emotion, in contrast, understands emotion as a dialectic of "self" and "world" and seeks to return emotion to the field of political theory and political action.

Anger, for example, is a response to a sense of violation, to a sense of unjustified violation of the self and of what the self cares for. While anger is always a response to a sense of violation, not every instance of anger is political. Still, I want to pursue the possibility that more often than not anger does have a hidden political dimension and thus must be understood as a clue to suppressed social relations. Anger clearly becomes political when it is the emotional response we feel in being dominated, whether momentarily by the isolated derogatory remark or injurious act or more pervasively and continually through systems of subordination. In this context, anger is a protest against violation; it is a demand for justice. Feminist anger is a paradigmatic case: it questions the "rationality" of the patriarchal social order and sees "reason," as Lyman suggests, purely as a "*rhetorical* claim by the dominant about their legitimacy" (67). In an effort to characterize the social and political origin of anger, Nietzsche defines anger as the "pathos of subordination" (see Lyman 62). In a society in which many suffer, on a daily basis, the indignities of poverty, sexism, racism, and heterosexism, there are likely to be many angry people who feel a pervasive and daily sense of violation. Yet, we do not often hear a collective expression of their anger, for it is continually channeled, through the work of ideology, into a self-destructive adaptation to subordination expressed as an internalization of anger—that is, rage. Nietzsche calls this condition of repressed anger *ressentiment*—an impotent, often unconscious rage—which he contends is the dominant political emotion of modernity.[6] Lyman suggests that *ressentiment,* properly understood, is a political neurosis that "creates a dramaturgy of revenge out of the everyday world, but this revenge is acted out unconsciously as a latent motivation hiding beneath seemingly ordinary speech and action" (63).

Shame should also be considered in any discussion of the pathos of subordination. Indeed, shame and anger together may form the heart of *ressentiment.* Psychologists and sociologists increasingly identify shame as the "master emotion" in this culture, or, as Robert Karen puts it, "the unseen regulator of our entire affective life" (40). Bartky defines shame as "the distressed apprehension of the self as inadequate or diminished" (86). It is the recognition that, as Karen suggests, "one is at core a deformed being, fundamentally unlovable and unworthy of membership in the human community. It is the self regarding the self with the withering and unforgiving eye of contempt" (43). In his study of the relationship between shame and extreme acts of sadistic violence, James Gilligan explains that violence can only be understood as the consequence of shame, which, he says, is tantamount to "soul-murder." Like anger, shame is social and intersubjective, a dialectic of self and world: "It requires if not an actual audience before whom my deficiencies are paraded, then an internalized audience with the capacity to judge me, hence internalized standards of judgment" (Bartky 86). As Foucault has pointed out in his study of a highly stratified, deeply bureaucratized disciplinary society, shame is an especially effective instrument for keeping people in place, for transforming a social relation into a psychological symptom. Yet, repressed shame and anger will find expression in revenge — whether it be in minor, seemingly insignificant acts or in heinous crimes such as mass murder and genocide.[7]

Bitterness, too, may be understood as a dialectic of self and world. According to Lynne McFall, bitterness expresses and bears witness to the disappointment of a person's important and legitimate hopes. The world, as it were, has given us reason to hope, to expect a certain outcome, and we are bitter when legitimate hope is disappointed. Bitterness may express itself as sorrow and anguish or intense animosity. Bitterness may be active or passive; it may be object-directed or become a pervasive affective attunement to the world, a state that characterizes the entire person. In whatever form it takes, bitterness is an emotion that is routinely silenced. Yet, as McFall reminds us, this is a society that ensures that many are poor and even homeless, that even more are members of despised minorities, and that more than half the population are members of a despised majority (that is, women). In short, it thereby ensures the existence of a number of justifiably bitter people whose *legitimate* expectation of fair, equitable, and humane treatment is routinely disappointed (153). But we won't hear bitter words as *political* speech; we typically condemn bitter speech as the complaint of those who are unwilling to forgive and forget and move on. Still, bitterness is, as McFall argues, "a necessary reminder that something hoped for and greatly valued has been lost." Thus, if given its political voice, bitterness becomes "a form of moral accounting, of naming the losses," of bearing witness and telling the truth about social injustices (156).

While not every experience of anger, shame, or bitterness can be traced to structures of subordination, these emotions often do have a political dimension and thus must be understood as potential clues to suppressed social relations. Anger, shame, and bitterness express a sense of loss: violation as a kind of loss and the loss of trust that accompanies violation; loss of a sense of self-worth; loss of a legitimate hope; loss of legitimate and beloved standing in the world (see Jordan). Structures of subordination — such as sexism, racism, classism, and heterosexism—produce, in generation after generation, a profound and determining experience of loss that is often unconscious and unnamed and misrecognized. This loss must be acknowledged and mourned; however, without the language to adequately name and understand the social and political dimension of our affective lives, this loss cannot be mourned. Frustrated or inadequate mourning becomes melancholia and, like *ressentiment,* expresses itself psychically as revenge against the self. Thus, instead of political action, what we too often see is a kind of political depression that, without a proper language to give it expression, can only be relieved (however inadequately) through the magic that mutes political protest by transforming it into a psychological symptom. How else are we to explain the silence of the vast majority of the world's peoples who live in conditions of impoverishment, subordination, and exploitation?

In an economy of scarcity such as the one we find in the United States, where the top one percentage of the population *reasonably* expects to get more obscenely wealthy in the coming years at the expense of others, we must find the political will to tap what must be a vast resource of private sorrow that can be repoliticized and used to make significant social change.[8] As many feminist theorists have argued, emotion is an important resource for political resistance and social change. In fact, it may be the indispensable element of social movement. This view opposes that of traditional political theorists who have argued that social change comes about either through a drive to fulfill self-interest or, in the model of John Rawls or Jürgen Habermas, through rational deliberation. That is, both of these competing models assume that political change is driven in one way or another by rational means. In contrast to these interpretations of how politics works, feminists and political philosophers such as Chantal Mouffe stress that much more central to political change is the role of what Mouffe terms "passion." She claims that passion is what moves people to act in politics: "It's not that reason and interests have no place, but I think that these are not the main motives for people to act. It's what I call 'passion.' Outrage, anger, empathy, sympathy, and those kinds of emotions are part of the same family in criticizing the rationalist model" (Worsham and Olson 197). Maintaining that reason and self-interest are not the basis for collective identification, Mouffe asks the key question, "What makes people crystallize into a 'we,' a 'we' that is going to act politically?" (197).

Writing and the Pathos of Theory

In the women's liberation movement of the late 1960s and early 1970s, consciousness raising was the key strategy for giving political voice to private sorrow. "Speak pains to recall pains" is a Chinese proverb that guided the feminist technique of consciousness raising and the effort to build the kind of solidarity that is necessary for making social change (see Morgan xxvi). During this time, feminist theory and feminist writing in general arose out of concrete social and political situations, out of the human feeling that comprises much of the content of the experience of subordination (Morgan xx). Although the successful institutionalization of feminism in the American academy makes it possible for feminist writing today to be both merely academic and profoundly arhetorical—that is, when it is produced and read with no understanding of the social and political context from which it arises and to which it speaks—feminist theory nonetheless offers a glimpse of intellectual work at its best.

What feminist theory has shown us is that it is possible to oppose the pathos of subordination and oppression through the pathos of theory. That is to say, theory that arises from and addresses concrete social and political situations has the power to illuminate the political dimension of human suffering. Feminist theory has sought to articulate a language for understanding the political dimension of emotion and thereby transform private sorrows into, as Clifford Geertz says, "a public possession, a social fact, rather than a set of disconnected, unrealized private emotions" (232). Feminist theory has sought to make mourning possible at the social level by creating a public language for grief and rage, a language that converts the aggression that too often is acted out at a personal level through melancholia and *ressentiment* into a self-conscious (self-conscious because self-critical) energy that works on changing the world. Although theory alone does not bring about social change, feminist efforts to come to terms with the real world, to remember and to tell of unacceptable losses, are driven by an understanding that grief and rage are, as McFall reminds us, our highest ethical imperatives (158).

My own engagement with feminist theory—and feminist writing more generally—has illuminated the connections between emotions and ideology and academic work and intellectual work. These connections suggest several important implications for the field of composition studies. If composition studies is going to be more than an academic enterprise, a purely service profession, then we must revalue the intellectual content of our work. If we are truly committed to rhetoric and composition as intellectual work, then we must engage writing on its very material and political levels. In particular, we must begin to reconceive the workings of ideology so that it is no longer cast as an imposition of ruling class ideas or assumptions. We must detail the ways that ideology makes its appeal through emotion to bind us to particular ways of life that make the affective (and effective) work of ideology almost invisible to us. And if we truly value work directed toward effecting social and political change, then it is incumbent on us as intellectuals to continue the "deadly serious" work of making "really free" places, lives, and identities. This work of composition, as Marx suggested, requires the most intense exertion.

Notes

1. I realize, of course, that I'm being somewhat polemical here by making what some have termed the "critical intellectual" the paradigm for all intellectual work. However, in this short essay, I want to focus on the difference between academic work and intellectual work rather than digressing into a discussion of different types of intellectuals.

2. I place "really free" in quotation marks to suggest that this is only a way of speaking and thereby to indirectly qualify the nature of the claim that I am making. I do not believe that the making of "really free" places, lives, and identities is ever fully achieved or accomplished, though it remains the utopian goal of intellectual work as I define it here.

3. Since no one escapes the workings of ideology, I use the universal "we" here and elsewhere in this essay even though such usage has been criticized as leading to an erasure of difference. Although individuals are constituted as subjects quite differently according to the specific ideologies of, say, gender, race, class, and sexuality that are in play in a given culture, at some level the general process of subject formation is much the same. See Althusser for a discussion of the process of subject formation that informs this essay.

4. For more on the social and political dimension of emotion, see Bartky, *Femininity* 83–98; Ferguson; Foucault 194; Lyman; Rosaldo; and Sennett and Cobb.

5. Elshtain makes another point germane to this discussion. She links the triumph of therapeutic culture and the narcissistic subject to the demise of the public intellectual and the public sphere. Her discussion suggests to me that we might question the simultaneous emergence of a renewed anxiety over the role of intellectuals in society at the same time that we also see a trend in academic writing that focuses on "the personal" in uncritical ways. I would add that a similar phenomenon is manifest in composition studies, where there is a trend away from social constructionist theory and back toward expressivism and a preoccupation with "authentic voice" and "personal experience." In

other words, the narcissistic subject that is constituted and supported by therapeutic culture may have found a way to convert true intellectual work into a form of academic writing that simply seeks self-validation through an obsession with "the personal" rather than seeking to worry the world and ultimately to change it.

6. See especially the first essay, "'Good and Evil,' and 'Good and Bad,'" in Nietzsche's *Genealogy*.

7. In "Going Postal," I argue that emotion is the key to both relatively minor acts of symbolic violence and to mass murder and genocide. See also Scheff and Retzinger.

8. Butler suggests that many political movements are "fueled by the sense of a loss that has already taken place or that is expected to take place," and she links mourning and melancholia to political action (Olson and Worsham, "Changing" 750). She also suggests that the recent surge of anti-intellectualism in the academy might be explained by the fact that in the humanities, people have lost a sense of their value to and influence in society. She implicitly identifies anti-intellectualism among some academics as a kind of *ressentiment* that they turn on their colleagues (733–34). Her remarks are illuminating for their relevance to the dramaturgy that takes place in composition studies between different factions in the "theory-practice split."

Works Cited

Althusser, Louis. "Ideology and Ideological State Apparatus (Notes towards an Investigation)." *Lenin and Philosophy*. By Louis Althusser. Trans. Ben Brewster. New York: Monthly Review, 1971. 127–86.

Bartky, Sandra Lee. *Femininity and Domination: Studies in the Phenomenology of Oppression*. London: Routledge, 1990.

Benjamin, Jessica. *The Bonds of Love: Psychoanalysis, Feminism, and the Problem of Domination*. New York: Pantheon, 1988.

Deleuze, Gilles. *Nietzsche and Philosophy*. Trans. Hugh Tomlinson. New York: Columbia UP, 1983.

Ferguson, Ann. *Blood at the Root: Motherhood, Sexuality, and Male Dominance*. London: Pandora, 1989.

Foucault, Michel. *Discipline and Punish: The Birth of the Prison*. Trans. Alan Sheridan. New York: Vintage, 1979.

"The Future of the Public Intellectual: A Forum." *Nation* (12 Feb. 2001): 25–35.

Geertz, Clifford. *The Interpretation of Cultures*. New York: Basic, 1973.

Gilligan, James. *Violence: Our Deadly Epidemic and Its Causes*. New York: Putnam, 1996.

Giroux, Henry A. *Impure Acts: The Practical Politics of Cultural Studies*. New York: Routledge, 2000.

Jordan, June. "Where Is the Sisterhood?" *Progressive* 60.6 (1996): 20–21.

Karen, Robert. "Shame." *Atlantic Monthly* Feb. 1992: 40–70.

Lyman, Peter. "The Politics of Anger: On Silence, Ressentiment, and Political Speech." *Socialist Review* (May-June 1981): 55–74.

McFall, Lynne. "What's Wrong with Bitterness?" *Feminist Ethics*. Ed. Claudia Card. Lawrence: UP of Kansas, 1991. 146–60.

Merod, Jim. *The Political Responsibility of the Critic*. Ithaca: Cornell UP, 1987.

Morgan, Robin, ed. *Sisterhood Is Powerful: An Anthology of Writings from the Women's Liberation Movement.* New York: Vintage, 1970.

Nietzsche, Friedrich. *The Birth of Tragedy and the Genealogy of Morals.* Trans. Francis Golffing. New York: Doubleday, 1956.

Olson, Gary A., and Lynn Worsham. "Changing the Subject: Judith Butler's Politics of Radical Resignification." *JAC* 20 (2000): 727–65.

———. "Staging the Politics of Difference: Homi Bhabha's Critical Literacy. *Race, Rhetoric, and the Postcolonial.* Ed. Gary A. Olson and Lynn Worsham. Albany: State U of New York P, 1999. 3–39.

Rosaldo, Michelle. "Toward an Anthropology of Self and Feeling." *Culture Theory: Essays on Mind, Self, and Emotion.* Ed. Richard A. Shweder and Robert A. LeVine. Cambridge, Eng.: Cambridge UP, 1984. 137–57.

Scheff, Thomas J., and Suzanne M. Retzinger. *Emotions and Violence: Shame and Rage in Destructive Conflicts.* Lexington, MA: Lexington, 1991.

Sennett, Richard, and Jonathan Cobb. *The Hidden Injuries of Class.* New York: Vintage, 1972.

Watkins, Evan. *Work Time: English Departments and the Circulation of Cultural Value.* Stanford: Stanford UP, 1989.

Worsham, Lynn. "Going Postal: Pedagogic Violence and the Schooling of Emotion." *JAC: A Journal of Composition Theory* 18 (1998): 213–45.

Worsham, Lynn, and Gary A. Olson. "Rethinking Political Community: Chantal Mouffe's Liberal Socialism." *Race, Rhetoric, and the Postcolonial.* Ed. Gary A. Olson and Lynn Worsham. Albany: State U of New York P, 1999. 165–201.

11

Holdin It Down: Students' Right and the Struggle over Language Diversity

KEITH GILYARD

M Y ORIGINAL INTENTION for my contribution to this important volume was to write a laid-back essay cataloging recent efforts to imple-
ment the controversial resolution "Students' Right to Their Own Language,"
which was adopted at the 1974 CCCC convention in Anaheim.[1] The field of
composition has never developed a consensus on how such a "right" could
be ensured in colleges and universities, and the field's response has been
enigmatic at best relative to the key claim of the document that to rule particular language varieties unacceptable amounts to the exertion of social
dominance by the powers that be over marginalized groups. Despite the
checkered history of the "students' right" era, however, the resolution itself
suggests possibilities for critical pedagogy, especially around issues of language and hegemony, that should not be dismissed. Thus, it is always in order
to check in on those working in the spirit of this groundbreaking statement,
those "holdin it down," which really means lifting up their practice to secure
gains in thinking about teaching and linguistic diversity. Of course, I would
not be able to mention everyone, just a cadre of scholars whose recent work
I happen to know. My preference, also, was for things to remain relatively
static until I finished my review of the intellectual work in this area. But I
should have known better. New battles, some unanticipated, continually arise
on the ideological terrain surrounding "students' right." I find myself, therefore, absorbed in responding in an edgy way to new attacks on Ebonics
(given that this language variety and its speakers have been the primary
metaphor for language activism connected to the CCCC resolution) and in
considering the argument and reception of Stephen Parks's new book *Class*

Politics: The Movement for the Students' Right to Their Own Language. These are now my entry points, although I will still wind up by identifying a community of practitioners and theorists, of whom Parks himself is one, who are pushing forward in productive ways.

The Struggle over Language Rights

In the June 2000 issue of *Middle American News,* Nicholas Stix, a steadfast opponent of language rights for African Americans and an instructor at Baruch College, opened his article "The Language of Hate" by asking, "Which language do you speak—Ebonics or the Language of Wider Communication? Of which nation are you a citizen—Amerika or Afrika?" He follows by stating that "prior to 1997, most Americans would have been baffled by my opening." Some of us still are. Why would most Americans be asked these questions? Ebonics is not the native language variety of the nation's majority, nor would most Americans expect to be questioned about their national citizenship. Besides, when did Africa, however one spells it, become a nation? The best thing about Stix's sloppy lead is that it accurately indicates the quality of his entire piece. He rants that every word of the Oakland School Board's original proposal was a lie and asserts that Ebonics is a story of racist hatred, scholarly fraud, and cowardice. He then posits that support for Ebonics results directly from the influence of the Nation of Islam's founder, Wallace Fard, whose Black nationalist rhetoric, Stix surmises, spurred the Black Power movement, which white professors like J. L. Dillard, author of *Black English,* chose to serve with "psuedo-linguistics." This is the historical stage for the so-called Ebonics hoax that is now supposedly being "perpetrated by a tiny number of well-to-do, influential, mostly black university professors and racist public school teachers and administrators."

Next, Stix unveils shopworn, simplistic, and misinformed criticisms of the Linguistic Society of America's 1997 "Resolution on Ebonics."[2] Here is his own original contribution: "Can one then do physics and philosophy in Ebonics? Please." It is a peculiar verbal barb, given the fact that one can indeed do physics and philosophy in Ebonics or any other language variety. *No one* seriously argues this point. But as evident by now, Stix isn't much about logic. He goes on to misrepresent the overall work of John Rickford, whom he considers the most influential linguistics professor in support of Ebonics, and insists that there is no research that connects African American English to Africa. After dismissing all language scholars with whom he dis-

Isn't this the same name calling?

agrees, including Wayne O'Neil, Lisa Delpit, and myself, he turns for the ultimately authoritative pronouncements to his undergraduate students, none
of whom would ever have to take courses to become linguists because they
already know more than all the leaders in the field. After all, he has a Black
student at Baruch College named Karen Thompson who has declared that
"there is no Ebonics! It's bad English!" Stix saves his most sinister remarks
for last as he argues that "Ebonics hustlers" are exploiting Black ghetto youth
for their own material gain and will be responsible to a degree for whatever
murder and mayhem occurs in such inner-city neighborhoods.

Kix is for kids ☺

    In the final analysis, intellectually speaking, Stix is for kids. Very little
investigation will reveal that one should not ponder for too long the idea of
a strong connection between the Black Muslims and J. L. Dillard and that the
Black Powerists can hardly be reduced to a single political, economic, or
social bloc that endorsed separatism as a total solution. Similarly, the idea
that Dillard practiced "pseudo-linguistics" can be quickly dispelled. Obviously, the creole hypothesis, the one supported by Dillard, is not the only way
to explain the existence of African American English; dialect geographers
and the like do exist. But the creole hypothesis as an overall conception is
considered quite a powerful explanation in professional language circles. It
certainly is not considered "pseudo," as the action of the Linguistic Society of
America indicates. What one hopes is that any student who has Stix as an
instructor poses to him the question of who the racists and haters really are.
Are they the educators who consult respectable scholarship about Black dis-
tinctiveness (which in and of itself is never the cause of failure in school) in
order to address educational crises among Black students, or the critics who
spout "sillygisms" designed to conceal their motive of maintaining a Euro-
centric stronghold on educational and cultural politics?   ———
    As Theresa Perry points out, what is obscured by folks "who be trippin'
like Stix" is that the Oakland School Board was motivated largely by the
above-average performance of African American students at Prescott Elementary School, the only school in the Oakland school district where the
majority of teachers had opted to participate in a standard English profi-
ciency program of the type the board was proposing districtwide. Also
obscured is how the standardized language variety often produces humili-
ated consciousness in African American students, limits their possibilities for
self-expression, and has been a vehicle to accomplish far more murder and
mayhem than any contemporary linguist could manage. Echoing the "Students' Right" resolution, bell hooks notes that "it is difficult not to hear in

standard English the sound of slaughter and conquest" (169). She further observes that African American Vernacular English creates room for "alternate cultural production and alternative epistemologies" and thus is an indispensable tool in helping the marginalized to challenge domination and to recover themselves through language (171–75). I hear several criticisms of bell hooks, but none that suggest that she's to blame for violence in the 'hood. Stix, self-anointed white protector of Black students, had already flipped over his hole card in an earlier article, a review (appearing in the April 2000 issue of *Ideas on Liberty*) of Sandra Stotsky's *Losing Our Language: How Multicultural Classroom Instruction Is Undermining Our Children's Ability to Read, Write, and Reason*. Stix equates multiculturalism, whether it's about Ebonics or not, with evil and endorses Stotsky's book resoundingly.

The most important point about Stix's views is that they find expression in media outlets and remind progressive educators that they must actively and continually contest for an audience. It is certainly gratifying and productive to converse with fellow travelers, but it is also crucial to remember that the counter rhetorics circulating in public discourse are not simply opposing but are indeed persuasive. If we are to have a shot at swaying the likes of Karen Thompson, and I believe we have a great chance, we have to extend our discursive reach. For those whose negative views about language diversity are not calcified, such activity matters. For example, the CCCC Language Policy Committee recently surveyed CCCC and NCTE members regarding their views on language diversity. Findings reveal that a significant number of teachers are unaware of CCCC policies on language diversity and that verbal commitment to language diversity often does not translate into classroom practice. However, the results also indicate that course work in linguistic diversity does have a significant impact on teachers' understanding and attitudes.

The Struggle over Language Diversity

The data from the CCCC language survey point to the value of educational efforts aimed at demystifying language attitudes. An important part of such a program is to convey a sense of the broad social experiences and intellectual activity that inscribe present work in vernacular educational theory so that folks can clearly see that Ebonics and "students' right" proposals are but cases in point that have been advanced in reasonable ways. In fact, two decades before the "Students' Right" resolution, UNESCO maintained the legitimacy of the approach implied. In the 1953 monograph *The Use of Vernacular Languages in Education* it was argued that the mother tongue was an appropriate medium of instruction at all levels of education. UNESCO officials knew that there were social, political, and economic questions attached to that assertion about language. There always are. But the point I am pressing here is that pedagogy linked to a positive view of language variation is not some latter day fad being promoted, as some in the media would depict it, by a small band of Afrocentrists and their multiculturalist allies. The International Group for the Study of Language Standardisation and the Vernacularization of Literacy operates out of England, not Oakland. Members of the group also sound a lot like bell hooks. As Andrée Tabouret-Keller writes:

> We cannot avoid being concerned with what is being spread by literacy. The most favourable circumstance for the mass of ordinary people to become literate, either in the vernacular or in some standard language, would be the genuine utility of such literacy for those aspects of social and political life with which they are concerned. (327)

The sentiment expressed by Tabouret-Keller is part and parcel of Stephen Parks's project to provide an in-depth story of the politics that produced the actual "Students' Right" resolution and to advocate that the most progressive aspects of those politics should inform contemporary work by compositionists. Parks is right that, as he points out in his introduction, the focus in composition historiography has been on an individual's scholarly production at the expense of a full examination of such production relative to specific political organizations. In contrast, his own history firmly links innovations in composition theory and pedagogy to the work of groups like the Black Panthers and the New University Conference. It is a very promising line of inquiry, but his criticism of previous accounts and his subsequent vision yield mixed results that have implications for his ability to participate in the types of coalitions that he seeks. Almost exclusively archival in method, Parks's work constructs an interesting history relative to the development of the watershed CCCC statement in question. In his narrative, the New University Conference comes off as a fairly heroic collection of liberals and progressives hamstrung in their efforts by somewhat conservative members of CCCC and NCTE. There is more than a little truth in that view; however, his history fails to account adequately for the motives of various central figures involved in the formulation of the "Students' Right" resolution. Parks has deemed archival work—mainly just minutes of meetings and a handful of letters—to be sufficient despite the fact that he is dealing with such a recent moment in history and despite the fact that most of the people involved in framing the resolution are around and available for interview. I am not at all suggesting that any historian should be reduced to parroting informants' self-reports. Self-reports are sometimes suspect data. But they are also potentially useful data, and it is startling that a researcher would ignore them. In this case, I am sure that consultation with Geneva Smitherman would have kept Parks from so glibly misreading her.

In his chapter "Black Power/Black English," Parks refers to remarks made by Smitherman, who in 1972 argued that demonstrating to students that language is power may be a way to convince them that "the pen is mightier than the Molotov cocktail" and who in 1977 posited that some instances of Black Power rhetoric were examples of selling wolf tickets (109). Parks concludes that Smitherman was "redefining African American culture away from the political violence and unrest that had marked the 1960s" (109). He adds that she was devaluing the commitment of Black Power participants and was unable to imagine that the Black English used in classrooms could lead to policies, like socialism, that they articulated (110–11). What Smitherman, a pivotal figure in the "Students' Right" developments, actually attempted was far more nuanced than Parks has the experience to discern. Fully enmeshed in the cultural politics of the times, she was reflecting the complexities of Black rhetorical and political engagement. Such engagement is never simply "violence-not violence" or "socialist-not socialist." The African American community has never been that simple, nor has its communication. "Insider" and "outsider" messages were encoded all the time. As the saying went back in the day, "Those who know don't say, and those who say don't know." Such engagement also rubs up personally against the tragedies of political participation. African American scholars and activists who emerged from the crucible of the 1960s were also the ones whose family members and close friends bore the brunt of the nation's political violence. These scholars and activists filed through more funeral parlors than they care to remember and were not subsequently going to enter classrooms to glorify violence, which is not, in any event, the litmus test for progressive Black political activities. While Smitherman did not openly endorse all manifestations of Panther-style activism (would she have reached all the people like Parks if she had?), she did not negate radical possibilities in her rhetoric and certainly understood the transformative potential of literacy in general and African American English in particular. She saw language as a political weapon and knew also that even the Black Panthers spent as much time producing and peddling their newspapers as they did engaging in other activities. Furthermore, to understand the "woofin" that some of the bloods were doing back then is not to devalue the commitment of Black Powerists as a group. Only detached researchers need to talk about them as an undifferentiated mass. Smitherman *knew* these people and, therefore, was in a position to distinguish between mere boastfulness and stone-to-the-bone seriousness. When I first read her passage in *Talkin and Testifyin* about "woofin," the memories haunted me, but I nodded in affirmation of the passage's accuracy.

Not surprisingly, Smitherman has a different take on the political and organizational milieu that led to the "Students' Right" resolution. Rather than seeing the New University Conference as essential, she contends that CCCC had been concerned with student language rights virtually from the outset. In *Talkin That Talk,* she identifies the work of Donald Lloyd in the early 1950s—work associated with the "new linguistics"—as generative. By the late 1960s, Smitherman argues, Blacks were at the forefront of rainbow coalitions that were pushing a human rights agenda not only within CCCC but within other organizations, such as the American Psychological Association, the American Sociological Association, the Speech Communication Association, the American Bar Association, and the American Speech and Hearing Association. In her view, the symbolic turning point for CCCC was the assassination of Martin Luther King Jr., which occurred while the CCCC annual convention was underway in Minneapolis. This event dramatically highlighted the dismal record of CCCC relative to people of color and led, in Smitherman's estimation, to the centrality of the "race/Color" component in subsequent discussions of linguistic difference (381). The following December, Ernece Kelly edited a special edition of *College Composition and Communication* featuring Black scholars who addressed issues of language, politics, and pedagogy. To Smitherman, it was a logical progression from the fervor of 1968 to the "Students' Right" resolution, a statement that, in her words, "represented a critical mechanism for CCCC to address its internal contradictions as the resistance of the Black Liberation Movement called the Question of justice in all areas of American life—including language and education" (384). Looking back, Smitherman concludes that while vitally important as a touchstone, the goals of the "Students' Right" resolution have never fully been instantiated, that too often the impetus is still to "remake those on the margins in the image of the patriarch, to reshape the outsiders into talking, acting, thinking, and (to the extent possible) looking like the insiders" (398).

Of course, the versions by Parks and Smitherman are not mutually exclusive. The New University Conference did have a presence in CCCC. It is also possible to have been a language activist in CCCC, and a more progressive one than Parks would characterize you, without having been inspired directly by the New University Conference. The main point to make here, however, is that Parks silences African American scholars; this is an unfortunate turn, one that is ironic given Parks's comments about white scholars and African American students. He sensitively and cogently demonstrates that the impetus for political struggle by white leftists often stemmed from the interplay of their liberal and radical imaginations and Black suffering. Just as Richard Wright had opined that "the Negro was America's metaphor" (24), people like Jerry Farber and Ken Macrorie, in order to gain political legitimacy, employed the oppressed, vernacular-speaking Black as their primary trope. Parks correctly notes, however, that this type of argument, exemplified for example by Farber's student-as-nigger rhetoric, often trivialized the exploitation of African Americans and was forwarded more in the service of individualism than in the spirit of collective struggle that embraced Blacks. But although Parks is wary of misappropriating the experiences of African American students, he uses scholars like Smitherman as objects, speculates about their motivation, and constructs a history *about* them while ignoring the chance to incorporate them as speaking subjects in his study. Other informants who would have been available to Parks include Marianna Davis, Jim Hill, Vivian Davis, and Ernece Kelly. They did not have the research teaching load and support that Smitherman had and thus could not have the same impact as writers. But they contributed mightily as consultants, committee volunteers, and forum participants.[3]

Presumably, Parks wants to form alliances with some key African American members of organizations like CCCC, but he has compromised this goal given his description of Black involvement in the "Students' Right" resolution. In fact, the NCTE/CCCC Black Caucus sent a letter to the executive director of NCTE (the organization that published Parks's book) objecting to the publication of *Class Politics*.[4]

The Politics of Language Rights: A New Millennium Crew

Despite the shortcomings in Parks's work (and one definitely should not be dismissive of the measure of rigor that does mark his work), he formulates a vision (which is very much like the one Smitherman has held all along) of the continuing relevance of the "Students' Right" resolution. I hope it gains wide acceptance:

> The SRTOL [the "Students' Right" resolution] emerged from a struggle to link the university, the community, and the students' language. The instantiation of that legacy would be courses and programs which provide students an opportunity to engage in the difficult work of recognizing the culture of power and finding the alliances, programs, and struggles that expand who has power in that culture. Indeed, at a moment when corporations are developing an expanding role in defining and supplying "educations" to their workers, to have in place a reminder of how knowledge should serve the political empowerment of citizens seems particularly important. That is, perhaps the role of the university can serve as a reminder that education is about more than economic efficiency. (247–48)

Significantly, this call for linking composition work to a more authentic democracy already lines up with the current intellectual activity of an interesting interdisciplinary and international group of academics, some of whom I have previously mentioned. I would add to this group Romy Clark, Roz Ivanič, Lesley Milroy, Terry Meier, Arnetha Ball, Ted Lardner, Eleanor Kutz, Tom Fox, Charles Coleman, and Elaine Richardson.

Clark and Ivanič, both affiliated with Great Britain's Lancaster University, stress the importance of problematizing discourse choices and of paying attention to the ways in which such choices construct readers and writers and convey political viewpoints. As part of this process,

> learners should be encouraged to make choices as they write that will align them with social and political values, beliefs and practices to which they are committed, if necessary opposing privileged conventions for the genre and thereby contributing to discoursal and social change. (231)

Milroy, a University of Michigan professor who hails from England and is steeped like Clark and Ivanič in the British tradition of sociolinguistics, continues to interrogate "standard-language ideology," which she contends is rooted in the United States because of a complex history of enslavement, guilt, and a legacy of racism, largely in race and ethnicity. We continue to need up-to-date analyses of language ideology as well as courses that privilege such information. One example is Language and Culture, Meier's graduate offering at Wheelock College. The overall purpose of the course, as she states it, is "to deepen students' understanding of the complex relationships among language, culture, and identity and to have students reflect on the implications of those connections for their current or future work with children in schools" (119). As we know from examining the CCCC language survey, such insight should not be restricted to those planning to teach children.

Ball and Lardner—of Stanford University and Cleveland State University, respectively—are also concerned with teacher knowledge. They propose *teacher efficacy* as the most useful construct; this model "places affect at the center and in doing so opens up and addresses questions of motivation and stance which are prior to and underlie curricular designs or pedagogical technique" (478). Writing pedagogy, then, should not fail to foreground the influences of teacher, student, and site (482). In a subsequent essay about teacher preparation, Lardner expands on the notion of teacher efficacy and describes, by highlighting the voices of his students, how the attendant dynamics may play out in the classroom. He reaffirms the need to examine context in detail, arguing that

> technical analyses of "nonstandard" English and their yield of facts cannot resolve the ideological dilemmas entailed in teaching writing to "nonmainstream" students, and the activity of teaching writing can neither be adequately reflected on nor practiced without considering these politics. (126)

Kutz has been designing both education and composition courses for many years at the University of Massachusetts in Boston, and she continues to build in a sophisticated manner upon the fundamental assumption that no language variety is inherently better or worse than another. She understands that the situation for students relative to the learning of academic discourses is a specific instance of what we all face as we try to join alternate language communities. That is,

> our successful participation in those communities will have a lot to do with whether we're invited into the conversation and treated with tol-

erance and respect as we gradually acquire a new discourse, or whether we're kept outside the conversations that would support that acquisition until we demonstrate a mastery that we can't achieve without participation. (137)

Emphasis on tolerance and access also mark recent scholarship by Tom Fox, a professor of English at California State University in Chico. As he does in a chapter in this volume, Fox critiques the use of bureaucratic standards, which often employ language as the pretext to exclude people of color from higher education. He shares and reads generously, yet critically, some of the powerful writing produced by his students, texts that might be deemed unacceptable by those overly concerned with adherence to formal conventions. Fox's students produce examples of what Coleman calls *interlanguage* or *interdialect* writing, essays that reflect the developing but incomplete mastery of standardized English. Continuing the kind of the linguistic analysis that has admirably informed composition theory, Coleman, a professor at the City University of New York, points out that we all write with accents, with a certain set of prosodic features (487). He concludes that "interlanguage/interdialect theory may be helpful because it allows us to see a class of student errors as growth" (498). Elaine Richardson, former student of both Lardner and Smitherman and my colleague at Penn State, is presently engaged in research that amplifies the thinking of Coleman, Fox, and the others about language variation and composition pedagogy.

The "Students' Right" resolution remains an important template for composition studies. It serves to historicize, ground, and focus discussions about language politics, and it provides a rationale or support for emerging scholarship, teaching, and political organizing. The most vital question now before us and on the horizon is whether a twenty-first-century crew of scholars, teachers, and community workers can achieve new levels of progress relative to the resolution's most radically democratic aspects.

Notes

1. The resolution reads: We affirm the students' right to their own language — the dialects of their nurture or whatever dialects in which they find their own identity and style. Language scholars long ago denied that the myth of a standard American dialect has any validity. The claim that any one dialect is unacceptable amounts to an attempt of one social group to exert its dominance over another. Such a claim leads to false advice for speakers and writers, and immoral advice for humans. A nation proud of its

diverse heritage and its cultural and racial variety will preserve its heritage of dialects. We affirm strongly that teachers must have the experiences and training that will enable them to respect diversity and uphold the right of students to their own language.

2. A resolution affirming the Oakland School Board's decision as "linguistically and pedagogically sound" was passed at the meeting of January 3, 1997.

3. In a personal correspondence to me dated November 28, 2000, and reprinted here with the permission of Steve Parks, Parks agreed that I was accurate about the short-comings of his book. He informed me that he had originally proposed a book, modeled on Teodori's *New Left*, that would have included ample oral histories, including inter-views with Geneva Smitherman, Vivian Davis, and Juanita Williamson. However, he could find no publisher, including NCTE, who thought such coverage of the SRTOL was important. So the project became more a history of the 1960s. Parks does not feel he is the person to write about the Black Caucus, though he would like to collaborate with members of the organization to get a fuller history of the SRTOL told. He closed by stating: "What I'm really saying is that one response to this situation would be a brief flare up of journal articles between parties. This always strikes me as half a step. I'm hoping I can gain the trust of those in the Black Caucus to be able to participate in a structural answer to the deeper issues—the collection and publication of voices tradi-tionally excluded from our canon, the need for a full accounting of the SRTOL that accurately represents the complexity out of which it grew. Although I doubt at this point that they would cite my book as an example of this, my sense is that we both agree with the general aim. I always knew my book was incomplete, and, as a consequence, always intended to work beyond the book for the full story. It sounds like the Caucus letter is working for this larger goal. Maybe I can work with them to create structural solutions."

4. The letter was written April 28, 2000, by Demetrice Worley, president of the NCTE/CCCC Black Caucus, to then Executive Director Faith Schullstrom. Copies were sent to NCTE President Jerry Harste, NCTE President Elect Anne Ruggles Gere, and NCTE Director of Special Programs Sandra Gibbs.

Works Cited

Ball, Arnetha, and Ted Lardner. "Dispositions Toward Language: Teacher Constructs of Knowledge and the Ann Arbor Black English Case." *College Composition and Com-munication* 48 (1997): 469–85.

CCCC. "Language Knowledge and Awareness Survey." Urbana, IL, 2000.

Clark, Romy, and Roz Ivanič. *The Politics of Writing*. London: Routledge, 1997.

Coleman, Charles F. "Our Students Write with Accents—Oral Paradigms for ESD Students." *College Composition and Communication* 48 (1997): 486–500.

Farber, Jerry. *The Student as Nigger: Essays and Stories*. New York: Pocket, 1970.

Fox, Tom. *Defending Access: A Critique of Standards in Higher Education*. Portsmouth, NH: Boynton/Cook, 1999.

hooks, bell. *Teaching to Transgress: Education as the Practice of Freedom*. New York: Routledge, 1994.

Kutz, Eleanor. *Language and Literacy: Studying Discourse in Communities and Classrooms.* Portsmouth, NH: Boynton/Cook, 1997.

Lardner, Ted. "Item 50: Dialect Diversity and Teacher Preparation." *Situated Stories: Valuing Diversity in Composition Research.* Ed. Emily Decker and Kathleen Geissler. Portsmouth, NH: Boynton/Cook, 1998. 119–27.

Macrorie, Ken. *Uptaught.* New York: Hayden, 1970.

Meier, Terry. 1998. "Teaching Teachers about Black Communications." *The Real Ebonics Debate: Power, Language, and the Education of African American Children.* Ed. Theresa Perry and Lisa Delpit. Boston: Beacon. 117–25.

Milroy, Lesley. "Standard English and Language Ideology in Britain and the United States." *Standard English: The Widening Debate.* Ed. Tony Bex and Richard J. Watts. London: Routledge, 1999. 173–206.

Parks, Stephen. *Class Politics: The Movement for the Students' Right to Their Own Language.* Urbana, IL: NCTE, 2000.

———. Letter to the author. 28 Nov. 2000.

Perry, Theresa. "I 'on Know Why They Be Trippin": Reflections on the Ebonics Debate." *The Real Ebonics Debate: Power, Language, and the Education of African American Children.* Ed. Theresa Perry and Lisa Delpit. Boston: Beacon, 1998. 3–15.

Rickford, John, and Russell Rickford. *Spoken Soul: The Story of Black English.* New York: Wiley, 2000.

Smitherman, Geneva. "Black Power Is Black Language." *Black Culture: Reading and Writing Black.* Ed. Gloria M. Simmons and Helene Hutchinson. New York: Holt, 1972. 85–91.

———. *Talkin and Testifyin: The Language of Black America.* Boston: Houghton, 1977.

———. *Talkin That Talk: Language, Culture, and Education in African America.* London: Routledge, 2000.

Stix, Nicholas. "The Language of Hate." 2000. <www8.bcity.com/differentdrummer>.

———. "Losing Our Language." 2000. <www8.bcity.com/stixandstones/>.

Tabouret-Keller, Andrée. Conclusion. *Vernacular Literacy: A Re-Evaluation.* Ed. Andrée Tabouret-Keller et al. Oxford: Clarendon, 1997. 316–27.

Tabouret-Keller, Andrée, et al., eds. *Vernacular Literacy: A Re-Evaluation.* Oxford: Clarendon, 1997.

UNESCO. *The Use of Vernacular Languages in Education.* Paris, 1953.

Wright, Richard. *White Man, Listen!* Garden City, NJ: Doubleday, 1957.

Part Four

Philosophical Inquiry

12

From Segregated Schools to Dimpled Chads: Rhetorical Hermeneutics and the Suasive Work of Theory

STEVEN MAILLOUX

> *Attorney Klock:* What I'm saying, sir, is this: that you cannot be in a situation of using the word "interpret" to explain anything that a court does. The word "interpret" cannot carry that much baggage.
>
> *Justice Souter:* But . . . it seems to me that you, in effect, go to the opposite extreme that you're excoriating the Florida Supreme Court for, and say they can't interpret at all.
>
> —Oral Argument for *Bush v. Gore* (2000)

IN *TOM SAWYER ABROAD*, Tom argues confidently that "the trouble about arguments" is that "they ain't nothing but *theories* after all, and theories don't prove nothing, they only give you a place to rest on a spell" (67). William James spins the same tropes differently, claiming that theories are "instruments, not answers to enigmas, in which we can rest. We don't lie back upon them, we move forward, and, on occasion, make nature over again by their aid" (32). The intellectual work we call "rhetorical hermeneutics" follows, among other things, such theoretical movements, treating theories as temporary rest stops and as tools for moving along. In doing so, it traces some of the historical ways that theoretical arguments appear in different cultural sites, noting how they get used and abused in their various rhetorical travels (see Said). More broadly, rhetorical hermeneutics is an interweaving of *rhetorical pragmatism* in contemporary theory debates and *cultural rhetoric studies* in ongoing historical practice. Because

I am somewhat taken with sloganizing, I have described this project as "the use of rhetoric to practice theory by doing history."[1] To illustrate, I will discuss not only argument as theory but theory as argument and theories in arguments—that is, how theory *does* prove something, and one thing it proves is that both Tom and James are right about theory.

Rhetorical hermeneutics, like the cultural rhetoric studies of which it is a part, travels well through many disciplinary domains in the human sciences; but because of the textual traces archived for certain interpretive fields in manuscript, print, microfilm, and digital media, rhetorical hermeneutics is especially at home in disciplines dealing with scriptural, legal, and literary texts. All these archives can be approached through *reception study,* the interpretive history of how events, texts, figures, and other cultural bits are used at different times and places, and the specific ways they are rhetorically established as meaningful and appropriated in different contexts for different purposes. One well-trodden archival path is the reception of *Adventures of Huckleberry Finn,* which has been praised as the quintessential expression of democratic equality and true American freedom and condemned as a producer of juvenile delinquency and a perpetrator of racist stereotyping.[2] In one especially ironic reception a few years ago, a certain school in Virginia removed *Huckleberry Finn* from its curriculum, and this book banning made it into the national press, at least partly because of the school's name: Mark Twain Intermediate. "The book is poison," declared the assistant principal. "It is anti-American; it works against the melting pot theory of our country; it works against the idea that all men are created equal; it works against the 14th Amendment to the Constitution" (qtd. in Sager A-1).

The legal event that helped create the cultural politics in which this reception of *Huckleberry Finn* and the Fourteenth Amendment took place involved an earlier application of that same constitutional amendment, the U.S. Supreme Court decision in the 1954 segregation cases, *Brown et al. v. the Board of Education of Topeka et al.* Here I will practice some rhetorical hermeneutics by doing a partial reception study of the Fourteenth Amendment's equal protection clause, focusing on just two moments in that interpretive history: *Brown v. Board of Education* and *Bush v. Gore.* Both opinions have been criticized for allowing politics to interfere with legal interpretation. This historical "coincidence" will allow me to develop rhetorical hermeneutics' double thesis about the role of theory in interpretation: first, that a certain kind of theory doesn't work, doesn't prove anything (this is a claim about theory as foundationalist project); and second, that a certain kind of theory does work, does prove something (this is a related claim about theory as rhetorical practice).

Rhetoric, Interpretation, and the *Brown* Case

The *Brown* opinion famously turned on its construal of the equal protection clause of the Fourteenth Amendment (1868): "No State shall . . . deny to any person within its jurisdiction the equal protection of the laws." In *Plessy v. Ferguson* (1896), the Supreme Court had interpreted this clause as allowing "equal but separate" public facilities for different races. More than a half century later in *Brown,* the Court argued against this separate but equal doctrine, declaring, "Separate educational facilities are inherently unequal" (*Brown* 347). To see how the Court rhetorically achieved this reinterpretation, we can look first at the theoretical moments in the *Brown* opinion, those moments in the argument when the Court commented self-reflexively on its own interpretive practices. In the 1954 decision, the Court began with the question of whether arguments from intention could resolve the dispute over the constitutionality of racially segregated schools. Each side claimed that the historical evidence for intent supported its case, but the court remained unpersuaded: "This discussion and our own investigation convince us that, although these sources cast some light, it is not enough to resolve the problem with which we are faced. At best, they are inconclusive" (*Brown* 489).

The Court was prepared for this turn of hermeneutic events, however. In its 1953 directions for reargument, it had requested counsel for both sides to address the question: If the intention of the framers or the adopters of the Fourteenth Amendment cannot be discovered, "is it within the judicial power, in construing the Amendment, to abolish segregation in public schools?" (*Brown* 345). In other words, if historical investigation is inconclusive, can the Court interpret the Fourteenth Amendment as rejecting the doctrine of "separate but equal"? In the *Brown* opinion delivered a year later, the Court answered its question with an emphatic "yes" and justified its interpretive practice in the decision's most important theoretical moment:

> Our decision . . . cannot turn on merely a comparison of . . . tangible factors in the Negro and white schools involved in each of the cases. We must look instead to the effect of segregation itself on public education. In approaching this problem, we cannot turn the clock back to 1868 when the Amendment was adopted, or even to 1896 when *Plessy v. Ferguson* was written. We must consider public education in the light

of its full development and its present place in American life throughout the Nation. Only in this way can it be determined if segregation in
public schools deprives these plaintiffs of the equal protection of the
laws. (492–93)

So in this moment of methodological self-reflection, the Court announced
a crucial decision about what it would use as the relevant interpretive framework for its construal of the Fourteenth Amendment. The Court did not
interpret the equal protection clause within the historical context of its adop-
tion or its most famous application but rather within the mid-twentieth-
century situation of American education. What the Court then determined
was that separate means unequal and that, therefore, state-imposed segregation in public schools violated the equal protection clause of the Fourteenth
Amendment and must come to an end.

How was this theoretical moment received in the aftermath of *Brown*?
Quite predictably, there was an abundance of praise and blame reported in
the popular press. Outraged responses included those that accused the
Supreme Court of creating law rather than merely interpreting it. Governor
Herman Talmadge of Georgia claimed that the justices "had blatantly . . .
usurped from the Congress and the people the power to amend the Constitution and from the Congress the authority to make the laws of the land."
Senator James O. Eastland of Mississippi predicted that the South would "not
abide by or obey this legislative decision by a political court" (qtd. in Kluger
710). The General Assembly of South Carolina passed a resolution that
declared, "If the Court in the interpretation of the Constitution is to depart
from the sanctity of past decisions and to rely on the current political and
social philosophy of its members to unsettle the great constitutional principles so clearly established, the rights of individuals are not secure and government under a written Constitution has no stability" ("Joint" 101). The
exact ideological nature of the Court's purported fall into partisan politics
was even more specifically characterized by some of its critics. Circuit Judge
Tom P. Brady of Mississippi attacked the Court for accepting the views of
"left-wing Liberals, . . . Marxian Christians in our churches, and . . . Neo-
Socialists, teachers and preachers in the schools." And Eastland added to his
attack the charge that "the country has entered an era of judicial tyranny"
and that "the Court has responded to a radical, pro-Communist political
movement" (qtd. in Blaustein and Ferguson 8).[3]

Besides such receptions noted in the mass media, there began a calmer
interpretive history of *Brown* within professional law journals. In one of the

earliest law journal articles, "Toward Neutral Principles of Constitutional Law," Herbert Wechsler also charged the Court with allowing politics to influence its decision. Wechsler defined the issue of enforced segregation in *Brown* not as a problem of discrimination but as an issue about freedom of association. Thus he asks:

> Given a situation where the state must practically choose between denying the association to those individuals who wish it or imposing it on those who would avoid it, is there a basis in neutral principles for holding that the Constitution demands that the claims for association should prevail? (34)

Wechsler answered that the legal argument in *Brown* failed to provide such a basis.

Wechsler made his critique of *Brown* at the service of a broader theoretical project: the proposal of a general hermeneutics that establishes "the standards to be followed" in interpreting the constitution (10–11). His theory prescribes that judges must decide cases "on grounds of adequate neutrality and generality, tested not only by the instant application but by others that the principles imply." If "neutral principles" are ignored, he claims, the Court becomes nothing more than "a naked power organ" transforming the Constitution into "the partisan of a particular set of ethical or economical opinions" (12, 19).[4] Wechsler's theory of neutral principles aims to ensure that the Court avoids this fall from legal adjudication into political ideology. And because the Court did not avoid this danger in 1954, Wechsler reluctantly rejected the *Brown* opinion, an opinion that he claimed did not "rest on neutral principles" (17).

Nearly fifty years after the *Brown* decision and its initial controversy, the case continues to be cited within court opinions (including, most recently, a *Bush v. Gore* dissent), and the theoretical issues raised in its reception continue to be discussed in legal and popular culture.[5] One of those issues remains the question of whether theoretical constraints can prevent the collapse of legal interpretation into partisan politics, a question that assumes the viability of the law/politics distinction. A rhetorical hermeneutics here argues that such worries are both inevitable and unnecessary—inevitable given the theoretical assumptions about the Supreme Court, legal adjudication, and party politics in the United States, but unnecessary because politics and interpretation cannot be separated by theory or anything else. Both the issue of interpretive constraints and the worry over collapsing law into politics become problems for theorists, especially when they misunderstand theoretical moments such as those in the *Brown* decision—that is, when they believe that self-conscious reflections within one's arguments are something more than rhetorically specific, historically situated uses of theory to extend and justify those arguments. Rhetorical hermeneutics suggests instead that theories within legal arguments should not lead to general hermeneutic theories about all legal constructions. They should not lead to foundationalist attempts to ward off the purported dangers of interpretive anarchy and political determinism.

Rhetorical hermeneutics rejects such foundationalist efforts by replacing a general hermeneutics with rhetorical histories. Rather than proposing still another theory of how to define and constrain individual interpreters and their relations to independent texts, instead of aiming for an abstract theoretical account of interpretive practice that would provide normative rules supposedly guaranteeing the discovery of correct meanings, rhetorical hermeneutics replaces a confrontation model of interpreter and text with a conversational model of arguments among interpreters (see Rorty 170–71). Theories governing textual confrontations become histories of interpretive conversations. More exactly, general hermeneutic descriptions and prescriptions become rhetorical analyses of specific historical arguments about texts. These historically situated reception studies about historically situated textual arguments cannot escape the configurations of power-knowledge that are constitutive of both the interpretive context of historical description and the interpreted context of the history described. Thus, a rhetorical hermeneutics embraces a kind of Foucauldian neo-pragmatism that, for example, argues for a complex imbrication of legal adjudication and political formation. Put too simply, rhetorical hermeneutics claims that all interpretation involves rhetoric (we make our interpretations through figure and argument) and that all rhetoric involves politics (power relations both condition and are affected by our arguments); therefore, interpretation, including legal adjudication, is not completely separable from politics.

But to make the interpretation/politics distinction problematic does not mean that just anything goes in legal (or any other kind of) interpretation, as Wechsler and others fear. Arguments are always situated in specific historical circumstances that include (in the case of law) relevant legal precedents, agreed upon facts, modes of judicial argumentation, and other contextual conditions, all of which make certain arguments appropriate or persuasive and others inappropriate or unconvincing at particular moments.

Thus, pointing to words in a statute, describing legislative intent, noting changing historical conditions, or laying out one's interpretive framework can all count as valid tactics in a court opinion. Making such rhetorical moves does not in itself signify that judges believe in a foundationalist theory of interpretation; it just means that they are playing the serious game of legal interpretation. At certain times during a theoretical moment, judges might temporarily step into another overlapping game called "philosophy" or "theory of jurisprudence" and suggest that their own theory is "universal" or "objective." But even this move does not invalidate the rhetorical efficacy of their judicial arguments; it only adds another potentially persuasive (for a foundationalist) or unpersuasive (for an anti-foundationalist) aspect to the judge's interpretive rhetoric. Pointing to general rules of construction or explaining one's interpretive method—"going meta" in a judicial argument—is simply part of that interpretive argument, a part that I have referred to as the theoretical moment of a legal text.

Some neo-pragmatists, however, contend that theory has no consequences (see Mitchell). They argue, and I agree, that if theory is defined as a general account of interpreting that provides guidelines for guaranteeing correct interpretations, theory is impossible and can't do what it desires. It cannot become a foundationalist hermeneutics outside of and ruling over the untidy domain of interpretive practices in such a way that it absolutely constrains those practices. That is, foundationalist theory does not have the consequences of its foundationalist claims. In this limited sense, theory is inconsequential. However, this neo-pragmatist argument is not the general rejection of *all* theory it is sometimes taken to be. Rather, it is a narrowly defined claim about one specific type of theory. There are other sorts of theories with other sorts of consequences. Moreover, what looks like foundationalist theory, when inserted into historically situated legal and critical arguments, does have consequences of a very rhetorical kind. Theoretical moments in these cases function as part of the suasive attempt to prove or disprove, support or challenge a specific interpretive argument. Only when these theoretical moments get extracted from their historical context of persuasive activity and become the basis of foundationalist theorizing do theorists run into trouble. Only then does Mark Twain's wry observation—that theories don't prove nothing—apply (see Mailloux, *Rhetorical* 155–64).

Theories in arguments often do make for very effective rhetorical practice within legal and other interpretive disciplines. Rhetorical practices are the discursive form of micropractices making up the social arrangement of power-knowledge within those disciplines at certain historical moments. The rhetorical power of any judicial opinion effectively organizes the argumentative energies functioning within particular sociohistorical contexts — disciplinary and extra-disciplinary — in which textual meanings are established. The upshot of this Foucauldian neo-pragmatism, what I'm calling rhetorical hermeneutics, is a reworking of the law/politics distinction. The distinction does not pay its way if we use it as part of a general legal hermeneutics that declares the political out of bounds. The legal is always a form of rhetorical politics, and rhetorical-legal practices are always embedded both in institutional traditions, like legal precedent, and in larger social formations, like cultural politics. For a rhetorical hermeneutics, an essentialist distinction between law and politics does no useful work. However, the law/politics opposition might prove useful at specific historical moments for particular legal arguments. It may be theoretically misleading to separate law and politics in general, but it is exactly this distinction that some conservative arguments cited in attacking the *Brown* opinion. In a cultural context in which law is assumed to be above politics, the legal/political distinction might well perform quite important rhetorical work in a legal argument. But when that work becomes the basis for a *theory* that attempts always and everywhere to separate politics and law, a misguided, ahistorical foundationalism is the unfortunate result.

I have to admit, however, that it is often quite difficult to resist the "theoretical urge" to elaborate a foundationalist hermeneutics, especially when faced with theoretical moments in arguments with which you strongly disagree. Take, for example, the Joint Resolution of the General Assembly of the State of South Carolina, passed in February 1956, that condemned the Supreme Court for the *Brown* decision. The resolution argued that the Court disregarded legal precedent and "the plain language of the Fourteenth Amendment" and that this action "constitutes a deliberate, palpable, and dangerous attempt to change the true intent and meaning of the Constitution." At one point, the assembly declared, "This action of the Court ignored the principle that the meaning of the Constitution and of its Amendments does not change. It is a written instrument. That which the Fourteenth Amendment meant when adopted it means now" ("Joint" 101–2).

We can regard this theoretical moment of the resolution in two very different ways: as a budding foundationalist theory or as a supporting rhetorical strategy. As a piece of embryonic foundationalism, removed from its rhetorical context, it looks like the beginning of an intentionalist theory very similar to that of E. D. Hirsch and its "permanent meaning" versus "changing significance" distinction (see Hirsch, "Meaning" 202; and *Validity*). But as a rhetorical strategy, the resolution's theoretical moment occurs as part of an anti-*Brown* argument. I may be tempted to launch into a theoretical challenge to the assembly's theory of meaning, but I would be better advised to stick to the case rather than the theory, if I want to address the argument. Or if I do attempt to theorize, I should do so in an anti-foundationalist rhetorical mode and not engage in an essentialist debate over intentionalism or formalism.

One lesson of rhetorical hermeneutics, then, might easily be stated: rhetoric should always be the focus, whether discussing abstract hermeneutic theory or analyzing theoretical moments within concrete arguments. Let me use a final example to tease out what such lessons might help us to understand about specific cases; this one is another, more recent reception of the equal protection clause of the Fourteenth Amendment. It is as surprising as it is troubling. Unfortunately, rhetorical hermeneutics can only describe the surprise; it can't, by itself, remedy the trouble.

Standards of Interpretation and *Bush Versus Gore*

In its effects, *Bush v. Gore* determined the final outcome of the 2000 presidential election. Perhaps the most surprising part of the majority's argument was its appeal to the equal protection clause of the Fourteenth Amendment. The issue before the Court was whether to reverse the Florida Supreme Court's ruling that ordered a manual recount of the November 4, 2000, election ballots in each of the state's voting precincts. The *per curiam* opinion focused on arguments about reading dimpled and hanging chads: "The question is . . . how to interpret the marks or holes or scratches on an inanimate object, a piece of cardboard or paper which, it is said, might not have registered as a vote during the machine count" *(Bush)*. The Court worried over how such interpretations would take place uniformly across different precincts. The justices agreed on the legislative standard to be applied: "Florida's basic command for the count of legally cast votes is to consider the 'intent of the voter.'" But how was this consideration to be carried out? "The problem inheres in the absence of specific standards to ensure its equal application." "Equal application" would, in the Court's view, guarantee equal protection of an individual voter's rights: "equal weight accorded to each vote and the equal dignity to each voter." The Court used this theoretical moment in *Bush v. Gore* to justify its finding that since no standards for equal application were in place, the Florida Supreme Court's judgment to continue the recount should be reversed and the case "remanded for further proceedings not inconsistent" with the U.S. Supreme Court's opinion.

The hermeneutic rule regarding voter intent and the legal principle of equal protection organize the theoretical moment of *Bush v. Gore,* and the rule and principle were cited as the basis for the specific decision about standards of interpretation. The Court held that "the formulation of uniform rules to determine intent" was "practicable" and "necessary," but "the want of those rules here has led to unequal evaluation of ballots in various respects." The Court cited as evidence information from the Florida opinion: "Should a county canvassing board count or not count a 'dimpled chad' where the voter is able to successfully dislodge the chad in every other context on that ballot? Here, the county canvassing boards disagree." Such evidence led the Court to conclude that a lack of interpretive standards results in arbitrary relativism: "As seems to have been acknowledged at oral argument, the standards for accepting or rejecting contested ballots might vary not only from county to county but indeed within a single county from one recount team to another." Thus, for the Court majority, a lack of uniform interpretive standards ultimately entailed unequal treatment of individual votes and a violation of the equal protection of voters.

Much has already been said and written about this unusual appropriation of the Fourteenth Amendment: that it was a creative or unprecedented or cynical application of the equal protection clause.[6] I will add only one point to conclude this brief demonstration of rhetorical hermeneutics. Did politics influence the Court's decision in *Bush v. Gore*? There seems to be as little doubt in this case as in *Brown*. Is there a way of separating out the politics from the legal interpretation? Not according to rhetorical hermeneutics. Does this ironically leave us in a position analogous to that of the Floridians interpreting chads as hypothesized by the Court majority, with no absolutely clear distinctions, no uniform standards, and thus interpretive anarchy? Well, yes and no. Theoretical distinctions between politics and interpretation cannot be made universally, and no general set of standards comprehensively governing all interpretations can ever be found. Still, interpretive rules as heuristic guidelines often come in handy, and their recognition can in fact become necessary for achieving argumentative success in certain situations. And, of course, there is politics and there is politics. Though there might be no general way for distinguishing in principle where appropriate interpretation ends and objectionable politics begins, there are contextualized ways of judging when bad rhetoric is replacing good, which is to say (among other things), when unpersuasive arguments are replacing persuasive arguments.

Of course, any such judgment is itself a function of later interpretive arguments within other contexts of power-knowledge relations. That is, any
attempt to argue that another argument is unconvincing—that it is simply
political self-interest crudely asserted rather than persuasively argued—is
itself open to further challenge within another context. Theory as argument,
theory in arguments, must withstand the same rhetorical scrutiny. When it
does, then indeed it proves something. As an attempt at theory, one thing
rhetorical hermeneutics tries to prove is this: it's interpretation all the way
down; rhetoric all around; and, yes, ideology here there and everywhere.

Notes

1. See Mailloux, *Reception;* also see Cain.

2. See Mailloux, *Rhetorical;* also see Arac.

3. On the relation of rhetoric to ideology, see Mailloux, *Reception:* ideologies are "sets
of beliefs and practices furthering socio-political interests in certain periods and locations; these ideological networks define positions within cultural conversations where
they appear as strategic arguments and rhetorical figures" (100).

4. Wechsler is quoting from *Otis v. Parker,* 187 U.S. 606, 609, U.S. Supreme Court,
1903.

5. See essays in Levinson and Mailloux; Lagemann and Miller; Sarat; Martin. For the
citation in *Bush v. Gore,* see Justice Breyer's dissent.

6. Here are two sample comments from "What We'll Remember in 2050: Nine Views
on *Bush v. Gore.*" First, a guardedly positive view:

> It was unfortunate that the majority of the court had to go to the equal-
> protection clause, which hasn't been applied in voting cases before this and
> has potential for future mischief if it comes to be supposed that equal protec-
> tion requires each vote to have the same power. That would run counter to
> our federal system. But I think the five conservative justices agreed to using
> the equal-protection clause in order to get two more votes, from Breyer and
> Souter, and that was a reasonable and statesmanlike thing to do in the cir-
> cumstances. (Harvey J. Mansfield, Professor of Government, Harvard
> University)

And, then, a more negative evaluation:

> The most devastating parallel [between the 1876 and 2000 elections] is the
> central role that race—especially the meaning of the "equal protection" clause
> of the 14th Amendment—played in shaping the outcome in both cases. . . .
> The heart of the irony is that large portions of those [Florida] votes that were
> invalidated, not counted, or prohibited were black votes. . . . Was there an
> issue of "equal protection" in this election? It would seem so. Only it was not
> the one the court identified. The smoldering ember in this election dispute is
> the likelihood that minority voters in 2000—as in 1876—will once again see
> themselves as the primary victims of an election they view as stolen. (William
> H. Chafe, Dean of the Faculty of Arts and Sciences, Duke University)

Works Cited

Arac, Jonathan. *Huckleberry Finn as Idol and Target: The Functions of Criticism in Our Time*. Madison: U of Wisconsin P, 1997.

Blaustein, Albert P., and Clarence Clyde Ferguson Jr. *Desegregation and the Law: The Meaning and Effect of the School Segregation Cases*. 2nd ed. New York: Vintage, 1962.

Brown v. Board of Ed. 345 U.S. 972. U.S. Supreme Court. 1953.

Brown v. Board of Ed. 347 U.S. 483. U.S. Supreme Court. 1954.

Bush et al. Petitioners v. Gore Jr. et al. 531 U.S. n.p. U.S. Supreme Court. 2000.

Cain, William E., ed. *Reconceptualizing American Literary/Cultural Studies: Rhetoric, History, and Politics in the Humanities*. New York: Garland, 1996.

Hirsch, E. D. "Meaning and Significance Reinterpreted." *Critical Inquiry* 11 (1984): 202–25.

———. *Validity in Interpretation*. New Haven: Yale UP, 1967.

James, William. *Pragmatism*. 1907. Cambridge: Harvard UP, 1975.

"A Joint Resolution of the State of South Carolina, 14 Feb. 1956." *Desegregation and the Supreme Court*. Ed. Benjamin Munn Ziegler. Boston: Heath, 1958. 100–103.

Kluger, Richard. *Simple Justice: The History of* Brown v. Board of Education *and Black America's Struggle for Equality*. New York: Knopf, 1976.

Lagemann, Ellen Condliffe, and LaMar P. Miller, eds. *Brown v. Board of Education: The Challenge for Today's Schools*. New York: Teacher's College P, 1996.

Levinson, Sanford, and Steven Mailloux, eds. *Interpreting Law and Literature: A Hermeneutic Reader*. Evanston: Northwestern UP, 1988.

Mailloux, Steven. *Reception Histories: Rhetoric, Pragmatism, and American Cultural Politics*. Ithaca: Cornell UP, 1998.

———. *Rhetorical Power*. Ithaca: Cornell UP, 1989.

Martin, Waldo E., Jr., ed. *Brown v. Board of Education: A Brief History with Documents*. Boston: Bedford, 1998.

Mitchell, W. J. T., ed. *Against Theory: Literary Studies and the New Pragmatism*. Chicago: U of Chicago P, 1985.

Otis v. Parker. 187 U.S. 606. U.S. Supreme Court. 1903.

Plessy v. Ferguson. 163 U.S. 537. U.S. Supreme Court. 1896.

Rorty, Richard. *Philosophy and the Mirror of Nature*. Princeton: Princeton UP, 1979.

Sager, Mark. "Mark Twain School Trying to Censor Huck." *Washington Post* 8 Apr. 1982: A1+.

Said, Edward. "Traveling Theory." *The World, the Text, and the Critic*. Cambridge: Harvard UP, 1983. 226–47.

Sarat, Austin, ed. *Race, Law, and Culture: Reflections on Brown v. Board of Education*. New York: Oxford UP, 1997.

Twain, Mark. *Tom Sawyer Abroad; Tom Sawyer, Detective*. Ed. John C. Gerber and Terry Firkins. Berkeley: U of California P, 1982.

Wechsler, Herbert. "Toward Neutral Principles of Constitutional Law." *Harvard Law Review* 73 (1959): 1–35.

"What We'll Remember in 2050: Nine Views on *Bush v. Gore*." *Chronicle of Higher Education* 5 Jan. 2001: B16.

13

Paralogic Rhetoric: An Overview

THOMAS KENT

THE TERM "paralogic rhetoric" is something of a misnomer. The term suggests that different types of rhetoric exist—such as an Aristotelian rhetoric or an expressivist rhetoric or social-constructionist rhetoric—when I really mean to describe only a condition of rhetoric. By "rhetoric," I mean the study of the production and reception of discourse, and by a "condition" of rhetoric, I mean that both the production and the reception of discourse are paralogic in nature. In general, *paralogy* (a term I appropriated from Jean-François Lyotard's *The Postmodern Condition*) refers to the moves we make within the give-and-take of communicative interaction. These moves cannot be predicted in advance of any communicative situation, nor can they be codified or conventionalized in any meaningful way. Of course, the germ of this idea has been around for quite a while. For example, a somewhat similar and certainly more familiar rendering of this idea appears in the distinction between *langue* and *parole*, where *langue* corresponds to the underlying system of rules in a language game and *parole* corresponds to the moves we make when playing the game. Another example would be John Austin's understanding of the performative nature of language, where what matters for communication is language-in-use and not an underlying grammatical structure. However, I should also note an important difference between paralogy and these two examples: unlike structuralist linguistics or speech-act theory, a paralogic conception of language-in-use suggests that no rules or even conventions exist at either the synchronic or the diachronic level that control or determine in advance the efficacy of our utterances.

This view of rhetoric—what I will persist in calling a *paralogic* rhetoric, even with the term's attendant baggage—has been influential in several recent and significant studies in the area of composition studies (see, for example, Dasenbrock, Dobrin, Ward, and Yarbrough). I will not attempt to summarize this important work, but I will attempt to outline below what I take to be the general features of a paralogic rhetoric as these features apply to writing and to the intellectual work of composition scholarship. First, I will outline briefly five presuppositions that inform a paralogic conception of rhetoric and writing (or at least my understanding of these presuppositions), and then I will move on to discuss two practical ramifications for the area of composition studies that derive from this view of rhetoric.

Five Presuppositions

Broadly conceived, a paralogic rhetoric endorses an anti-foundationalist and neo-pragmatic view of knowledge formation, and it holds that communicative interaction—and not simply the acquisition of a language—constitutes a necessary condition for the formation of belief, meaning, and human understanding. Stated a bit differently, a paralogic rhetoric holds that we believe and understand others only through our communicative interactions with them, and in order to believe and to understand others, we do not need to employ the same language or even belong to the same discourse community as others. Each of the five presuppositions outlined below follows from this fundamental axiom. I need also to point out that although I employ the term "rhetoric" to include both the production and the reception of discourse, in my discussion below I will concentrate only on writing and not on the other myriad forms of discourse production and reception.

Writing Is a Kind of Communicative Interaction

On the surface, this assertion resembles a truism, but in many contemporary accounts of writing, the act of writing appears as a thing-in-itself, most often as a process of one kind or another that can be reduced to a system and then taught. A paralogic rhetoric understands writing to be a specific kind of communicative interaction that shares features with other kinds of communicative interactions, although writing is clearly different from speaking, sign language, painting, music, or other forms of communicative interaction. However, the primary motive for the act of writing consists in communication, given of course that what we desire to communicate through writing may entail a very wide range of intentions. Consequently, in order to understand more completely the act of writing, we need to consider the nature of communicative interaction.

Communicative Interaction Is Thoroughly Hermeneutic

To make sense of different semiotic systems no matter how elementary a particular system might be, we must possess the ability to interpret the signs employed in that system. In our everyday existence, this interpretive activity generally goes unnoticed. In a sense, interpretation becomes transparent or "automatic" in our everyday lives. On the other hand, the act of interpretation becomes foregrounded and often more difficult when we are forced out of our habitual behaviors and made to encounter communicative situations that require us to ponder the intentions of others or to make sense of an unfamiliar sign or sign system.

Whether it is transparently automatic or foregrounded, effective interpretation, and consequently effective communication, requires at least three elements: a language user, another language user, and a world we share with others. We may say then that without other language users and a world we share with other language users, no communication or understanding would be possible. Within this triangle, we employ what Donald Davidson calls "passing theories" (or what I have called "hermeneutic guesses") in order to interpret the intentions of others as well as to interpret events in a world that we inhabit with others. When we enter a communicative situation, we guess about the meanings, beliefs, and intentions held by other language users, and these guesses in most everyday situations prove to be highly accurate. In fact, they do not appear to be guesses at all. However, even in the most mundane communicative situation, our guesses about what another person means to communicate obviously may be wrong. Therefore, these hermeneutic guesses are always temporary, tentative, and contingent. A guess that works in one situation may not work in another. As a kind of communicative interaction, the act of writing partakes of this kind of hermeneutic guesswork.

Writing Requires Hermeneutic Guesswork

When we write, we make guesses — often highly accurate guesses — about the strategies that others will employ to understand our utterances. This guesswork cannot be reduced to a process or a system that will allow us to predict in advance of a particular communicative situation the success of our utterances. Certainly, our knowledge and understanding of the complexities of a particular communicative situation — what is often called the "rhetorical context" — will help us make more efficacious guesses, but nothing can ensure in advance that our intentions will be understood by another language user. Clearly, however, the more we know about other language users and the world we share with them, the more efficient our communication will be. As Davidson points out, we tend to speak and write as our neighbors speak and write, and our knowledge of one another's habits and social conventions obviously makes communication more efficient, but possessing this knowledge still does not ensure that our utterances will be understood. When we write, we employ our interpretive ability to predict as best we can the strategies that others will employ to read our work, and this interpretive guesswork allows us to make decisions about every aspect of document production, from decisions about exigence and purpose all the way down to decisions about genre, syntax, and even word choice. In everyday writing situations, these choices may be relatively easy, and we may not even see our choices as choices. In less "automatic" and more troublesome interpretive situations, however, our decisions about the most effective means of document production always become more problematic and difficult.

In the give-and-take of hermeneutic guesswork that accompanies every act of writing, we are not bound by convention or by any preexisting social system of norms, although knowledge of these conventions or social norms will undoubtedly make our acts of writing more efficient, as I pointed out above. Because writing is a thoroughly hermeneutic activity and therefore not convention-bound, we do not need to imagine ourselves to be prisoners of a discourse community. We do not require the social-constructionist formulation of a unified (and some would say stultifying) community that shares a terministic screen or set of social conventions that shapes and determines how we understand others and the world. From the perspective of a paralogic rhetoric, the difficulty that we encounter when we attempt to understand strangers and their unfamiliar languages is different only in degree and not in kind from the difficulty we encounter when we try to understand our neighbors. For the paralogic rhetorician, ethnocentrism is not an issue; we simply must expend more interpretive energy understanding strangers. We are not required to see the world differently when we move from one community to another, nor do we even need to learn a new language. We well may need to exercise the virtues of patience and tolerance when attempting to communicate with strangers, but no epistemological problem exists that prohibits our understanding of the intentions and beliefs of those who occupy spaces outside our community. With enough time and tenacity, we can understand strangers just as completely as we understand our neighbors or even ourselves. This anti-ethnocentrism grows out of the view that all understanding derives from communicative interaction and that no understanding of any sort can take place without other language users and a world we share with others. When we consider the act of writing as a kind of communicative interaction, then, this recognition of the other becomes paramount.

Writing Requires Interaction with Others

Because understanding would be impossible without communication—that is, understanding would be impossible without the interaction among a language user, other language users, and a shared world—writing cannot take place without a sense of what I shall call, following Emmanuel Levinas, "Otherness." Writing forces us to engage the ubiquitous singularity, strangeness, or "Otherness" of other language users, and, as a consequence, we are forced to confront our assurance of our own selfhood, for our sense of selfhood comes into being only through our encounter with Otherness, the encounter with conditions and lives outside ourselves. In other words, we know ourselves precisely because we exist in a communicative relation with others and a world we share with others. This encounter with Otherness, as a totality and not as a single thing or individual, allows questions of ethics to emerge. Only through our relation with other language users and with a world we share can we even imagine what a better life might be. From this perspective, we must give ethics priority over ontology because, as paradoxical as it sounds, only through the intervention of Otherness can we even imagine the nature of being. What we have in this triangular relation, then, is a way of imagining our being-in-the-world, for only through communicative interaction with others and with the world do we discover who we are and what is important to us.

When we write, we cannot avoid an encounter with Otherness. We cannot avoid being thrown into relations with others, and these relations may be very close and comfortable, or they may be distant and uncomfortable. Of course, when we find ourselves close and comfortable with others—usually our neighbors—the easier we find communication to be, for when we communicate with people like ourselves, we can take a variety of semantic shortcuts and assume a great deal of common ground. However, even when we communicate with our neighbors, we know what to write and how to write it only because we know ourselves relative to them. When we produce any kind of written text, we cannot avoid responding to and interacting with others, and through this interaction, we define ourselves—including our ethics—by situating ourselves in some relation to others. When we understand the act of writing as an ongoing and open-ended communicative activity, writing can be viewed no longer as simply a skill that we learn and master, a skill that can be reduced to a system or process and then taught.

Writing Is Not a Process

Because writing partakes of the give-and-take and sometimes the rough-and-tumble of communicative interaction, and because this interaction is thoroughly hermeneutic, writing cannot be reduced to a system or a process that can be codified in any meaningful way. Of course, when we need or desire to produce a written text, we may and often do apply composing guidelines or heuristics that may very well help us make decisions about how others will interpret our documents, but these guidelines and heuristics just as surely may fail us. Because the hermeneutic guesses we make when we write a specific document may not work when we write a second similar document, we can never be sure that the process or system we used initially will prevail a second time around. However, the more knowledge that we garner from the hermeneutic guesswork we employ in a particular writing situation—that is, the more we know about the interpretive strategies employed by others—the more likely we will be to produce documents that others will understand in the ways that we intend the documents to be understood. Unfortunately, no process exists or could exist that ensures understanding on the part of our readers. Certainly, we may employ heuristics and rules of thumb to help us in our production of written texts—guidelines such as "think about your reader's needs" or "make the reader's work easy" or "employ an appropriate style"—but these rubrics, as helpful as they might be, do not constitute a description of the writing act in any meaningful sense of the term.

Two Ramifications

If we take seriously the claims outlined above, I believe that we are required to rethink the practice of writing as it now exists in our educational institutions. I cannot outline here all of the pedagogical and institutional ramifications that derive from a paralogic rhetoric, but I would like to discuss briefly two of the more important and obvious ramifications.

Writing Cannot Be Taught

If writing cannot be reduced to a process or system because of its open-ended and contingent nature, then nothing exists to teach as a body-of-knowledge. Writing's greatest quality—and its greatest liability—is its open-endedness, its deferral of meaning, its ability to efface authorship. Writing communicates only when it is comprehended within an open-ended and therefore uncodifiable relation among other language users and the world. As an aside, I would just say that this triangular relation is not the same as *situatedness,* for this term suggests, for many people, that the specific situation or *context* within which writing occurs may be recovered. It cannot be. No such thing as "context" exists if context means what some composition theorists seem to mean by the term: a recoverable rhetorical situation that determines or shapes understanding. Although we cannot recover context and then teach students how to write "in context," we certainly may teach and students certainly may learn something we might designate as a "text grammar," a body of knowledge that relates how a text works and how readers read texts, and this information no doubt will help us in our hermeneutic guesswork. However, as I indicated previously, we may know all there is to know about how texts work and how readers read, and we still may create documents that fail to communicate effectively.

In my claim that writing cannot be taught, I want to be clear that I do not claim that *composition* cannot be taught, for no doubt exists that we can teach issues dealing with the composing process—issues such as semantics, style, cohesion, genre, and so forth. However, composition—understood here primarily and narrowly to mean the study of the composing process—is not the same as writing; writing is a kind of communicative interaction while composition aims primarily to disclose the elements that constitute the composing process. Because writing is a kind of communicative interaction, and because communicative interaction partakes of hermeneutic guesswork that cannot be reduced to a codifiable process, the act of writing is not equivalent to the composing process or to a text grammar, and we should not confuse the concepts. Although composition—especially in the form of a text grammar—may be taught effectively and should be a requirement in every college student's curriculum, I believe that we would be better served if we simply dropped the idea that writing can be taught as a codified body of knowledge.

The Need for Institutional and Pedagogical Reform of Writing

A second important practical ramification that derives from a paralogic rhetoric is the need for change both in the way we position writing within our educational institutions and in the way we think about writing in our classrooms. If we believe that writing is a crucial—albeit open-ended—form of communication, then obviously nothing confines writing to English departments within our colleges and universities. Writing may occur everywhere in the academy, just as oral and visual communication may occur everywhere. Nowadays within the academy, however, writing is frequently viewed as a set of skills and not as a kind of communicative interaction, and instructors in courses outside of English departments seldom imagine themselves to be active participants in the production of their students' written work. If writing requires the active participation of others, as I have suggested, then administrators and faculty need to rethink the position of writing in the academy. Writing occurs or should occur everywhere across the university curriculum, and to produce effective writing—a text that genuinely communicates a writer's intentions—instructors should understand that they need to participate actively in the give-and-take produced by the written projects they assign, even if the instructor is not the intended reader of a document. This change in institutional understanding about the nature of writing will not come quickly or easily, for such a change asks every instructor in every course to view writing assignments as open-ended communication and not as an exercise to be corrected, graded, and then put away.

Another institutional impediment that prevents us from thinking of writing as a kind of communicative interaction crops up in English departments, a place where one would think that the conception of writing-as-communication might be championed. Many English faculty fear that if writing becomes part of every course within the university, the English department will be saddled with teaching multiple sections of dreary and mind-numbing composition courses where "composition" means only remedial instruction in grammar and the conventions of written discourse. All the interesting course content would occur in *writing* courses, courses that include literature or history or social and cultural issues where students are thrown into authentic communicative interactions with others. However, I don't believe that composition instruction needs to focus exclusively on stylistic issues. I believe that composition courses might be structured around the idea of a "text grammar," as I mentioned previously. Such a course would focus primarily on the problem of how written texts operate, and at the center of such a course would be centripetal issues related to cohesion (how texts hang together) and centrifugal issues related to genre (how texts are formed). This kind of course certainly would include instruction about the grammatical conventions of written English, but the focus of such a course would be the elements of textual production, not exclusively issues dealing with style. And obviously English departments are especially prepared to teach such courses.

On the other hand, *writing* should be part of every course in the academy, although clearly some courses might emphasize writing more than others. I believe that within the academy (outside of humanities departments mostly) an unacknowledged fear exists that writing is dangerous, and I believe that this fear is well founded, for the most part. Writing is dangerous in the sense that it places the instructor in the middle of things. When writing occurs in classroom settings, the instructor is implicated in the give-and-take of communicative interaction if for no other reason than the instructor must evaluate a student's written texts. When an instructor becomes an active participant in assignments that actually require writing — that is, assignments that require communicative interaction among the student, other language users, and a world the student shares with others, including the instructor — the instructor cannot disappear behind a veil of aphorisms regarding the composing process. The instructor must assume the role of collaborator and relinquish at least some of the authority that goes with the role of *teacher*. By confronting the assurance of the teacher's own selfhood as a teacher, writing allows questions of classroom and institutional ethics to come into being, especially questions about grading and evaluation in general. In addition, we can easily understand the implications raised by a paralogic rhetoric for relations of power within the classroom and within the academy, for university instructors, especially instructors outside of humanities departments, are generally loathe to relinquish to students their power to authorize interpretation both in the production and the reception of texts. Nonetheless, if we take seriously the demands placed upon our institutions and our classrooms made by a paralogic rhetoric, then change is inevitable, for we can no longer imagine writing to be a skill, process, or system that we can teach and then abandon.

To conclude, the kind of paralogic rhetoric that I am advocating here represents one of the numerous approaches to the movement that has come

to be called "post-process theory." Attempting to move beyond the still
dominant writing-process paradigm in composition studies, a paralogic
rhetoric understands communicative interaction to be necessary and even
sufficient for the formation of human understanding, and because writing
constitutes one of the most important forms of communicative interaction,
a paralogic rhetoric seeks to investigate how writing helps us to understand
ourselves and our social positions in relation to other language users and to
a world we share with these language users. Perhaps even more important,
a paralogic rhetoric seeks to investigate how we may become better hermeneutic guessers, better communicators, and consequently better neighbors.
And much work remains to be undertaken in these endeavors.

Works Cited

Dasenbrock, Reed Way. "Do We Write the Text We Read?" *College English* 53 (1991): 7–18.

Davidson, Donald. "A Nice Derangement of Epitaphs." *Truth and Interpretation: Perspectives on the Philosophy of Donald Davidson.* Ed. Ernest LePore. New York: Blackwell, 1986. 433–46.

Dobrin, Sidney I. *Constructing Knowledges: The Politics of Theory Building and Pedagogy
in Composition.* New York: State U of New York P, 1997.

Lyotard, Jean-François. *The Postmodern Condition: A Report on Knowledge.* Trans. Geoff
Bennington and Brian Massumi. Minneapolis: U of Minnesota P, 1984.

Ward, Irene. *Literacy, Ideology, and Dialogue: Towards a Dialogic Pedagogy.* Albany: State
U of New York P, 1994.

Yarbrough, Stephen R. *After Rhetoric: The Study of Discourse Beyond Language and
Culture.* Carbondale: Southern Illinois UP, 1999.

14

Writing and Truth: Philosophy's Role in Rhetorical Practice

BARBARA COUTURE

PERHAPS THE MOST MEMORABLE line in the blockbuster film *A Few Good Men* is Jack Nicholson's rejoinder to Tom Cruise's courtroom search for "the truth": "You want the truth? You can't handle the truth." It's a line that I have thought about now and then in the context of the work that I do both as a scholar in rhetoric and composition and as an academic dean. My last book, *Toward a Phenomenological Rhetoric*, was a response to a line of inquiry in our profession that I believe sidesteps the very human search for "the truth." I argued against the more popular view that a search for "the truth" is, at best, an epistemological anachronism—a holdover from the days when people believed that absolute truth was attainable (see Herrnstein Smith)—and at worst a misguided quest pursued by ideologues and hapless student writers (see Neel). I claimed that a search for the truth is at the core of the acts of writing and reading, and, furthermore, that claims about the ephemeral relationship of language to reality and the instability of meaning often are mistakenly applied to invalidate or deny that search. If I were to characterize the line of inquiry that my book and the work that I am doing now represent, I would say that I am exploring philosophy's role in rhetorical practice. My interest, however, is even more specific than that: I wish to explore philosophical conceptions of truth and truth telling as these have an impact on our practice and teaching of speaking and writing.

Truth and Truth Telling

To pursue truth telling may seem an esoteric line of inquiry for the classroom teacher who has the day-to-day charge to help students master the written sentence, apply and practice particular rhetorical genres, and competently address a variety of audiences. Nonetheless, I believe that scholarship that explores the relationship of writing to truth could not be more practical. My work as an academic dean demonstrates this verity nearly every day. Let me give a single example in which a question of "the truth" was at the core of interpreting a written exchange.

Not too long ago, I was asked to act on a case in which a faculty member was broadly distributing "factual" information that purported to summarize the validity of another faculty member's professional publications. The faculty member whose work was maligned argued not only that the facts reported were untrue but also that the reports were intended to be damaging and thus contributed to a lack of collegiality within the department. The consensual resolution to this problem hinged not only upon whether the "facts" reported told the truth but also upon a faculty member's right and obligation to disseminate, outside of the departmentally sanctioned processes of faculty evaluation, information that would call into question the work of another. Our eventual resolution to this dilemma reflected a judgment about the relationship between truth and goodness, the appropriate balance between, on the one hand, protecting the right to disseminate information in a situation in which truth is in dispute and, on the other, contributing appropriately to the collegial atmosphere of a workplace environment. In short, the controversy spoke to the concept of truth as a human value, as a concept that draws us together in a collaborative and, in my view, ultimately charitable enterprise of reaching common understanding within a system defined as just by all concerned.

While a human concern to find and share the truth is universal, at the same time, a variety of human standards for declaring a written statement accurate, valid, or true direct our written and spoken expression. When we make a claim to truth, we are also making a claim to an affiliation, to our association with a group of fellow human beings who hold similar standards for making such a claim. Scientists and engineers, for instance, expect factual claims to be linked to professional standards for careful observation and adherence to the scientific method of inquiry. Scholars of language and literature base and evaluate claims to truth on their affiliation with critical, rhetorical, or linguistic theories. But also at the core of human expression is something more universal than these separate claims to affiliation: a universal desire for the truth. Working from this premise, my line of inquiry explores the implications of this human value—that is, the desire for truth— for our production and evaluation of speaking and writing.

If I were to characterize the task that I set out for myself as a particular kind of intellectual problem, I would say that I am trying to reconcile a human value, an abstract ideal, with our physical effort to enact that value in our communication, a material practice. In my view, academic disciplines reflect boundaries defined by standards of abstract reasoning—explored especially, for instance, by scholars of philosophy, mathematics, and aesthetics—and properties of material objects and practices, studied by researchers in such fields as biology, geology, linguistics, physics, architecture, and engineering. The kind of problem that I am addressing crosses the boundaries of disciplines devoted to abstract reasoning and material practices because I am attempting to reconcile an intellectually defined concept with the physical reality of actual material practices.

The scholarship that informs my work, in particular, represents a line of inquiry that investigates the relationship between abstract concepts of ideal order and the material order we experience in physical objects and human practices. Three areas of scholarship explore this nexus as it relates to the problem of reconciling truth with rhetorical practice: phenomenological epistemology, philosophies of rhetoric, and moral theories of truth. Each of these categories represents scholarship that explores the link between abstract reasoning and experienced reality. Phenomenological epistemology, for instance, links abstract conceptions of knowledge and being with the human experience of knowing and living; philosophies of rhetoric combine theories of knowledge and truth with the categories and kinds of linguistic expression; and moral theories of truth combine definitions of truth with moral judgments of defined human behaviors. This charge to combine definition of an abstract concept with the human application or realization of that concept characterizes all of these areas of inquiry. It also is at the crux of the epistemological question they ask: Is truth an abstract ideal outside of or beyond human expression, or is truth integral to human expression? In the remainder of this discussion, I shall attempt to describe briefly each of these lines of inquiry, demonstrating what I believe is their relevance to my project of relating truth to writing. I will conclude with a speculative summary of how continued study of the problem of relating truth to writing might improve the teaching of writing.

Three Lines of Inquiry

Phenomenological epistemology, as I am defining it, covers a broad line of inquiry. Although some scholars who relate knowing to human experience mark an intellectual break between the phenomenological theory of Edmund Husserl and Jacques Derrida's post-structuralist response, I include all of this work under the broad term "phenomenological epistemology." These theories of knowledge all call into question the concept "objective knowledge," declaring that all knowledge is learned and created intersubjectively or inter-linguistically. In short, knowledge does not exist outside of human experience, whether you believe that experience is recorded in the human conscience (as do the phenomenologists) or generated through linguistic interchange (as do the post-structuralists). Although an abundance of scholarship in philosophy and critical theory can be included in the phenomenological project, I shall summarize here only the perspectives of Edmund Husserl and Jacques Derrida, who represent opposing "takes" on the phenomenological project.

Phenomenology as a named line of inquiry begins with the work of Edmund Husserl, who broke with the Cartesian tradition of separating the consciousness of a single individual from the world outside the individual. It is from this tradition that we derive our popular distinction of objective and subjective observation, the former being free of individual perspective, reflecting the world "out there," and the latter reflecting the perspective of the individual observer. Husserl broke with that tradition by claiming that there is no world that can be known outside of the subjective observer. This is not to say that there is no real world, but rather to say that all that we know about the world is our conscious sense of it through standing in relation to it. Hence, the path to true knowledge lies in our careful and accumulated conscious sense of the observed world. Husserl claimed that in order to come to perfect understanding, we must practice a complex process of attending called the "phenomenological reduction," whereby we "bracket" our preconceptions of the world and observe "things in themselves" as they appear directly to our consciousness. Even the concept of "objective validity" is, in

Husserl's terms, a subjective construction, derived from a consciously developed conceptualization of what objectivity is, and validated through intersubjective contact with things of the world and others in it. Husserl idealized a future pacific world of observers who might intersubjectively work together toward a common understanding, toward truth, through practicing together the phenomenological reduction (see, for instance, "Phenomenology").

Jacques Derrida's work in many ways is a response and reaction to Husserl's phenomenological project. He indeed credits Husserl with demystifying the Cartesian paradigm that suggests that there is a world "out there" that can be defined beyond our capacity to define it. But in Derrida's view, he did not go far enough. While Husserl did let go of the notion of a stable reality that can be defined beyond our human experience, he did not let go of the notion of stable meaning. Husserl's conceptualization of the phenomenological reduction presumed a conscious process by which a stable meaning might be realized through a person's intersubjective evaluation of his or her experience and interactions with others within the human consciousness.

Derrida posited that no such thing as consciousness exists wherein stable meaning might be housed or developed. In fact, consciousness itself is an artifact of language. Consciousness arises from our reaction to the differences that are inherent in language as it cues meanings and to the constant deferrals that language imposes on meaning as it is developed through linguistic interchange (see "Differánce"). Much of Derrida's work addresses a variety of problems that are encountered when we attempt to define "meaning," and he continues to explore how language figures in our quest for stable meaning — in short, our quest for truth. One more recent and quite interesting take on this problem appears in *Archive Fever*. Here, Derrida offers a phenomenological description of the historical archive, speculating about our interpretation and knowledge of Sigmund Freud as his archive "speaks" about him and through him. Derrida's speculations provoke such questions as these: Has the archive overtaken what we know to be the man? Does it tell us who is Sigmund Freud? Where does the truth about him lie? Does the archive build a truth all its own?

The phenomenological project to define truth in human experience and various reactions to it intrigues me because this scholarship elaborates truth as a human value expressed through our interactions with others. Husserl presents a notably optimistic projection of our prospects of achieving truth through the material practice of intersubjective communication. He spent the greater part of his life attempting to articulate an intellectual process through which we could come to fully understand the world through inter-subjective contact. Derrida, on the other hand—while often accused of advocating the nihilistic futility of achieving reliable meaning, and, consequently, of endorsing radical relativism—also optimistically projects language as a dynamic practice filled with possibility for creation and renewal. It is language that allows us to enjoy a vibrant present; the death of language is none other than our own death (see, for example, "Speech and Phenomena"). Continued exploration of the phenomenological perspective, I believe, allows those of us who practice and teach writing to develop greater insight into the ways that intersubjective interaction develops valued meaning.

Under the category "philosophies of rhetoric," I count those kinds of scholarship that link rhetorical practices to theories of truth or ways of knowing. Two philosophers whose work in this area bears relationship to my own interests are Richard Rorty and Jürgen Habermas. Both scholars concern themselves less with the relationship between language and truth than with the relationship between established or typical rhetorical practices and the development of shared beliefs and values.

I have found most fruitful Rorty's conception that knowledge is defined by alternative approaches to reasoning, approaches also defined by differing rhetorical practices. Briefly, Rorty argues that knowledge about the world can be validated by the different purposes it serves. The scientist who is seeking to verify reliable perceptions of the world and its workings is concerned with making a distinction between established facts and speculative theories, and this will be reflected in the way that he argues for or defends a theory as supported by fact. The humanist who is seeking to reveal something about human nature has greater interest in developing an ever-elaborated conception of our environment and ourselves than in distinguishing between a stable fact and a questionable theory; more important is the capacity of language to reveal something about ourselves. Humanist scholars, as Rorty suggests, have little interest in following established criteria for verifying fact. Rather, they are interested in developing criteria for validity that are relevant to those who will live by, appreciate, or use what they have to say. Rorty has tried to define a new conception of reasoning in language, one that reflects the various rhetorical methods by which we reach a common truth (see "Science as Solidarity"). He likewise has tried to characterize and define the human need to seek truth as this need is reflected in our practice of constantly "recontextualizing" belief—that is, adjusting what we believe to account for new information and our interactions with others (see "Inquiry as Recontextualization").

Another approach to reconciling rhetorical behavior with the desire to seek and define common belief is reflected in Jürgen Habermas's work to define a theory of communicative interaction. Habermas has tried to "organize" a social approach to truth seeking that reliably recognizes and acknowledges diverse interests. Working from a phenomenological premise that truth is developed intersubjectively, Habermas attempts to determine "rules" that lead a group of interactants, conversing together, to discover the truth. He has great faith in the rhetorical power of argument to lead us to a common belief that respects the interests of all who have a stake in it, and he makes this social criterion, in effect, his criterion for truth. For Habermas, congruence with logical principle—of deductive or inductive proof—following the principles of scientific reasoning forms a rational standard for the validity of a stated idea, and consensus forms a moral standard for reconciling the views of individuals whose views differ in attempts to reach an agreement. His research—at least in the context of this intellectual problem of defining a productive form of argument—has centered on the capacity of argument to develop beliefs that have common acceptance and respect across diverse groups participating in a common forum. I find work like that of Rorty and Habermas (and the "philosophies of rhetoric" they have developed) to be important to my project because this scholarship defines the place of rhetoric in the human project of constructing a shared belief or a shared value— something that might be construed as truth.

Although the work of Rorty and Habermas has addressed the relationship between moral values and standards of truth, it has not had the direct focus of defining truth as a moral value, a third area of inquiry that I have found important to my project of relating truth to writing. Two scholars of importance to me here are Alasdair MacIntyre and Emmanuel Levinas. In his well-known work, *After Virtue,* MacIntyre explores how our conceptions of truth relate to moral purpose. In MacIntyre's view, Enlightenment rationalism— that is, our belief in empirical proofs as forming the foundation for scientific knowledge—cannot lead us to truth because it is too limited. Rationalism defines the world and humanity on the basis of what we say and do, without any consideration of what we *ought* to say and do. In the Aristotelian cosmos that preceded the Enlightenment, MacIntyre reminds us, true or right beliefs and actions were related to humanity's established moral value. When the merit of someone's actions or beliefs is assessed solely according to an external rational standard for adequacy, without regard for whether those actions or beliefs reflect and respect a shared understanding of the function of human existence, these actions or beliefs have no moral value. Furthermore, without an evaluation of individual acts and claims in terms of a larger existential purpose, we have no foundation upon which to build beliefs that are shared truths among all human beings.

While MacIntyre's focus is defining truth as a human value related to a moral conception of humanity's purpose on earth and on developing a theoretical basis for moral action, Levinas's work focuses on knowledge and human existence as these are defined by our relationship to others. In attempting to define this relationship, Levinas comes to the conclusion that a selfless, uncompromising care for and attention to the needs of others is essential to our self-development and to our capacity to understand the truth of our existence. Levinas's work articulates a dynamic relationship between self and other that, it may appear, often defies articulation. This articulation is particularly difficult in a world that subscribes to the Cartesian assumption that knowledge exists on the outside, either captured in a world that we see through a "glass darkly," as it were, or defined by an infinite order that is beyond our reach. For Levinas, knowledge is being, a phenomenon that subsumes us and is realized in our perpetual act of relating. The total expression of this being is realized in a selfless relation to an other. In short, Levinas argues against the philosophical stance that being exists before beings, a stance that omits the fact that we experience and understand being only through our face-to-face encounter with others. This conception of being differs radically from a conception that defines the infinite—that is, knowledge beyond our own being—as something fundamentally prior to the relationship between self and other. Furthermore, it radically differs from a conception of self that defines an individual without reference to another; the self, rather, is distinguished only in one's unique responsibility to respond to another: "The I is bound up with the non-I as if the entire fate of the Other was in its hands. The unicity of the I consists in the fact that nobody can respond in its place" (Levinas 18).

According to Levinas, our moral conscience, as it were, develops as our sense of interdependency develops, as we understand that we can only be realized and recognized as independent because of our responsibility to others. We exist, therefore, in a charitable dependence upon others because they are like us, dependent on us, and thus the same. In distinguishing his development of this I-Thou relationship, as we have seen it more familiarly developed by Martin Buber, Levinas notes:

> Moral consciousness is not invoked here as a particularly commendable variety of consciousness but as the concrete form taken by a movement within the Same in the face of the Other, a movement that is more fundamental than freedom but that returns us to neither violence nor fatality. (20)

For Levinas, the "idea of the infinite" is grounded in being and defined by the endless responsibility of beings for one another, a responsibility that virtually *is* the perpetual nature of being.

Both MacIntyre and Levinas have worked from the premise that we cannot separate any question of truth from a moral obligation to address truth in human experience as a human value. This moral responsibility both legitimizes our existence and obligates us to respect and embrace others. MacIntyre's approach is rhetorical, defining our moral existence in terms of our characterization of human value; Levinas's approach is ontological, grounding moral consciousness in a theory of the beginnings and endings of being.

Truth and Rhetorical Practice

Having now summarized three lines of inquiry that I have found useful to my project of relating truth to writing, I shall conclude with a few words about what I hope continued work on such a project might achieve. I have no naïve hope that before I leave this earth I will have found the golden goose—that is, the "answer" to the characteristically human quest to find "the truth." I do, however, hope that I might articulate for writers and teachers of writing the issues that are at stake when we teach rhetorical argument—that is, when we define the particular way in which writing is bound up with our human conceptions of truth and moral value. To put aside this reality when teaching students does them and ourselves a terrible disservice because it puts aside what I regard as the most important function of writing: that is, to keep us together.

I will conclude with one more example of the possible application of philosophical studies of the relationship between truth and writing to this larger project of "keeping us together." Just yesterday, I was shown a copy of a departmental newsletter before it was to be distributed to our alumni. The chair had written an opening letter that addressed a new university-wide initiative and that suggested a power struggle between people in power (such as university administrators) and those who are affected by that power (students and faculty). This was the first expression that I had seen of the chair's views on this matter. Should the newsletter go out and be read by our alumni, by me, and by our university's executive officers, some readers may assume that a "voice" is not being listened to. But this voice was never "voiced" in the community that is responsible to one another for the particular initiative at hand. The chair may be speaking the truth. Must it therefore be publicly expressed? And to whom? And for what purpose? In short, what is our responsibility to make claims to truth, regardless of our investment in "the Truth"? The editorial piece, rhetorically, is quite effective. It may, in fact, also evoke a helpful response—for instance, broad discussion of the initiative under question. But will it also build for the writer a sense of self in relation to the others to whom it was written that is richer, more substantial, more knowledgeable than before it was written? Will it build a sense of what it means to be human, standing in relation to others also seeking the truth?

Answers to questions like these might be argued without end. My fear, however, is that they are not being argued or even talked about because attention to questions like these takes much time to consider, time away from lessons on rhetorical modes, audience analysis, revising techniques, and the like, and time away from the business of pushing papers, writing memos, and just getting things done. Yet, too, I wonder that if we did spend more time addressing philosophically our investment in truth as we write, might our writing do what it ultimately is designed to do? Might our writing bind us together in a common quest for truth, a meld that may do more to increase understanding than can be accomplished by what is said or written? I wonder.

Works Cited

Couture, Barbara. *Toward a Phenomenological Rhetoric: Writing, Profession, and Altruism.* Carbondale: Southern Illinois UP, 1998.
Derrida, Jacques. *Archive Fever: A Freudian Impression.* Trans. Eric Prenowitz. Chicago: U of Chicago P, 1996.

———. "Differánce." *Speech and Phenomena* 129–60.

———. *Speech and Phenomena and Other Essays on Husserl's Theory of Signs.* Trans. David B. Allison. Evanston, IL: Northwestern UP, 1973.

———. "Speech and Phenomena: Introduction to the Problems of Signs in Husserl's Phenomenology." *Speech and Phenomena* 3–104.

Habermas, Jürgen. *Moral Consciousness and Communicative Action.* Trans. Christian Lenhardt and Shierry Weber Nicholsen. Cambridge: MIT P, 1990.

Herrnstein Smith, Barbara. *Contingencies of Value: Alternative Perspectives for Critical Theory.* Cambridge: Harvard UP, 1988.

Husserl, Edmund. "'Phenomenology,' Edmund Husserl's Article for the *Encyclopedia Britannica* (1927)." Revised trans. by Richard E. Palmer. *Journal of the British Society for Phenomenology* 2 (1971): 77–90. Rptd. in *Husserl: Shorter Works.* Ed. Peter McCormick and Frederick A. Elliston. Notre Dame: U of Notre Dame P, 1981. 21–35.

Levinas, Emmanuel. "Transcendence and Height (1962)." *Emmanuel Levinas: Basic Philosophical Writings.* Ed. Adrian T. Peperzak, Simon Critchley, and Robert Bernasconi. Bloomington: Indiana UP, 1996. 11–31.

MacIntyre, Alasdair. *After Virtue: A Study in Moral Theory.* 2nd ed. Notre Dame: U of Notre Dame P, 1984.

Neel, Jasper. *Plato, Derrida, and Writing.* Carbondale: Southern Illinois UP, 1988.

Rorty, Richard. "Inquiry as Recontextualization: An Anti-Dualist Account of Interpretation." *The Interpretive Turn: Philosophy, Science, Culture.* Ed. David R. Hiley, James F. Bohman, and Richard Shusterman. Ithaca: Cornell UP, 1991. 59–80.

———. "Science as Solidarity." *The Rhetoric of the Human Sciences: Language and Argument in Scholarship and Public Affairs.* Ed. John S. Nelson, Allan Megill, and Donald N. McCloskey. Madison: U of Wisconsin P, 1987. 38–52.

15

Seeing in Third Sophistic Ways

VICTOR J. VITANZA

M ETAPHORS FOR SEEING are plentiful. As the cliché goes, *seeing is understanding*. We often say, "Oh, I see!" The predominant image used yesterday for the new visual technology known as television was the eye. (CBS, a modernist network, uses the eye as its logo.) The image used today in the new technology known as the WWW, a postmodernist network, is again the eye. Yes, we live in a predominantly visual culture, but how, when, and what we see with our eyes and through various media are radically different.

Incipient paradoxes for seeing are everywhere. As the cliché goes, *a way of seeing is a way of not seeing*. Those of us in rhetoric and composition attribute this cliché to Kenneth Burke; those in criticism, to Paul de Man, who with an additional twist says that there are critics whose "moments of greatest blindness with regard to their own critical assumptions are also the moments at which they achieve their greatest insight" (109). But there is the ancient paradoxical mythos of being blind when seeing, and becoming a seer when blind. Variations on this mythos include Tiresias and Oedipus.

Thus far, I have pointed to metaphors and paradoxes for seeing. Now I want to turn to other modernist notions of "seeing." In *Ways of Seeing,* John Berger writes:

> When we "see" a landscape, we situate ourselves in it. If we "saw" the art of the past, we would situate ourselves in history. When we are prevented from seeing it, we are being deprived of the history [that] belongs to us. Who benefits from this deprivation? In the end, the art of the past is being mystified *because* a privileged minority is striving

to invent a history which can retrospectively justify the role of the ruling classes, and such a justification can no longer make sense in modern terms. And so, inevitably, it mystifies. (11; emphasis added)

Berger discusses "seeing" as a matter of ideology and mystification.

Continuing Berger's discussion of modernist notions of seeing, Fredric
Jameson, in *Signatures of the Visible*, discusses Alfred Hitchcock's film *Rear
Window*, in which the narrative metaphor is a subject "seeing" an object, or
is, as Jameson writes, an expression of the

> scopophilic impulse [which] is not merely contained by . . . a psychic
> subject; [but it also] becomes what allows a narrative to segment into
> the distinct or semi-autonomous events of this or that viewing. When
> the psychic subject disappears altogether, however, . . . we are . . . in full
> postmodernism, at which point the analysis of scopophilia as a symp-
> tom and even an ideological stance becomes pointless. Postmodern
> specularity needs no motivation: . . . a subject obsessed with looking
> does not have to be "constructed" since there are no longer any cen-
> tered subjects of that sort in the first place: looking is everywhere and
> nowhere in the "society of the spectacle." (216–17)

Theory, Theoria, Spectacle, Theatre, Seeing

The four authors that I have quoted or alluded to speak of "seeing" and either
implicitly or explicitly refer to a subject or agent who sees. But each author
illustrates more than just seeing, for each stresses a different way of *seeing*
and *not seeing* and "seeing." (For the lack of a third term, I am at this point
simply repeating but placing the word "seeing" in quotation marks. I will
return to this third meaning.)

Each is putting forth a way of seeing or *theorizing* (or if I may purpose-
fully misspell, theor*eye*zing). But what does seeing have to do with theorizing? To answer this question, let us turn to the history of the word *theory*.
Raymond Williams points out that the history of the word and key term is
associated with spectacle and sight:

> The earliest English form was *theorique* (C14), followed by *theory*
> (C16), from [immediate forerunner] *theoria*, [Late Latin], *theoria*,
> Gk — contemplation, spectacle, mental conception (from *theoros*, Gk —

spectator, [ultimate traceable word] *thea,* Gk—sight; cf. theatre). In C17 it had a wide range: (i) spectacle: "a Theory or Sight" (1605); (ii) a contemplated sight. . . ; (iii) scheme (of ideas). . . ; (iv) explanatory scheme. (316)

George Kennedy translates Aristotle's definition of rhetoric as "Let rhetoric be [defined as] an ability, in each [particular] case, to see the available means of persuasion" (36; Kennedy's bracketed terms). In a lengthy footnote, Kennedy points to the word *"dynamis,"* saying that it signifies "ability, capacity, faculty, and potentiality," and the word *theoresai* signifies "to see." Together, then they signify "ability to see" (36-37).

I Am a Theorist

As a member of the field of rhetoric and composition, I have always (all ways) considered myself to be a theorist, a theoretician. I am solely, yet boundlessly, concerned with theorEYEzing. When I write "boundlessly," I mean that I leave behind on occasion systematic, alienated seeing—that is, I leave (as I write in "Three Countertheses") "homogeneity and arborescence" behind, and *by choice* (150). At least, this has been my intention. I cavort with the strangeness within words (within the material conditions of the *logos*) and for whatever ethical and political purposes I believed I must attend to— namely, to leave the spectacle of "presuppositions and the State" (that which has heralded the accomplished nihilism that Capital has thrust upon "us") for the spectacle of the *logos* without presuppositions and the State. I have done this cavorting in the name of a "third sophistic" (see Agamben, *Coming* 79-83).

Now, however, I am beginning to see that "our" *home of systematic seeing* (by way of the conceptual starting places or inventional *topoi* such as Aristotle's twenty-eight or Burke's five) will not for long remain a metatopos where "I" or "we" might return to after a dark drunken night out of town on the virtual Ovidian woods, cavorting with wild, savage *polylogoi*—that is, with all that has been excluded. I used to believe that it was possible after leaving the *polis* of systematic seeing to spend some paraproductive time in the *pagus* of thought—that wild, savage border zone where the excluded thirds and their ways of seeing dwell—and then when done to return, with insights, to the *polis* so as to make it more inclusive. I still believe that such excursions are valuable, but they soon will be impossible. Let me be unequivocal in making this point: I no longer believe that the *polis* will continue to be such a familiar, perhaps redeemable place; for the *polis*, which has been determined by the negative, is disappearing. The polis/pagus distinction is disappearing! Why? Put simply—as Jean Baudrillard, Paul Virilio, and so many others have been prophesying—because of the diminishing power of the negative to maintain identity by way of binaries. No quick injections of massive rounds of the negative will exclude the returning middles and thereby fix the collapsing binaries. No neo-pragmatisms will re-negate the excluded middles, or thirds, that are returning to collapse and then widely disperse the formerly dynamic duos. As the *polis* goes, so goes the sub-ject(ed)/object(tified). What will de/form the coming community is without any notion of antithesis but only remainders. Whatevers!

Let me explain further, but to do so, I will first sketch out my attitudes as I have *practiced* them (as in a political praxis), and then explain, by pointing, to the inevitable, imminent loss of what we refer to as the *polis* (local and global) and all that is part and parcel of it. I can but be sketchy and point to recent *sightings*, given the limits of space (which is ever collapsing around and on "us") and the ever-growing briefness of the hour.

A Theorist of Third Sophistic Ways of "Seeing"

As a theorist/writer of third sophistic ways of "seeing," I have used three *a*conceptual starting places, which I will represent here in a systematic way and thereby engage in a performative contradiction, as is expected in our field (or any educational field) when writing for scholarly publication. The three are *misrepresentative antidotes, dissoi-paralogoi,* and *theatricks.*

Each of these potential radical multiplicities is an alternative "seeing" (theorEYEzing) different but without any notion of the negative that would allow for the topos of difference (or similarity, more, less, etc.). These three can take people to the fringes of dyadic or binary systemic SEEing, which is the foundation of traditional philosophical rhetoric (SEEing, writing, speaking, thinking). It is difficult for most people to view these aconceptual starting places, for they will receive them semiotically across the negative. But this is understandable, for it is in the negative where we live and dwell (our home and nostalgia, our *polis*). Let me explain *these three* some more.

The first, *misrepresentative antidotes,* wages a perpetual war of denegation against "representative anecdotes" (Burke 59–126) or against grand narratives or negative essentialisms and customs (nature/culture), whether naïve or strategic-provisional. (The tragic-cum-farcical-cum-comedic war being waged is against the semioticians of the negative.)

The second, *dissoi-paralogoi* (a dis/uniting of sophistic *dissoi logoi* and paralogy), wages perpetual war against dialectic (of any kind), against didactic, and against *dissoi-logoi* by moving from one and two to an explosion of *threes* or "some more" (excesses, *dissoi-polylogoi*).

The third, *theatricks* (based on pragmatics), wages perpetual war against the conditions that establish T/truth and A/author/ity. Whereas *sentences* deal in truth claims and whereas *utterances* (speech acts) deal in authorial-performatives, theatricks (*theos*-tricks, "soundance" with sound and rhythm and slashing [or the virgule, /] over meaning, and farce cum comedy over tragedy) wage perpetual-paganistic war (on sentences and utterances) through third sophistic trickery and ruse after ruse. The fodder for this war is mined from the *pagus*.

These three have their sources in the SEEing performed variously by nonOedipal SEERs—specifically, for example, in the last century, from Georges Bataille and Paul Feyerabend through Gilles Deleuze and Félix Guattari to Jean-François Lyotard and Giorgio Agamben. These three, therefore, are not unique to me, nor are they new. These three have always already been available but forbidden (i.e., placed under the hortatory and philosophical negatives) by *what* counts as (mathematically correct) SEEing, theorizing, thinking.

Let us sum up by seeing that these three are not determined by a *restricted economy* but are de-determined by what Bataille calls a *general economy,* which would allow "us" *the ability "to see"* outside the binaries, "to see" what's been repressed, suppressed, oppressed because of the conditions of exclusion known as identification, noncontradiction, and the excluded middle. "We" would have done better to stick with the paralogics of the excluded Middle Ages (see Agamben, *Coming* 52–57)!

A quick example might remind us that for centuries, only men were considered fully formed, correct human beings. Only men were considered subjects (agents). Women were considered mistakes, not fully formed men, objects—hence, the structure of violence known as Subject/Object or more specifically Man/Woman, with *Man* privileged and *Woman* only a supplement.

The opposite *(dissoi logoi)* of this would be Woman/Man, which is a seeing by reversal and the refounding of a way of seeing that had been delig-

itimized with the coming of rational man. The process of this reversal of seeing can be called a *negative deconstruction,* which is still deeply indebted to a
restricted economy and to repression, suppression, oppression — that is, to
the conditions for the possibilities of what can be seen as Being and as Good.
As Being Good! Nothing changes by way of this process except the shift in
power over the opposing group; all of the *ressentiment* remains.

We are left with the question, however, Are these the exhaustion of the
conditions of possibilities for the sexes? The answer is nes and yo; that is,
the answers can be *yes,* if we allow our seeing to be determined by the
conditions of the *negative* or the *positive,* which is an incipient negative (i.e.,
a restricted economy); or it can be *no,* if we allow our "seeings" to be de-
determined by the negative — that is, by a third way of "seeing" called a *non-
positive-affirmative* (i.e., by a general economy). This way allows for "us to
see" third sexes (or intersexes) such as hermaphrodites, merms, ferms, and
so forth (see Fausto-Sterling). These sexes are not eccentric or showcase odd-
ities, for these sexes are now well into discussions on sexuality and civil rights
and equal opportunity in such commonplace, conservative publications as
Time and *Newsweek.*

Our third sophistic ways of "seeing" in the above example have moved
from *binary construction* through *negative deconstruction* or an imminently
reversible binary *(dissoi-logoi)* to *affirmative deconstruction (dissoi-paralogoi).*
For strategic-political reasons, many women who are concerned with theorEYEzing the "feminine" would not have "us" see in this manner/ism. What
still remains to be liberated is not only the term "man" (even in the face of
the ends of man) but also the term "woman," while other more strange terms
remain in a state of oppression. Imminent reversibility (M/F, F/M) leads but
to thirds. It is crucial to understand, however, that I am not using thirds in
the sense that Victor Turner is; I am not using them as a "liminal space," or
a space of transformation between now and then. There is no sense of *then*
(time as we know and have experienced it) after the collapse and dispersal of
all into remainders. If a "we" is to be in-between — and yes, there is a coming
community — it is not a hybrid "we" or "they," which would only be a thinking determined by the negative. There will have been no determination. And
yet, I will foreshadow and say that Turner is close to seeing the coming
"whatever beings," for these beings that are radical singularities live in a radical finitude.

The lists of threes, or third ways of seeing — the great horde of the excluded middle — is growing and becoming immense, if not endless and with

excess. We have yet to imagine what it might be like to see all that Aristotle labeled bad in terms of "excess" and "defect" (*Nicomachean Ethics* 1106b). I have discussed these ways previously as a paragenealogy of third positions (see "Threes").

A Third Sophistic Imminently Realized

Like a reporter at the late hour of a collapsing civilization, I must hurriedly write that a set(less) of third sophistic conditions is at play now. The jig is up! A yet wilder cavorting is almost upon "us." I can but report in a telegraphic style from this point on, knowing that I will be interrupted and cut short. But while the telegraph and its special kind of writing will have been interrupted, there is nonetheless the other writing that I am doing here: the writing of potentialities, faxing potentialities. I would rather be a "student" at (of) Tiananmen than a cyborg. What I am saying is that while I could opt for Donna Haraway's cyborg monsters—which I have in the past—I prefer instead to opt for the future perfect in yet another form(less). I am leaving behind Haraway's discussion of technology and going on with Giorgio Agamben's rereadings and rediscoveries of *techne, dynamis, potentialities* (see his *Potentialities*). I am leaving what is an ever *incipient* Victorian view of restricted economics, industrial revolutionary economics, and am un/headed along the borders (Lyotard's *pagus,* Derrida's *parergon,* and Agamben's *para-deigma*) for a general economy according to Agamben. While I would feign becoming a "student" at (of) Tiananmen, I would also practice (with) Bartleby's preferences—that is, his preference Not to Not. I would become, as Agamben suggests, s/he who "writes nothing but its potentiality to not-write" (*Coming* 37).

All is disappearing, and there is little to see, to theorEYEze. How does one write the disappearance? One cum three FAXes: along the borders, the threshold, where inside and outside collapse! As a reporter of this implosion and radical dispersal (it has been unbeknownst to me that I was its reporter!), I often used French sources. Now I turn to my own, Italian-Sicilian sources—eventually leaving them, too, behind, leaving identity.

According to Agamben, in *The Coming Community,* the coming beings are "whatever beings." (Yes, the coming community is inevitable! Border crossings to get bits and pieces of it to take home are no longer possible. The *pagus,* after all is said and undone, is in a manner of speaking coming home. I prefer to live in the pagus.) "Whatever beings" are not particular (i.e.,

species) or general (genus); instead, they are a set(less) of radical singularities (in the paralogic of the excluded Middle Ages, a.k.a. the *manere* [27]).
Their "in-difference with respect to properties is what individuates and disseminates singularities" (19). Hence, their indifference is their very whatever
being. Like Ulrich, in *The Man Without Qualities,* they are in-between—that
is, neither negative nor positive, but nonpositive affirmative, as I have been
saying I have been "seeing." They give accounts; they count: one, two, some
more. In this manner *(manere),* whatever beings leave behind all presuppositions and the State. Agamben writes that whatever beings "experience their
own linguistic being—not this or that content of language, but language
itself, not this or that true proposition, but the very fact that one speaks" (83).
The spectacle (accomplished nihilism) does not speak for them; they speak
without and beyond the spectacle: *in language itself!*

Agamben asks—just as "we" (who live with predispositions and the State)
would ask:

> What could be the politics of whatever singularity, that is, of a being
> whose community is mediated not by any condition of belonging
> (being red, being Italian, being Communist) nor by the simple absence
> of conditions (a negative [i.e., denegated] community, such as that
> recently proposed in France by Maurice Blanchot), but by belonging
> itself? A herald from Beijing carries the elements of a response. (85)

In belonging itself! But for "us" this belonging—or anything called a politics
based/less on this belonging—is so difficult to understand since it is a
belonging without a predisposition or State, a politics without taking a stand;
after all, the very word *understand* itself is a stasis, status, State word! (see
Burke 21, 23.) Whatever singularities have no understandings. They do not
ask or demand or fight for *recognition*—among themselves, or with "us."

There is not a belonging to something but a reflexive belonging itself,
which means a belonging without the negative. I can but ex-claim what
Agamben exclaims: This is a community without propositions as supports
that need, in turn, further scaffolding and support, even when it realizes that
it is scaffolding all the way down to radical finitude. Such a community in
need of supports is but a house of cards when confronting the community
without the negative that is the coming community.

Whatever beings are post-Lacanian, post-Žižekean subjects that are not
subjects but whatever singularities. Yes, "a herald from Beijing carries the
elements of a response" to our question concerning "What could be the

politics of whatever singularities"? Unlike Lacanian subjects, unlike Oedipal subjects, whatever beings do not make *demands*. Agamben writes:

> What was most striking about the demonstrations of the Chinese May [Tiananmen] was the relative absence of determinate contents in their demands (democracy and freedom are notions too generic and broadly defined to constitute the real object of a conflict, and the only concrete demand, the rehabilitation of Hu Yao-Bang, was immediately granted). ... *The novelty of the coming politics is that it will no longer be a struggle for the conquest or control of the State, but a struggle between the State and the non-State (humanity), an insurmountable disjunction between whatever singularity and the State organization.* This has nothing to do with the simple affirmation of the social in opposition to the State that has often found expression in the protest movements of recent years. Whatever singularities cannot form a *societas* because they do not possess any identity to vindicate nor any bond of belonging for which to seek recognition. (85–86)

The key words are *determinate contents, demands, identity,* and *recognition.* The absence of these words and what they conceptualEYEze signal that the Hegelean and Kojèvean principles of *subject/object in a struggle unto death for recognition* are no longer present, since the determinate negative has been set aside for the absolute negative (i.e., denegation) — in other words, since subjectivity/objectivity has been set aside for a third or whatever singularity or sovereignty.

However, a modernist reporter, Patricia Harkin, has written critically, as so many other modernist reporters have, not about Chinese students but about Hoosier students:

> When the postmodern Hoosier rhetor [student] has a contradiction pointed out to her [in an argument], then, she is less likely to contemplate the cognitive dissonance as a spur to invention and more likely simply to say "whatever." The postmodern Hoosier reinvents the "whatever" genre. (496–97)

Here are two communities blind to the other and colliding: one dead, yet teaching; the other, in its incipient formlessness, mutating. As Agamben says:

> Whatever is constituted not by the indifference of common nature with respect to singularities, but by the indifference of the common

and the proper, of the genus and the species, of the essential and the accidental. Whatever is the thing *with all its properties,* none of which, however, constitutes difference. In-difference with respect to properties is what individuates and disseminates singularities, make them lovable *(quodlibertable)*. (*Coming* 19)

Harkin has her greatest insight in her blindness: reinventing by way of "whatever." Yes! Whatever beings intuit that the principles of identity, non-contradiction, and excluded-middle (all the principles of negation informing re/invention) are the very principles that exclude, that disallow the thing with all its properties, that disallow radical singularities, themselves as such, in community.[1]

When asked, What is it that you want? *(Che Vuoi?)* by the aging political-pedagogical fathers and mothers, whatever singularities do not answer. After all has been said and undone, they are *whatever beings.* They prefer not to be in the present reactionary community, prefer not to be complicit in employing the principle that excludes, prefer not to not be in the coming community. In the "interworld" (97). In Limbo. Living there, abandoned by God and Satan, Generals and Pedagogues, abandoned beyond good and evil and with "guilt and justice behind them . . . the life that begins on earth after the last day is simply human life" (6-7).

Note

1. What I am suggesting is that, yes, there is a method of invention for a "whatever genre," and one that is more ethically-politically sound for the coming "whatever beings." See my beginning efforts to exemplify it in "From Heuristic to Aleatory Procedures."

Works Cited

Agamben, Giorgio. *The Coming Community.* Trans. Michael Hardt. Minneapolis: U of Minnesota P, 1993.

———. *Potentialities: Collected Essays in Philosophy.* Ed. and trans. Daniel Heller-Roazen. Stanford: Stanford UP, 1999.

Aristotle. *Nicomachean Ethics.* Trans. Terence Irwin. Indianapolis: Hackett, 1985.

———. *On Rhetoric: A Theory of Civic Discourse.* Trans. George A. Kennedy. New York: Oxford UP, 1991.

Baudrillard, Jean. *Simulacra and Simulation.* Trans. Sheila Faria Glaser. Ann Arbor: U of Michigan P, 1994.

Berger, John. *Ways of Seeing.* 1972. London: BBC and Penguin, 1985.

Burke, Kenneth. *A Grammar of Motives.* Berkeley: U of California P, 1969.

De Man, Paul. *Blindness and Insight: Essays in the Rhetoric of Contemporary Criticism.* 2nd ed. Minneapolis: U of Minnesota P, 1983.

Fausto-Sterling, Anne. "The Five Sexes: Why Male and Female Are Not Enough." *The Sciences* (Mar./Apr. 1993): 20–25.

Haraway, Donna. "Manifesto for Cyborgs: Science, Technology, and Socialist Feminism in the 1980s." *The Socialist Review* 80 (1985): 65–108.

Harkin, Patricia. "*Rhetorics, Poetics, and Cultures* as an Articulation Project." *JAC* 17 (1997): 494–97.

Jameson, Fredric. *Signatures of the Visible.* New York: Routledge, 1990.

Virilio, Paul. *Open Sky.* Trans. Julie Rose. New York: Verso, 1997.

Vitanza, Victor J. "From Heuristic to Aleatory Procedures; or, Towards 'Writing the Accident.'" *Inventing a Discipline: Rhetoric Scholarship in Honor of Richard E. Young.* Ed. Maureen Daly Goggin. Urbana: NCTE, 2000. 185–206.

———. "Three Countertheses: Or, A Critical In(ter)vention into Composition Theories and Pedagogies." *Contending with Words: Composition and Rhetoric in a Postmodern Age.* Ed. Patricia Harkin and John Schilb. New York: MLA, 1991. 139–72.

———. "Threes." *Composition in Context: Essays in Honor of Donald C. Stewart.* Ed. W. Ross Winterowd and Vincent Gillespie. Carbondale: Southern Illinois UP, 1994. 196–218.

Williams, Raymond. *Keywords: A Vocabulary of Culture and Society.* Revised ed. New York: Oxford UP, 1983.

Part Five

New Directions

16

Body Studies in Rhetoric and Composition

SHARON CROWLEY

> Posthuman bodies are not slaves to master discourses but emerge at nodes
> where bodies, bodies of discourse, and discourses of bodies intersect to fore-
> close any easy distinction between actor and stage, between sender/receiver,
> channel, code, message, context.
>
> —Judith Halberstam and Ira Livingston, *Posthuman Bodies*

MODERN RHETORICAL THEORY assumes that "actors" "send" "messages" to "receivers" through "channels," all of which operate within lim-itable or describable "contexts." Composition studies takes the stability of the sender-message-audience relation equally seriously. That all parties to dis-cursive transactions are embodied remains unmentioned in either rhetorical theory or composition studies because both fields still cling to liberal-humanist models of the speaking subject—a sovereign, controlling disem-bodied and individual voice that deploys language in order to effect some predetermined change in an audience. This remains the case even though the feminist/postmodern announcement—that individuals are neither devoid of embodiment nor free of the linguistic/cultural contexts in which they circu-late—seriously compromises modernist notions about authors and rhetors.

In a posthumanist dispensation, to say that bodies are not containers of something-else-that-is-more-important (that is, to reject the modernist body) is not enough. Nor does it suffice to think of bodies as constructed by or within discourse (although even that minimal gesture disrupts the scene of composing typically depicted in both modern rhetoric and composition, since it disperses the "control" imagined to be operating within that scene away from authors or rhetors into language and culture). Posthumanists, though, take the further step of noticing that bodies—human and other-wise—are both the site and the aegis of the flow of power. As Halberstam and Livingston put it, "Posthuman bodies are the causes and effects of postmod-ern relations of power and pleasure, virtuality and reality, sex and its conse-quences. The posthuman body is a technology, a screen, a projected image" (3). The body both writes and is written upon; it is the scene as well as the aegis of representation.

Modern rhetorical theory and composition studies have yet to grapple with insights emerging in a field of discourse that may as well be called "body studies." For example, while the "writing body" is little noticed in composition studies, at the same time, compositionists anxiously and repeatedly write a phantasmic student body into their scholarship. In this essay, I review some recent scholarly work about bodies in the hope that readers of this collection will be motivated to rethink rhetoric and composition's clinging to a mod-ernist construction of the subject, a construction that after all supports a dis-criminatory and unfair distribution of intellectual, social, and political power.

Feminism and Bodies

Susan Bordo credits second-wave feminists with the discovery that female bodies are sites of representation in the political sense of that term—that is to say, second-wave feminists discovered that whose bodies get repre-sented, and where and how this representation occurs, is an effect of the cir-culation of power. According to Bordo, "neither Foucault nor any other post-structuralist thinker discovered or invented the idea . . . that the 'defi-nition and shaping' of the body is 'the focal point for struggles over the shape of power.' That was discovered by feminism, and long before it entered into its marriage with post-structuralist thought" (17). To bring her point home, Bordo quotes from a set of consciousness-raising exercises for men, devel-oped by second-wave feminists in 1971:

> Sit down in a straight chair. Cross your legs at the ankles and keep your knees pressed together. Try to do this while you're having a conversa-tion with someone, but pay attention at all times to keeping your knees pressed tightly together.
>
> Run a short distance, keeping your knees together. You'll find you have to take short, high steps if you run this way. Women have been

taught it is unfeminine to run like a man with long, free strides. See how far you get running this way for thirty seconds.

Walk down a city street. Pay a lot of attention to your clothing; make sure your pants are zipped, shirt tucked in, buttons done. Look straight ahead. Every time a man walks past you, avert your eyes and make your face expressionless. (19)

I quote this passage not to make the liberal and patronizing point that "You've come a long way baby." To the contrary, I suspect that even now many women readers will find their public behavior depicted in the last paragraph of the passage. I do want the citation from Bordo's work to point to the fact that in modern culture, women are particularly well placed to develop analyses and critiques of the body and of the regimes that govern bodily practices. Women's worth has been measured through and by their bodies: Are they virginal or not? Impregnable or not? "Attractive" or not? Negatively charged cultural constructions of women's bodies as both dangerous and fragile have forced women to become highly conscious of their bodies—the space they occupy in a room, on the street, in a crowd. As objects of the male gaze, women know very well what it means to occupy the position of "the other," even if they do not read the philosophical texts in which they are imagined as such.

The great contribution made to body studies by feminists is their articulation of the fact that bodies—and hence the flow of power—are intricately enmeshed in what Bordo calls "the 'micropractices' of everyday life": eating and cooking, cleaning house, wearing clothes, going to the doctor and the hospital, attending church or school. This attention to the social practices that produce and are produced by bodies occupied feminists of both the first and second waves who forcefully elaborated the ways in which everyday material practices are saturated with discriminatory politics. In the mid-nineteenth century, for example, Elizabeth Cady Stanton showed that marriage, divorce, inheritance law, and even the practices entailed in "citizenship" itself were saturated with patriarchal assumptions about what women "are" and could "do," as were the social codes that denied women the opportunity to speak in public or to participate in politics, to become educated, or to work outside the home. In Stanton's time, the female body was confined to a highly circumscribed round of activities centered on the home (women's bodies were literally confined as well by corsets and elaborate, expensive dresses that restricted movement).

The fact that public discourse typically assumes a male subject has made it necessary for feminists to interrogate the assumptions that inform public practices and rhetoric about them. The assumption that distinct public and private spheres exist, for example, animated nineteenth-century social thought, and it underlies a good deal of contemporary rhetorical criticism of public discourse as well. However, it is doubtful whether this theoretical distinction fits women's political practices; that is, it is doubtful that the "official" public sphere conceptualized by bourgeois theorists like Adam Smith in the eighteenth century and revived by Habermas in our own time was or is conceived as a place wherein women traffic. This is emphatically not to say that women did not participate in public practices in earlier periods, as they continue to do today.[1] But we should remember that the eighteenth-century coffeehouses—on which Habermas models his notion of the public sphere—denied access to women. Women were banned from appearing in public spaces without a suitable escort during the early decades of the nineteenth century, and women were denied access to public discourse de facto and de jure until first-wave feminists secured their rights to own property, legally represent their children, and vote. The connection between their inability to own property and their inability to claim legal jurisdiction over their own and their children's bodies was not lost on first-wave feminists such as Stanton. She and other first-wave activists struggled to establish legal and economic identities for women as beings who were not simply bodies or simply the property of fathers, husbands, brothers, or uncles.

First-wave feminists did not succeed in erasing women's bodies from the male imaginary as objects of desire; that struggle continues today, well beyond the major cultural impact wrought by the second wave. If first-wave feminists succeeded in inhabiting some public spaces with female bodies, neither they nor feminists of the second wave managed to locate or establish a space governed by women's discourse. Contemporary women cannot easily locate or inhabit a so-called "private space" that shields them from the effects of certain public discourses, such as those governing health care and reproduction, for example. Women are openly and sometimes violently harassed when they visit clinics where abortions are performed, and as I write this chapter antiabortion activists are promising to agitate for recall of the so-called "abortion pill," precisely because this new technology privatizes the decision to terminate a pregnancy. That is, women's bodies and their reproductive practices are still thought to be legitimate fodder for public discussion, which is in distinct contrast to the social response to men's bodies and reproductive practices. Consider, for example, that while men are crucial partners in teenage pregnancy and in prostitution, neither fathers nor "johns" are often named as responsible parties in public discussions of these activities.

Feminist scholars who are animated by both political and scholarly agendas continue to investigate the material conditions of reproduction, women's health, the circulation of disease, the distribution of justice, and other crucial issues affecting the construction, circulation, and control of bodies.[2] Efforts such as these are profoundly rhetorical (although, sadly, the feminist scholars who make them seldom recognize this fact). Feminists practice rhetoric when they attempt to have a voice in policy making and when they intervene in public practices. But feminists, including feminist scholars, also analyze the public rhetorics that affect women's bodies and practices not only in an attempt to understand how such bodies and practices are deployed but also in order to intervene into the power relations that produce and sustain them.

Postmodernism and Bodies

Postmodern thought also laid some important theoretical groundwork for the development of scholarly interest in bodies and material practices.[3] Credit for the insight that bodies are both the site and the object of representation is often given to Roland Barthes, who wrote, "The symbolic field is occupied by a single object from which it derives its unity. . . . This object is the human body" (214–15). Barthes might well have taken his cue from Freud, who comments on the constructive relation of the body to the ego as follows:

> A person's own body, and above all its surface, is a place from which both external and internal perceptions spring. It is seen like any other object, but to the touch it yields two kinds of sensations, one of which may be equivalent to an internal perception. . . . Pain, too, seems to play a part in the process, and the way in which we gain new knowledge of our organs during painful illnesses is perhaps a model of the way by which in general we arrived at the idea of our body. The ego is first and foremost a bodily ego; it is not merely a surface entity, but is itself the projection of a surface. (19–20)

Egos—identities—are bodily entities. Because of the way human perception works, the ego not only depends upon the body for its formation but also projects itself as an imagined body, as the surface it imagines itself "to inhabit." The body, then, is both the site and the mechanism that allows a human being to represent him or herself in language and behavior.

Barthes and Freud wrote out of a masculinist rhetorical tradition in which male bodies are virtually unrepresented—that is, the tradition of Western philosophy. The apogee (or nadir) of this tradition can perhaps be found in Thomas Hobbes's *De Cive,* where, according to Nancy Hirschmann, Hobbes "describes men as springing forth, virtually overnight, separate, discrete, and fully formed, like mushrooms—an image which conveniently does away with women's role in human reproduction" (37). On the other hand, this tradition hyper-represents female bodies, both as targets of male desire and as themselves representative of hidden or forbidden knowledge (Brooks, de Lauretis). While this asymmetry is now being remedied within feminist and other postmodern scholarship, (see Bordo's *The Male Body,* for example), it cannot be said, even yet, that male bodies have become objects of the cultural gaze with anything like the ease or frequency in which female bodies are still displayed for mass consumption.

Pasi Falk, author of *The Consuming Body,* argues that postmodernists' relentless resolution of dualisms into continua opened the way for the dissolution of the body/mind distinction (4). In the *Grammatology,* Jacques Derrida argued that such inherited dualisms privilege one term over the other, and he proposed a double move to countervene their effects; the first move asserts the importance of the formerly secondarized term, while the second demolishes the dichotomy itself. Body studies can be characterized as an example of the first deconstructive move insofar as it privileges the bodily or the embodied. Postmodernism in general has made the second move by displacing the body/mind dichotomy onto a continuum: Body$\longleftrightarrow$Mind. Seen this way, neither of the terms is privileged. This line of thought also opens a space for thinking about the relations that obtain between body and mind, and for speculating about the difficulty of distinguishing the limits of either in relation to the other.

Freud's analysis of the embodiment of perception and hence of ego, cited earlier, raises an interesting series of questions about both the "internal" and "external" limits of bodies. How do we mark "the inside" of a human body as opposed to its "outside"? Where, for example, does the "outside" of the human eye end or begin? At the eyeball? The iris? The retina? But, then, where does the retina begin and end? When I place two parts of my body together, say, touching thumb to index finger, both digits experience the

touch as both "inside" and "outside." To distinguish skin as the differentiat-
ing organ requires intense concentration, as well as my (learned) assumption
that the "skin" of my thumb is the same "skin" that covers my finger. And is
the mouth an "inside" or an "outside"? And as feminist theorists such as Luce
Irigaray and Monique Wittig remind us, female genitalia raise further interesting questions about the confidence with which we can distinguish
between bodily insides and outsides (the uncertainty of this bodily "boundary" may explain, at least in part, masculinist uneasiness about women's bodies). All of these considerations challenge the distinctions we like to make
between bodily insides and outsides as well as our habit of attaching our
sense of identity to the presumed limits of the body.[4] This attachment apparently attends the practice of organ donation. Very few people sign themselves
up as organ donors when they are issued drivers' licenses, and the bodies of
only about 10 percent of donors are made available to hospitals. Families, it
seems, are loathe to allow parts of their loved ones to become part of someone else.

Cultural anxiety about bodily boundaries exhibits itself in other ways as
well. Scholars who study exceptional bodies are investigating the ways in
which cultural-material practices shape and maintain what is included in the
category of "the normal body" and the cultural uses to which the category of
the "not-normal" is put (Davis, Thomson). Our culture seems to do its most
rigorous policing around the boundaries of the sexed body in an effort to
maintain a rigid distinction between male and female. In her study of her-
maphroditism, for example, Elizabeth Grosz notes that even though the existence and formation of external genitalia are the criteria most often used to
determine anatomical sex, there are at least six different combinations of
additional factors such as chromosomal sex, internal sex organs, and hor-
monal functions that combine to produce beings whose sex might be said to
be both female and male (59–60). A problem arises, says Grosz, not because
hermaphroditic bodies exist but because a restrictive system of sexual classi-
fication insists on a bipolar distinction between male and female. Within
such a regime, we do not celebrate the multiplicity of sexes "given" us by
"nature"; rather, we presume that people whose bodies do not clearly com-
ply with our bipolar definition of "true sexuality" are inadequately or inap-
propriately sexed, and we urge or force them to become one or the other. If
our presumption of bipolar sex is troubled by the range and variety of sexes
found in nature, it becomes even more troubling when we discover, as we do
when reading the work of historians of sexuality such as Ann Fausto-Sterling

or Thomas Laqueur, that "male" and "female" have not always been defined as they now are.

The Body⟷Mind continuum at least complexifies modern notions of identity and the self. Bodies are sexed, raced, gendered, abled or disabled, whole or fragmented, aged or young, fat, thin, and anorexic. In other words, bodies are marked in ways that carry a great deal of cultural freight. Identities are also marked by cultural constructions of bodies, and hence cultural evaluations of bodies extend to the subjects who inhabit them and with whose limits they are supposedly coterminous. Students of the new field called "whiteness studies" take this insight as their motivation, assuming that the cultural privilege accorded to bodies marked as racially white produces something that can be called "white identity" (Dyer).

Freud's elision of the body/mind dichotomy also suggests that the private mental space accorded to "the self" on modern models of identity, the space of fantasy, is produced to some extent by the body's being-in-culture. Slavoj Žižek notes that "at its most fundamental, fantasy tells me what I am to others" (9). That is to say, our fantasies, those wonderful or terrifying stories we weave about ourselves in our supposedly most private "interior" moments, are actually extensions of culture into that space formerly and mistakenly called "mind." Žižek argues that fantasy has a "radically intersubjective character" insofar as it is "an attempt to provide an answer to the question 'What does society want from me?' to unearth the meaning of the murky events in which I am forced to participate" (9). Hence, the rabidly racist fantasies advanced by white supremacists, say, are not simply graphic projections of

a mental force called "hatred" onto the bodies of others, as the traditional account would have it. Žižek reads such fantasies, rather, as the racist's attempt to cope with the realization that his identity, his body in fact, is not the founding center of the universe, that he inhabits a network of ideological and material relations that relate indifferently to his person.

So fantasy is constructed, at least in part, by ideology. Does fantasy at the same time construct ideology? In other words, do elements of fantasy (that is to say, desire) operate within dominant ideologies? Certainly, feminist thinkers have taken the psychoanalytic insight about the intersubjective nature of fantasy in overtly political directions. In her recent work, Zillah Eisenstein reminds us that shared fantasies have physical impact on empirical bodies. Arguing that racial and ethnic hatreds are projections of "fear of the other," Eisenstein writes that "hatred is not only color-coded but inscribed on such body parts as noses, hair, vaginas, eyes. . . . Bodies are always in part psychic constructions of meaning symbolized through coloring hatred on sexualized sites" (22). This is one reason why the enactment of ethnic and racial hatred in war or other violent episodes often involves rape and torture. The aim is not merely to inflict pain but actually to eradicate the enemy's subjectivity by invading, harming, and erasing his/her body (Scarry). Jacqueline Rose argues further that fantasy "fuels . . . the forging of the collective will. . . . You don't have to buy into Freud's account of hidden guilt to recognize the force in the real world of the unconscious dreams of nations" (3). Rose's primary example is Israel, where, she says,

> if you listen to one dominant rhetoric, it seems as if Israel cannot grant statehood to the Palestinians, not just because of felt real and present danger, but also because so great is the charge of fantasy against such a possibility that, were it to be granted, the nation would lose all inner rationale and psychically collapse in on itself. (4)

Rose's work causes me to speculate about the shared fantasies that motivate other nations' politics. The reunification of Germany seems to mark a triumph of national fantasy over impossible realities, while the American fantasy of super-powerhood rationalizes sending thousands of young bodies to Iraq, Panama, Rwanda, and Bosnia, either to make war or to keep the peace (which is which is not always clear).

Rhetoric and Body Studies

Rhetoric operates in discussions about which flag will fly over a state capital, who can protest outside an abortion clinic, who can buy and use a gun, who should pay for medications for the elderly, whether the habitat of the snowy owl should be preserved, whether persons of the "same" sex should be allowed to marry, and whether citizens of the United States should support the actions of the World Trade Organization. The rhetoric produced to resolve (or fail to resolve) issues such as these actually produces practices that either circumscribe or open new possibilities for the circulation of bodies within power. The study of actual rhetorical practices is the province of rhetorical criticism—a scholarly activity undertaken with much skill in departments of speech communication but virtually absent from composition studies, which could benefit, in my opinion, from attention to the ways in which teachers' and students' bodies and rhetoric about them circulate in classrooms and in the university. But body studies also contributes to rhetorical theory because of its habit of pointing up the interestedness of boundary drawing and distinction making. Distinctions and boundaries are never disinterested: when someone is named as a supporter of the Confederacy, a protestor, a homosexual, an environmentalist, or a patriot, someone profits from that distinction and, under capitalism, someone else pays for that gain. What I learn from body studies is that no body is disinterested. And that's why this work is central to rhetorical studies, which has always taken the study of partisanship as its province.

Notes

1. See Eley and Ryan for elaboration of this historical fact. My point is only that the "official" public sphere characterized in theory is a male or masculinized sphere. For arguments in support of this position, see Fraser, Hirschmann, and Pateman.

2. For feminist studies of these issues, see (for starters) the work of Wendy Brown, Drucilla Cornell, Irene Diamond, Nancy Fraser, Renata Salecl, and Susan Squire.

3. One needs to be careful here: a radical version of post-structuralist thought—what Teresa Ebert, among others, calls "ludic post-structuralism"—can be read to be hostile to materialism and the material.

4. For elaborations of this argument, see Jacques Derrida, "'Eating Well,' or the Calculation of the Subject: An Interview with Jacques Derrida," *Who Comes After the Subject?* ed. Eduardo Cadava, Peter Connor, and Jean-Luc Nancy (New York: Routledge, 1991): 96–119; and Pasi Falk, *The Consuming Body* (London: Sage, 1994).

Works Cited

Barthes, Roland. *S/Z*. Trans. Richard Miller. New York: Hill and Wang, 1974.

Bordo, Susan. *Unbearable Weight: Feminism, Western Culture, and the Body*. Berkeley: U of California P, 1993.

Brooks, Peter. *Body Work: Objects of Desire in Modern Narrative*. Cambridge: Harvard UP, 1993.

Davis, Lennard J. "Constructing Normalcy: The Bell Curve, the Novel, and the Invention of the Disabled Body in the Nineteenth Century." *The Disability Studies Reader*. Ed. Lennard J. Davis. New York: Routledge, 1997. 9–28.

De Lauretis, Teresa. *Alice Doesn't: Feminism, Semiotics, Cinema*. Bloomington: Indiana UP, 1984.

Derrida, Jacques. "'Eating Well,' or the Calculation of the Subject: An Interview with Jacques Derrida." *Who Comes After the Subject?* Ed. Eduardo Cadava, Peter Connor, and Jean-Luc Nancy. New York: Routledge, 1991. 96–119.

Dyer, Richard. *White*. London: Routledge, 1997.

Ebert, Teresa. *Ludic Feminism and After: Postmodernism, Desire, and Labor in Late Capitalism.* Ann Arbor: U of Michigan P, 1996.

Eisenstein, Zillah. *Hatreds: Racialized and Sexualized Conflicts in the 21st Century.* New York: Routledge, 1996.

Eley, Geoff. "Nations, Publics, and Political Cultures: Placing Habermas in the Nineteenth Century." *Habermas and the Public Sphere.* Ed. Craig Calhoun. Cambridge: MIT P, 1997. 236–58.

Falk, Pasi. *The Consuming Body.* London: Sage, 1994.

Fausto-Sterling, Anne. *Myths of Gender: Biological Theories about Women and Men.* 2nd ed. New York: Basic, 1992.

Fraser, Nancy. "Rethinking the Public Sphere: A Contribution to the Critique of Actually Existing Democracy." *Social Text* 25/26 (1990): 56–80.

Freud, Sigmund. *The Ego and the Id.* Trans. Joan Riviere. Ed. James Strachey. New York: Norton, 1960.

Grosz, Elizabeth. "Intolerable Ambiguity: Freaks as/at the Limit." *Freakery: Cultural Spectacles of the Extraordinary Body.* Ed. Rosemarie Garland Thomson. New York: New York UP, 1996. 55–66.

Halberstam, Judith, and Ira Livingston. "Introduction: Posthuman Bodies." *Posthuman Bodies.* Ed. Judith Halberstam and Ira Livingston. Bloomington: Indiana UP, 1995. 1–19.

Hirschmann, Nancy. *Rethinking Obligation: A Feminist Method for Political Theory.* Ithaca: Cornell UP, 1992.

Irigaray, Luce. *This Sex Which Is Not One.* Trans. Catherine Porter. Ithaca: Cornell UP, 1985.

Laqueur, Thomas. *Making Sex: Body and Gender from the Greeks to Freud.* Cambridge: Harvard UP, 1990.

Pateman, Carole. *The Sexual Contract.* Stanford: Stanford UP, 1988.

Rose, Jacqueline. *States of Fantasy.* Oxford: Clarendon, 1996.

Ryan, Mary P. "Gender and Public Access: Women's Politics in Nineteenth-Century America." *Habermas and the Public Sphere.* Ed. Craig Calhoun. Cambridge: MIT P, 1997. 259–88.

Scarry, Elaine. *The Body in Pain: The Making and Unmaking of the World.* New York: Oxford UP, 1985.

Thomson, Rosemarie Garland. "Introduction: From Wonder to Error—A Genealogy of Freak Discourse in Modernity." *Freakery: Cultural Spectacles of the Extraordinary Body.* Ed. Rosemarie Garland Thomson. New York: New York UP, 1996. 1–19.

Žižek, Slavoj. *The Plague of Fantasies.* London: Verso, 1997.

17

Delivering the Message: Typography and the Materiality of Writing

JOHN TRIMBUR

IN RECENT YEARS, those of us involved in the study and teaching of writing have been trying to adjust to life after the process movement. To be sure, the slogan "process not product" long ago lost any critical edge it might have possessed in the 1970s, and the once enabling notion that composing is the critical object of inquiry now seems, in Karl Marx's words, a "one-sided" view of the production of writing. One can no longer read, for example, Janet Emig's or Donald Graves's pioneer composing research without reading into it representations of their research subjects as gendered and racialized subjects of class society. And yet, the moment writing theorists are starting to call "post-process" must be seen not just as a repudiation of the process movement but also as an attempt to read into composition precisely the material conditions of the composer and the material pressures and limits of the composing process. As Robert J. Connors once remarked, the reason we feel we're living in a post-process era is that process has been so fully assimilated, so exhaustively read into and written over that we forget about the traces it has left in our theories and practices.

The dominant representations of writing typically offered by the process movement—voice, cognition, conversation—despite the crucial differences among them, all picture writing as an invisible process, an auditory or mental event that takes place at the point of composing, where meanings get made. In my contribution to this volume, I want to reread these dematerialized representations of writing in terms of the materiality of literacy, from the perspective that writing is a visible language produced and circulated in material forms. To put it another way, I want to suggest that the process movement's emphasis on the composer as the maker of meaning (whether that figure entails self-expression, mental activity, or participation in communal discourses) has obscured the composer's work in producing the resources of representation in order to signify at all, to make the special signs we call writing.

The Materiality of Writing

The line of thinking I propose holds that the figure of the composer we inherit from the process movement can still provide a generative topos in writing studies. The task, however, requires a thoroughgoing reconceptualization of the writer at work—one that locates the composer in the labor process, in relation to the available means of production. In certain respects, of course, such a project has already begun. No doubt the leading impetus to materialize literacy comes from the emergence of digital communication. Marshall McLuhan says that we can see human-made environments only once they have changed, and this is very much the case, I think, regarding the current shift from print to digital literacy. These changes in the technology of writing allow us to compare, say, mechanical means of production such as the typewriter or the Linotype machine and hot type of the late nineteenth-century print shop to the cool cybersurface and digital signals of the computer screen and digital signals. As Christina Haas points out, it is no longer quite so easy to treat the technologies of writing as transparent, to efface the material tools and embodied practices involved in the production of writing.

One of the main obstacles to *seeing* the materiality of writing has been the essayist tradition and its notion of a transparent text. (It is no accident that the process movement's favored genre has always been the essay, be it literary, journalistic, or academic.) I argued a few years ago that essayist literacy—from the scientific prose of the Royal Society to the essay of the coffeehouse and salon—emerged in the early modern period as a rhetoric of deproduction: a programmatic effort to reduce the figurative character of writing, minimize the need for interpretation, and thereby make the text more transparent ("Essayist"). What I was not aware of at the time, however, is how essayist literacy's compulsion to eliminate metaphor is linked to Old Testament warnings about graven images and to a Protestant desire to purge writing of all traces of visuality, a desire to replace, as Lester Faigley puts it, the "'mindless' auditory, visual, and olfactory credulity of Catholicism with the power of reason expressed in print" (174–75).

In Faigley's view, the notion of transparent text results from a great Alphabetic Literacy Narrative that runs through the work of Harold Innis, Jack Goody, Eric Havelock, and Walter Ong. This grand narrative identifies "'true' literacy" with the "abstract representation of sounds—a presupposition that subordinates syllabic and logographic writing systems and banishes pictographs and images to the status of illiteracy" (174). As the graphic design theorists J. Abbott Miller and Ellen Lupton say, "Westerners revere the alphabet as the most rational and transparent of all writing systems, the clearest of vessels for containing the words of speech" (21). By this account of literacy, the suppression of visuality in the alphabet's abstract coding system provides the groundwork for normative representations of both cultural and individual development as matters of overcoming a dependence on the visual that is taken to be immature, ephemeral, and manipulative. Accordingly, it should be no surprise that David Olson would want to make the essay into the culmination of alphabetic literacy precisely because it appears to transcend the visuality of writing by organizing the speech-sound abstractions of the alphabet into highly integrated grammatical and logical structures, forming self-sufficient, autonomous texts capable of speaking for themselves. The texts of essayist literacy, by Olson's account, appear to transmit meanings transparently, without reference to their mode and medium of production.

The fatal weakness of the Alphabetic Literacy Narrative and its commitment to textual transparency, however, is its scopophobia and how its fear of the visual causes it to align writing with speech. In this sense, the irony of the grand narrative is that it suppresses the full upshot of its own discovery—namely, that writing amounts to be less a recording of speech than a visual coding system that communicates by employing a range of nonphonetic elements such as spacing, punctuation, frames, and borders, not to mention the eccentricities in codes, such as in written English where different words can have the same sound (its/it's, meet/meat) and silent letters seem to defy phonetic strategies of pronunciation (might, paradigm). Haunted by suspicions of the visual (and hence of the visibility of writing), at just the moment when it elevates alphabetic literacy to a preeminent position in Western cultural history, the Alphabetic Literacy Narrative comes unglued, reminded by the very visuality of the alphabet, as Miller and Lupton say, that writing can only be a "faulty reflection of speech, an artificial by-product of the otherwise natural workings of the mind" (24).

Now, you don't have to be much of a Derridean (I'm certainly not) to recognize a metaphysics of presence at work in such disappointment with writing, the overwhelming sense that what promised to be the vehicle for rational
discourse is, in the end, a treacherous medium that continually betrays its
own ostensible transparency by thickening into metaphor and material
form. My view, perhaps uncharacteristically, is to follow Derrida out of the
morass created by the Alphabetic Literacy Narrative and to picture writing
not as a derivative of speech at all but instead as a typographical and rhetorical system of sign making. After all, as the turn-of-the-century Austrian
architect and graphic designer Alfred Loos put it so concisely, "One cannot
speak a capital letter" (qtd. in Helfand 50).

For post-process theorizing to rematerialize writing, we need to recast the
figure of the composer and its essayist legacy—to see writers not just as makers of meaning but as makers of the means of producing meaning out of the
available resources of representation. To understand more fully the work of
the composer in the labor process of writing, we must see, as Gunther Kress
has argued, that individuals do not simply *acquire* literacy but actually *build*
for themselves the tools to produce writing. As Kress shows in *Before Writing,* the multimodal activity of young children working with images, shapes,
letterforms, the directionality of writing, the page, and an emergent understanding of genre amounts to an active incorporation of sign-making tools
into their practices of signification. By the same token, instead of thinking of
writers as "users" who confront computers as machines that they must learn
to operate in order to write, we might think in terms of how individuals,
through the labor process of writing, appropriate the means of digital literacy, in highly variable ways, into their own repertoire of sign-making tools.
In either case, by locating the composer in a labor process that includes
assembling the means of making meaning, we can begin to see, as Kress suggests, how writing transforms the signifying resources at hand by consuming
them in the act of production and, in turn, how the material practice of writing transforms the composer's subjectivity and the world in which newly
made signs appear.

Typography and Writing Studies

The line of thinking I want to advance starts with the recognition that the
major images of writing from the process era (voice, cognition, conversation)
neglect the materiality and visuality of writing. The next step is to devise a

more adequate account. My claim is that studying and teaching typography as the culturally salient means of producing writing can help locate composers in the labor process and thereby contribute to the larger post-process work of rematerializing literacy. Typography, of course, has been a longtime topic in the writing curriculum. The problem is that, by and large, typography has been ghettoized in technical communication, where many compositionists think of it as a vocational skill. The concerns of typography—such as document design, page layout, fonts, infographics, and reading paths—are associated with at best commercial art and career training and at worst complicity with corporate culture. To put it bluntly, typography, for all practical purposes, has been assigned in the writing curriculum to the marketplace, at a far remove from the belletristic, critical, and academic work of the essay so cherished by the process movement.

There are good reasons to reconsider this marginalization and to bring typography into the mainstream of writing studies. For one thing, typography—quite literally "writing with type"—can help rematerialize literacy by calling attention to the visual design of writing, be it handwritten, print, or electronic. Typography enables us to *see* writing in material terms as letterforms, printed pages, posters, computer screens. It helps to name the available tools of representation that composers draw on to make their own means of production. For another, typography links writing to delivery—the fifth canon of rhetoric. Like typography, delivery has been neglected by the process movement, isolated from invention, arrangement, style, and memory, and, when mentioned at all, reduced to such afterthoughts as neat handwriting and manuscript preparation. From a typographical perspective, however, the visual design of writing figures prominently as the material form in which the message is delivered. That is, typography offers a way to think of writing not just in terms of the moment of composing but also in terms of its circulation, as messages take on cultural value and worldly force, moving through the Marxian dialectic of production, distribution, exchange, and consumption.[1] From the mass circulation of periodicals to the way junior high school girls write and fold the notes they pass in class (see Finders), the visual design of writing enters consequentially into the activity of composition.

Modern typography is associated with the rise of mass communication, consumer culture, and the society of the spectacle, with roots in both the popular culture of the metropolis and the agitations of the high modernist vanguard in art and politics. Typographical theory and practice developed largely within graphic design movements, from the art nouveau lithographs of Toulouse-Lautrec and Jules Cheret, William Morris, and the Viennese Secession at the turn of the previous century to the avant-garde of Futurism, Dada, and Soviet Constructivism, Jan Tschichold "new typography," Bauhaus, and the federal WPA posters of the 1920s and 1930s to the postwar ascendancy of Swiss Modern and its current postmodern challengers. Though now collected and displayed in art museums (see Friedman; Rothschild, Lupton, and Goldstein; and Lupton for catalogues of major exhibits), typographical work has typically occurred outside the art world, in the realm of commerce and politics—or, in some instances, such as with Futurism and Dada, as an anti-art.

Only recently has there been an organized academic investigation of graphic design theory and history. During the 1980s, the professional journals *Print* and *AIGA Journal of Graphic Design* started to feature historical and critical articles. *Visible Language,* founded in 1967 as the quarterly *Journal of Typographical Research,* and journals started in the 1980s such as *Design Issues* and *Journal of Design History* have worked to make typography and graphic design, along with other types of design, into respectable objects of scholarly inquiry. Victor Margolin gives a sense of design history from 1977 to 1987 in an important review essay ("A Decade"). Two textbooks, Philip Meggs's *A History of Graphic Design* and Richard Hollis's *Graphic Design: A Concise History,* and Robin Kinross's *Modern Typography: An Essay in Critical History* give overviews of graphic design movements and theories, and the three volumes of *Looking Closer* (edited by Michael Bieret et al.) collect both contemporary critical perspectives in the first two volumes and classic statements in the third. Book-length studies, such as Victor Margolin's *Struggle for Utopia* (a study of the Soviet constructivists El Lissitzky and Alexander Rodchenko, as well as the associated figure Laslo Moholy-Nagi) and Johanna Drucker's *The Visible Word: Experimental Typography and Modern Art, 1909–1923,* have started to appear, providing both critical accounts and an alternative to the expensive, coffee-table productions that contain extensive illustrations but little analysis—publications that have tended to dominate publishing on typography and graphic design.

I offer this quick bibliographical tour as an outsider to the field of graphic design and with considerable misgivings. What I hope to suggest is the intellectual ferment that is currently taking place around what we might call in its most general sense "design studies." There are two points to be made. The first is that graphic designers and typographers have started to interrogate design theory and history in ways that are potentially of great interest to those of us who work in writing. I will look at a few of the specific questions they raise in the final section of this chapter. The second point is more general, for it has to do with the relevance of the very notion of "design" to writing theorists.[2] Design studies and design history are relatively new interdisciplinary fields that take not only typography and graphic design as their objects of inquiry but more broadly "the conception and planning of all the products made by human beings" (Buchanan and Margolin x). In other words, "design" has to do with the work of architects, urban planners, engineers, computer scientists, psychologists, sociologists, anthropologists, marketing and manufacturing experts, as well as industrial and graphic designers and communication specialists (see, for example, Buchanan and Margolin; and Margolin, *Design*). The various efforts to identify a discipline of design that can organize such a range of activities into intelligible patterns go far beyond the scope of this paper. For our purposes, what is worth noting is the persistent quest in modern design theory for "the essential unity of all forms of making in the circumstances of a new cultural environment strongly influenced by engineering, technology, and commerce" (Buchanan 36).

Importantly this search for what Richard Buchanan calls a "new architechtonic art of design" emerges in the modern era not so much out of the profit motive of the market as from a utopian vision of the designer's relationship to mass production, on the one hand, and to the fine arts, on the other. As Walter Gropius says of the Bauhaus:

> Our guiding principle was that design is neither an intellectual nor a material affair, but simply an integral part of the stuff of life, necessary for everyone in a civilized society. Our ambition was to arouse the creative artist from his other-worldliness and to reintegrate him into the workaday world of realities and, at the same time, to broaden and humanize the rigid, almost exclusively material mind of the businessman. Our conception of the basic unity of all design in relation to life was in diametric opposition to that of "art for art's sake" and the much more dangerous philosophy it sprang from, business as an end in itself. (20)

Gropius's desire to "humanize" the business classes may sound naïve, particularly after so much of modernist design has been assimilated by advertising, mass media, the "corporate identity" programs of the postwar period, and the current "branding" campaigns of global capital. Nonetheless, like the aspirations of Morris, Lissitzky, and others to design for social ends, the Bauhaus's utopian goal of dismantling the boundaries between fine and applied art and of designing for social usefulness and the enrichment of everyday life still retains its critical edge.[3]

The desire to design for life has particular relevance to the study and teaching of writing. Not only does it emphasize the rhetoricity of design as deliberation and argument about the possible worlds we might construct, it also calls attention to genres of writing that have traditionally fallen outside the mainstream of writing instruction. As Walter Benjamin says:

> Significant literary work can only come into being in a strict alternation between action and writing; it must nurture the inconspicuous forms that better fit its influence in active communities than does the pretentious, universal gesture of the book—in leaflets, brochures, articles, and posters. Only this prompt language shows itself actively equal to the moment. (qtd. in Kinross xv)

If we substitute here the "universal gesture" of *the essay* for that of *the book,* we can read Benjamin's remarks as a pertinent critique of contemporary writing instruction (and the residual hold of its essayist legacy). Benjamin's notion of "prompt language" amounts to the design of messages for mass circulation, timely responses to the twists and turns of class struggle "actively equal to the moment." Long considered ephemeral and beneath notice by writing teachers, Benjamin's "inconspicuous forms" break with the "universal gesture" of the essay to deliver messages in the history of the contemporary. And in this light, typography and the visual design of writing can no longer be marginalized in the writing curriculum as afterthoughts or preprofessional training; they appear instead as essential elements in an emergent civic rhetoric. If anything, the call to write for the social good found in public and community service writing can help to materialize Benjamin's figure of the author-as-producer as a post-process representation to replace the process movement's composer as the essayist maker of meaning.

Typography in Theory and Practice

Three issues in typographical theory and practice seem to me to be of particular interest to writing studies: the narrativity of letterforms, the page as a unit of discourse, and the division of labor that produces written text. The comments that follow are meant to be suggestive rather than programmatic, to indicate some of the paths typography opens to further investigation in our own intellectual work.

The Narrativity of Letterforms

The history of letterforms is a complex one involving changing philosophies, technologies, and social uses of writing. In Gutenburg's fifteenth-century print shop, handmade letterforms imitated the calligraphy of the older scribal tradition. During the Renaissance, humanist designers departed from the naturalistic pen strokes of handwriting to fix the ideal proportions of the alphabet by using the tools of geometry; and in 1693, Louis XIV commissioned a study of the roman alphabet that imposed a rational grid on letterforms, resulting in the *romain du roi* that was meant to embody the authority of scientific method and bureaucratic power. Hopes for such an absolutist, idealized system of letterforms, however, disappeared within a century. According to Lupton and Miller, the Enlightenment typographers Giammbattista Bodoni and Françoise Ambroise Didot broke the "ancestral bond between contemporary typefaces and a divine classical past" by reducing the alphabet to "a system of oppositions—thick and thin, vertical and horizontal, serif and stem," in effect paving the way to an understanding of letterforms "as a set of elements open to infinite manipulation" (55). From the nineteenth-century proliferation of display type to modernist experimentalism and now the vast repertoire of computer fonts (including inexact and degraded forms and bi-fontal crossbreedings), the alphabet has changed, as Miller and Lupton point out, from a "pedigreed line of fixed, self-contained symbols" to a "flexible system of difference." The emphasis in typography has shifted "from the individual letter to the overall series of characters," exchanging the "fixed identity of the letter for the relational system of the font" (23).

What this shift enables us to see is the figurative, narrative character of letterforms. We might read, for example, Josef Alber's 1925 stencil typeface, Herbert Bayer's 1925 "universal," and Tschichold's "new typography" not simply as failed modernist master codes to produce a rational font out of standardized, interchangeable parts but also as expressions of technological and humanistic optimism about to be shattered by the atavistic nationalism of black letter type under Hitler's Third Reich. By the same token, we can find the story in the use of vernacular forms by current typographical designers such as Jeffrey Keedy, whose 1990 Manuscript "combines an anti-heroic amalgam of Modernist geometry and grade-school penmanship" to recall the "naïve yet normative scenario of learning to write"—an exercise that results "not only from external technologies but from the disciplinary socialization of the individual" (Lupton and Miller 24).[4] And finally, to bring things closer to home, we can read the manuscript conventions of the student essay as the story of the transparent text, where the neatness and clarity of standardized type on the printed page seek to efface the visuality of writing and bring the teacher-reader in direct and unmediated touch with the student's mind.

The Page as a Unit of Discourse

The standard units of discourse in writing instruction are the word, sentence, paragraph, and essay; and there is a sad—though now largely repudiated—history of arranging them as a developmental sequence. In the essayist tradition, the page itself is of little account, for as readers we are supposedly not looking at the visual design of writing but following the writer's thoughts. Typography, on the other hand, calls attention to how the look of the page communicates meaning by treating text as a visual element that can be combined with images and other nonverbal forms to produce a unit of discourse. Early printed books, for example, often sought to emulate the multimodal capacities of illuminated manuscripts by using borders, rules, columns, marginalia, textual inserts, and woodblock illustrations to design the page. Typography in the modern period has, in many respects, been eager to recover the visuality of the page from the monotony of standardized letterforms and dense monochromatic blocks of text by incorporating onto the printed page the available means of visual communication, from the engravings in such nineteenth-century periodicals as *Frank Leslie's Illustrated Newspaper* and *Harpers Weekly* to the mid-twentieth-century photo essays in *Life* and the computer infographics of *USA Today*. In addition, poets such as Stephane Mallarme, Guillaume Apollinaire, and Filippo Marinetti sought to free the word and the poetic line from the conventional horizontal and vertical structures of the printed page by mixing size, weight, and style of type and pasting letters and words in visual patterns to create nonlinear compositions. More recently, Dan Friedman's now famous design exercise, drawing on the mundane text of a weather report, raised questions about the emphasis on clarity, orderliness, and simplicity in the modernist use of the grid, rules, and information bands as the basis of page design to explore how "legibility (a quality of efficient, clear, and simple reading) is often in conflict with readability (a quality which promotes interest, pleasure, and challenge in reading)" ("Introductory" 139). And, with the advent of computers, designers such as Rudy VanderLans at *Emigre* magazine, April Greiman, and Katherine McCoy at Cranbrook Academy of Art have made use of the new digital technologies to give the page a formerly unimagined depth, layering and overlapping images and text in deep perspective in ways that confound the traditional opposition between seeing and reading and that call on reader/viewers to participate in making sense of the page.

The complicated relationship between reading and seeing text and image raises interesting questions for writing studies about how we might think about the page as a unit of discourse—about how, say, the juxtaposition of articles, photographs, and advertisements on a newspaper or magazine page creates larger messages than any single item can convey (see Kress, "Text," for an analysis of how the articles on a single newspaper page articulate complex and contradictory representations of poverty); about how "hyperactive" pages encourage browsing rather than reading (see Giovannini's warnings about the "capitulation of text to layout" [204]); and about how individuals find their own reading paths to negotiate the page. Finally, we might ask what is at stake in writing instruction by the common practice of taking articles and essays off the printed page on which they appear (along with other articles, images, and advertising) and reproducing them in handouts or anthologies.

Division of Labor

Typography was traditionally a craft, an artisan's labor that belongs to the print shop. In the early modern period, printing was often thought of as "black magic," and its secrets were guarded by guilds of craftsmen who passed their hermetic arts from master to apprentice. As printing spread, however, "a new occupational culture associated with the printing trades" began to appear, in which the print shop provided "a new setting for intellectual activity," and the master printer became a "hybrid figure"—by turns entrepreneur, lexicographer, editor, cultural impresario, sponsor of scientific research, and political activist—who "presided over the rise of a lay intelligentsia" (Eisenstein 24, 25). If printers like Benjamin Franklin played a central role in the scientific and democratic revolutions of the modern era, in the twentieth century, typography settled into the division of labor under corporate capital, becoming a career path for graphic artists in design studios, publishing, the media, advertising, and academia—another profession with its associations and publications.

I recount this brief historical overview to sketch a typical (if oversimplified) pattern of specialization in professional life and to suggest ways in which such specialization is now under pressure. With the rise of desktop publishing, the division of labor is beginning to flatten, and the distinctions between author, designer, and printer are starting to collapse. For example, the design, composition, production, and distribution of a memo or report may well be the continuous activity in virtual space of a single figure at a connected computer terminal. In the contemporary workplace, this is what new-age management gurus call "multitasking," where digital literacy overcomes the divisions of labor in the era of mechanical reproduction, eliminating secretarial pools and mimeograph machines and transforming managers into information designers.

But the pressure on specialization can do more than serve the ends of corporate restructuring. Benjamin's essay "The Author as Producer" anticipates the progressive possibilities inherent in a collapsing division of labor:

> What we require of the photographer is the ability to give his picture the caption that wrenches it from modish commerce and gives it revolutionary useful value. But we shall make this demand most emphatically when we—the writers—take up photography. Here, too, therefore, technical progress is for the author as producer of the foundation of political progress. (230)

Writing in 1934, Benjamin must have had in mind the work of revolutionary artists such as John Heartfield, whose photomontages used the airbrush, captions, and cut-and-paste techniques to turn the apparent transparency of the photograph into revolutionary messages ("prompt language") in the struggle against fascism (see Pachnickes and Honnef). At the same time, Benjamin raises questions for us today about how, with the rise of digital typography and online communication, we might imagine new possibilities for designers and authors to become producers, to take over the available tools of representation in order to transform the distribution and use of messages. Given the recent eruption of interest in visual culture within composition, Benjamin offers a way to think about how the study and teaching of writing might take up the visual (and the visibility of writing) as more than

just new texts and topics for theorists and students to write about in interpretive and critical essays—though I certainly endorse the value of such
work.[5] What remains to be seen, in theory and practice, is how typography—
the productive art of writing with type—can be "actively equal to the
moment."

Notes

1. For an extended argument on the importance of circulation to the study and
teaching of writing, see Trimbur, "Composition."

2. The notion of "design" is already seeping into writing studies, as a possible replacement for "composing." See Kaufer and Butler; Petraglia; and Cope and Kalantzis. The
view of "design" in this essay is aligned in important respects with the latter volume, but
I think, at this point, it is important to keep the idea of "design" an open one—to see
where it might lead us.

3. In this regard, see the three *Looking Closer* volumes (Bierut et al.) for the ongoing
discussion of the social responsibilities of graphic designers. Also see Daniel Friedman,
Radical, for an heroic attempt to join design and everyday life (as well as negotiate the
demands of modernism and postmodernism on the contemporary designer), and
Adbusters magazine and Web site <www.adbusters.org>.

4. In this narrative vein, typographer Jonathan Barnbrook has designed a Nixon
typeface "to tell lies" and Prozac to "simplify meanings."

5. *Reading Images: The Grammar of Visual Design* (Kress and van Leeuwen) provides,
in my view, the preeminently useful social semiotic analysis of the "look of the page,"
but I can't resist pointing out the irony that it "explains" visual structures in terms of
Hallydean linguistic ones.

Works Cited

Benjamin, Walter. "The Author as Producer." 1934. *Reflections: Essays, Aphorism, Autobiographical Writings.* Ed. Peter Demetz. New York: Schocken, 1978. 220–38.

Bierut, Michael, William Drenttel, Steven Heller, and D. K. Holland, eds. *Looking Closer:
Critical Writings on Graphic Design.* Vols. 1–2. New York: Allworth, 1994, 1997.

Bierut, Michael, Jessica Helfand, Steven Heller, and Rich Poynor, eds. *Looking Closer:
Classic Writings on Graphic Design.* Vol. 3. New York: Allworth, 1999.

Buchanan, Richard. "Rhetoric, Humanism, and Design." *Discovering Design: Explo-
rations in Design Studies.* Ed. Richard Buchanan and Victor Margolin. Chicago: U
of Chicago P, 1995. 23–66.

Buchanan, Richard, and Victor Margolin. Introduction. *Discovering Design: Explo-
rations in Design Studies.* Ed. Richard Buchanan and Victor Margolin. Chicago: U of
Chicago P, 1995. ix–xxvi.

Cope, Bill, and Mary Kalantzis, eds. *Multiliteracies: Literacy Learning and the Design of Social Futures.* London: Routledge, 2000.

Drucker, Johanna. *The Visible Word: Experimental Typography and Modern Art, 1909–1923.* Chicago: U of Chicago P, 1994.

Eisenstein, Elizabeth. "On the Printing Press as an Agent of Change." *Literacy, Language, and Learning: The Nature and Consequences of Reading and Writing.* Ed. David R. Olson, Nancy Torrance, and Angela Hildyard. Cambridge: Cambridge UP, 1985. 19–33.

Faigley, Lester. "Material Literacy and Visual Design." *Rhetorical Bodies.* Ed. Jack Selzer and Sharon Crowley. Madison: U of Wisconsin P, 1999. 171–201.

Finders, Margaret. *Just Girls: Hidden Literacies and Life in Junior High.* New York: Teachers College P, 1997.

Friedman, Daniel. "Introductory Education in Typography." *Visible Language* 7.2 (1973): 129–44.

———. *Radical Modernism.* New Haven: Yale UP, 1997.

Friedman, Mildred, ed. *Graphic Design in America: A Visual Language History.* Minneapolis: Walker Art Center, 1989.

Giovannini, Joseph. "A Zero Degree of Graphics." *Graphic Design in America: A Visual Language History.* Ed. Mildred Friedman. Minneapolis: Walker Art Center, 1989. 200–13.

Goody, Jack, and Ian P. Watt. "The Consequences of Literacy." *Comparative Studies in Society and History* 5 (1963): 304–45.

Gropius, Walter. "My Conception of the Bauhaus Idea." *Scope of Total Architecture.* Ed. Walter Gropius. New York: Colliers, 1962. 6–19.

Haas, Christina. *Writing Technology: Studies on the Materiality of Literacy.* Mahwah, NJ: Erlbaum, 1996.

Havelock, Eric. *The Literate Revolution in Greece and Its Cultural Consequences.* Princeton: Princeton UP, 1982.

Helfand, Jessica. "Electronic Typography: The New Visual Language." Bierut et al., vol. 2, 49–51.

Hollis, Richard. *Graphic Design: A Concise History.* London: Thames and Hudson, 1994.

Innis, Harold A. *The Bias of Communication.* Toronto: U of Toronto P, 1951.

Kaufer, David S., and Brian S. Butler, *Rhetoric and the Arts of Design.* Mahwah, NJ: Erlbaum, 1996.

Kinross, Robin. Introduction. *The New Typography: A Handbook for Modern Designers.* Jan Tschichold. Trans. Ruari McLean. Berkeley: U of California P, 1998. xv–xliv.

———. *Modern Typography: An Essay in Critical History.* London: Hyphen, 1992.

Kress, Gunther R. *Before Writing: Rethinking the Paths to Literacy.* London: Routledge, 1997.

———. "Text and Grammar as Explanation." *Text, Discourse, and Context: Representations of Poverty in Britain.* Ed. Ulrike H. Meinhof and Kay Richardson. London: Longman, 1994. 24–46.

Kress, Gunther R., and Theo van Leeuwen. *Reading Images: The Grammar of Visual Design.* New York: Routledge, 1996.

Lupton, Ellen. *Mixing Messages: Graphic Design in Contemporary Culture.* New York: Princeton Architectural P, 1996.

Lupton, Ellen, and J. Abbott Miller. "Laws of the Letter." *Design Writing Research: Writing on Graphic Design.* Ed. Ellen Lupton and J. Abbott Miller. London: Phaidon, 1996. 53–61.

Margolin, Victor. "A Decade of Design History in the United States, 1977–88." *Journal of Design History* 1.1 (1988): 51–72.

——, ed. *Design Discourse: History, Theory, Criticism.* Chicago: U of Chicago P, 1989.

——. *The Struggle for Utopia: Rodchenko, Lissitzky, Moholy-Nagy, 1917–1946.* Chicago: U of Chicago P, 1997.

Meggs, Philip B. *A History of Graphic Design.* 3rd ed. New York: Wiley, 1998.

Miller, J. Abbott, and Ellen Lupton. "A Natural History of Typography." Bierut et al., vol. 1, 19–25.

Olson, David R. "From Utterance to Text: The Bias of Language in Speaking and Writing." *Harvard Educational Review* 47 (1977): 257–81.

Ong, Walter J. *Orality and Literacy: The Technologizing of the Word.* New York: Methuen, 1982.

Pachnicke, Peter, and Klaus Honnef, eds. *John Heartfield.* New York: Abrams, 1992.

Petraglia, Joseph. *Reality by Design: The Rhetoric and Technology of Authenticity.* Mahwah, NJ: Erlbaum, 1998.

Rothschild, Deborah, Ellen Lupton, and Darra Goldstein. *Graphic Design in the Mechanical Age: Selections from the Merrill C. Berman Collection.* New Haven: Yale UP, 1998.

Trimbur, John. "Composition and the Circulation of Writing." *College Composition and Communication"* 52 (2000): 188–219.

——. "Essayist Literacy and the Rhetoric of Deproduction." *Rhetoric Review* 9 (1990): 72–86.

18

The Intellectual Work of Computers and Composition Studies

CYNTHIA L. SELFE AND RICHARD J. SELFE

IN THE CONTESTED and complex intellectual landscape of world-order changes resulting from the rise of the information age and the rapid development of networked societies, no territory seems less settled, more unstable, less sparsely mapped—and, at the same time, more promising and vigorous—than that formed by the intersection of technology and literacy, especially the area we will refer to in this chapter as "computers and composition studies."

Teacher/scholars drawn to this kind of work can be characterized by their commitment to the educational spaces of classrooms, writing centers, and literacy programs; by their interest in language studies, particularly the teaching of reading and composing (in the broadest sense of these terms and, increasingly often, in contexts that are not limited to alphabetic representation); and by their interest in the dynamic nature of language as it unfolds in new computer-based environments. Those who work in this area frequently also share an interest in exploring the relationships between humans and machines, as well as the social issues (agency, identity, humanity, responsibility) that those relationships throw into such sharp relief within the context of shifting postmodern sensibilities.

For us, some of the most interesting intellectual work in the field of computers and composition studies shares four characteristics:

> • A grounding not only in language studies but also in social theory. Given the fact that technology serves as a nexus of power, money, ideology, and political influence, it is not surprising that many scholars in

this field feel that scholarship concerning Marxism, cultural studies, ideology, and feminism possess great explanatory power. And given the ways in which recent technological systems have both shaped and been shaped by conditions associated with postmodernity, many scholars in the field of computers and composition are also influenced by the work of a range of postmodern theorists.

• A belief in social justice and the ability and responsibility of teachers to enact productive social change (even if only temporary, partial, and fragmentary) that will make the lives of certain groups of people (and thus of all people) better, more just, more equitable. By "certain groups," we mean particularly people of color; people labeled "illiterate," "underprepared," or "basic writers"; under-represented groups or groups who may hold positions counter to the dominant systems of power, particularly women, the lesbigay community, speakers of English as a foreign language, and the impoverished. Associated with this belief is an emerging understanding of the many difficulties associated with achieving social justice and enacting change and the tendential forces associated with stasis.

• A commitment to educational settings as potential venues for enacting productive social change — settings that include classrooms, schools and institutions, writing centers, educational sites in workplaces, and community literacy program. Paradoxically, this commitment is shaped by a sense of hope and optimistic pragmatism, even while it is tempered by skepticism. Influencing this work is the scholarship of critical pedagogists who understand the contributory role that educational systems and settings play in reproducing inequities along the related axes of race, class, gender, and orientation.

• An understanding of technology and technological systems as both a possible vector for enacting productive change, and a powerful force for resisting such change and continuing inequity. This belief rests on two understandings: first, that technology consists not only of machines (of computers, for instance) but also of a complexly articulated set of social formations; and, second, that, given these formations, technology, power, and literacy practices are linked at fundamental levels.

Given these related sets of beliefs, much of the work in computers and composition studies is pragmatically oriented. It has to do with studying, designing, and exploiting the productive potential of various forms of computer technology (systems, networks, the Web, individual machines, MOOs, list-servs, word-processing packages, computer-based classrooms) as possible vectors for critically informed pedagogical approaches or critically informed social action within the settings of classrooms, writing centers, educational institutions, community literacy programs, and workplaces. The goal for such work is, generally stated, to examine—with a critical eye—existing social and technological systems, educational practices and systems, and human language and literacy practices in order to better understand them and improve them.

Although the range of intellectual work undertaken by the scholar-teachers in computers and composition studies is considerable in its range and richly textured in its goals and methods, for the purposes of discussion in this chapter, we have selected work in only three areas: those which focus on educational issues, social/cultural issues, and issues of representation and identity. This work does not represent the whole of computers and composition, nor, necessarily, even the best work in this field. It is, however, the work that most interests us. We would caution, however, that even the work in these three limited areas contains many overlapping interests, topics, and approaches. As a result, this attempt to simplify the vigorous and unruly landscape of computers and composition studies is bound to fail, bound to misrepresent and underrepresent important elements.

Educational Issues

Perhaps the most immediate exigency for the intellectual work conducted in the field of computers and composition studies has to do with the pragmatic material reality of the American educational system, within which increasing numbers of students and teachers are being asked to use computers and networked systems in English studies, language arts, and composition classrooms; in writing centers; in educational institutions; in workplace education sites; and in community literacy programs. In these contexts, it is increasingly clear that literacy and technology are inextricably intertwined (at least within American culture) and that, as a result, individuals are no longer considered literate unless they know how to communicate in the officially sanctioned form of standard English and within electronic contexts. Given this context, many of the intellectual projects carried out in computers and composition have to do with discovering and designing effective instructional approaches that are based on sound theory and practice, and with critically reflecting on—and assessing—the efficacy of such approaches on different populations of students.

Working from this broad foundation, many scholars in computers and composition have explored the application of computers in a range of academic programs and instructional venues, including community literacy programs (Regan and Zuern); writing centers (Coogan; George; Grimm; Hobson; Inman and Sewell; D. Selfe); writing-across-the-disciplines and writing-in-the-disciplines programs (Riess; C. Selfe); interdisciplinary studies programs (Minock and Shor); distance-education programs (Stacey et al.); basic-writing programs (Conway); technical writing programs (Duin and Hansen; Selber; Sullivan and Dautermann); ESL programs (Susser; Pennington); and teacher preparation/professional development programs (Fey and Sisson; Moran, "From"; Yagelski and Powley).

Within these programs, scholar-teachers in computers and composition have explored the instructional potential of a wide range of specific computer-based environments, such as computer systems (Syverson); networks (Barker and Kemp; Bruce et al.; Porter); MOOs, particularly those designed specifically for language exchanges (Haefner; Haynes and Holmevick); list-servs (Cubbison; Selfe and Meyer); the Web (Gresham; Gruber; Harris and Wambeam; Hartley et al.; Mauriello et al.); e-mail (Hawisher and Moran; Moran, "Notes"); and computer-based classrooms and labs (Hawisher and LeBlanc; Kent-Drury; Galin and Latchaw; Palmquist et al.). A noteworthy collection in this vein is a recent work edited by Sibylle Gruber. This book offers composition teachers a range of Web-based assignments for a variety of authentic audiences and rhetorical purposes, and in a variety of formats (both text in its more conventional manifestations and in new kinds of hypertextual formats, and images).

As we have mentioned, much of the most interesting work in computers and composition studies is influenced by a paradoxical belief in both the goals of social justice and the power of systems that work against such justice. One particular strand of intellectual inquiry characterizes the tension between optimism and skepticism, enthusiasm and critical awareness, that marks this field. This work focuses on contested possibilities of creating computer-based learning environments that encourage increasingly democratic or egalitarian contexts for communicative exchanges (Castner; Gomez; Romano; Whitaker and Hill); increased understandings of discursively effective agency in feminist and multicultural contexts (LeCourt; Selfe and Selfe); the productive exercises of responsibility (Cooper; Janangelo); or an appreciation for difference along the related axes of race, class (Bennett and Walsh; Taylor), handicap (Buckley), sexual orientation (DeWitt; Janangelo; Woodland), and writing skill level (Crafton). In our estimation, it is this kind of effort that has laid the groundwork for much of the best debate and discussion in computers and composition for the last two decades.

We suspect that one of the most promising emerging strands of educational scholarship will focus on the intersection of technology and literacy. On the one hand, this work will be motivated by resistance to anti-technology stances of scholars such as Sven Birkerts and Barry Sanders, who perceive technology to be a fundamental contributory cause to growing levels of illiteracy in this country. On the other hand, it is inspired by the work of literacy scholars such as Deborah Brandt, Brian Street, Harvey Graff, David Barton and Mary Hamilton. Important to such work is a careful analysis of how individuals acquire, develop, and practice technological literacies, and what effect these literacies have on their daily lives.

Social/Cultural Issues

The general commitment that computers and composition scholars bring to issues of social justice and their understanding of technology as a potential vector for change in wider social venues also encourages them to undertake work that looks outward from the classroom. Often, such projects undertake examinations of complex and thorny social and cultural issues that are associated with technology use in everyday literacy practices and contexts.

One current thread of this work focuses on inequities related to the differential distribution of—and access to—computers within American culture along the related axes of race, class, age, and gender. This differential distribution affects performance not only in educational contexts but also in home and work contexts (Selfe, *Technology*). Building on the work of various scholars who have examined the connections between power and technology,[1] projects with this focus identify and examine problems that derive from differential access (Moran, "Access"; Reynolds and Lewis; Moran and Selfe); describe the social dynamics underlying large-scale national computer literacy initiatives (Selfe, *Technology*); look at the economic cost of computer use in community literacy programs (Grabill); point out the influence of sexism, classism, and ethnocentricity on the design of computer interfaces (Selfe and Selfe); and examine the effects of new technologies and new technological literacy expectations on individuals' daily practices (Merrifield et al.).

A related focus for the intellectual work that computers and composition scholars undertake has to do with the dynamic conditions of postmodernity and the changing nature of literacy practices generated within — and sometime in resistance to — these conditions. This work, has produced particularly productive examinations of the values that shape communication (especially those communicative exchanges that take place online) within the shifting conditions of postmodernity. For example, in a chapter of his *Fragments of Rationality,* "The Achieved Utopia of Networked Classrooms," Lester Faigley examines a group of students composing in an online synchronous discussion. This discussion, as Faigley points out, seems to reflect many of the characteristics associated with postmodernity, including fragmentation, alienation, contradiction, disaffection, the loss of authority, and a rejection of responsibility. In reply to this work, Marilyn Cooper speculates on how the same online exchange might be interpreted to illustrate not a rejection of responsible behavior but, rather, a shift in our understanding of the exigencies for responsibility in a world characterized by the conditions of postmodernity. Responsibility within such contexts, Cooper points out — building on the work of Michel Foucault and Zygmunt Bauman — rests on a personal "willingness" to relate to other humans, one motivated not by modernist authority figures or value systems rooted in Enlightenment values but, rather, by a personal "impulse to be responsive to and responsible for" others, a "willingness" to approach authentic problems arising from the postmodern condition (153). Other projects focusing on the postmodern contexts for and characteristics of online communication include work by Sirc; Sosnoski; and Guyer and Hagaman.

This attention to the social contexts associated with postmodernism has also encouraged some scholars in computers and composition studies to focus on the changing nature of workplaces in the contemporary era, especially those that use and depend on electronic exchanges. Often these projects — like many of those contained within Ann Duin and Craig Hansen's *Nonacademic Writing: Social Theory and Technology* or Patricia Sullivan and Jennie Dautermann's *Electronic Literacies in the Workplace* — build on foundational work in technical communication but employ situated methodologies designed to focus on local conditions affecting workplace communication in electronic venues. This same attention to situated workplace studies of electronic communications informs projects that look at community responses to corporate practices online (Gurak), that examine the coexistence of old and new technologies and the competing literacy demands that they generated in specific workplace settings (Haas), and that trace employees' efforts to use new technologies to negotiate and cope with organizational changes (Ziv). Other projects focusing on the workplace — such as Stuart Selber's collection, *Computers and Technical Communication: Pedagogical and Programmatic Perspectives,* and Kristine Blair's article about using microethnographies in workplace settings — suggest that the changing contexts for, and demands on, computer-based workplace communications in the postmodern age also have significant implications for technical communication programs in academic contexts.

If there is a topic of interest both to scholars who study computer-based communications in workplace settings and to those who study such exchanges in academic spaces, it is the dramatic changes that computer landscapes have occasioned in intellectual property concerns. A special issue of *Computers and Composition,* edited by Laura Gurak and Johndan Johnson-Eilola, focuses on these concerns and includes articles on changing attitudes toward fair use (Herrington; Shirk and Smith); publishing (Latchaw and Galin); citation and documentation issues (Leverenz); copyright (Logie; Walker); and the nature of plagiarism and collaborative authorship (Kitalong; Kolko).

Concern for social and cultural changes in the postmodern age has also provided the motivation for scholars' recent attention to global computing issues, especially as these issues intersect with studies of literacy in specific cultural settings. This work is given special exigency by the understanding — based on work by scholars such as Manuel Castells, Ronald Deibert, and Elizabeth Eisenstein — that computer technologies have both shaped and been shaped by postmodern contexts. Projects that focus on global issues include those that connect regional inequities in computer access to world-order economic changes that have caused increased poverty for certain peoples and parts of the world (Faigley, "Beyond"; Tu et al.; Wresch). Other projects — as represented in Gail Hawisher and Cynthia Selfe's collection, *Global Literacies and the World-Wide Web* — interrogate the myth of the global village by looking at Web-based literacy practices in specific cultural and social contexts, including those of Palau (Kitalong and Kitalong), Mexico (Romano et al.), Greece (Dragona and Handa), Cuba (Sullivan and Fernandez), Africa (Richardson and Lewis), and Japan (Sugimoto and Levin).

A focus on cultural and social contexts has also informed many historically based projects that individuals have undertaken in the field of computers and composition. In part, these projects have been inspired by the historical work in technology or language studies (Deibert; Eisenstein; Ong). From another perspective, however, their motivation is political in nature — often scholars undertaking such projects understand that ideology works to dehistoricize, to deny that "ideas and beliefs are specific to a particular time, place, and social group (Eagleton 59). These twin motivations, for example, shaped a book-length history of computers and composition as a field (Hawisher et al.). Projects in this category also include James Kalmbach's and Dennis Barron's historically based examinations of publishing technologies, the first of which focuses on the ideological ties between desktop publishing, typewriters, and liquid paper, and the second of which looks at the technologies of the pencil and the telephone in relation to the technology of the computer. Additional projects in this vein focus on the historical emergence — and cultural implications of — computer-based literacy forms such as hypertext, specifically how such forms may affect patterns of reading and writing, and, thus, of thinking.[2]

Representation and Identity

One of the most vigorous areas of intellectual work in the field of computers and composition involves recent projects clustering around issues of representation (both graphic and text-based representation) within computer-based environments. Because this work is often — albeit not always — shaped by concerns of social justice, it frequently focuses on problematic representations of gender, race, class, and sexual orientation.

Computer-based representations of gender, for example, have received a great deal of attention from computers and composition scholars. Often, these projects are informed by the work of feminist scholars and philosophers of technology that have identified the more conventional cultural narratives serving to limit women's relationships with technology.[3] Computers and composition scholars working from this base are frequently motivated by the possibility of finding ways to resist these conventional narratives or to write more productive narratives within computer-based communication systems and classrooms and on the Web.[4] Other scholars working on this theme have examined the gendered nature of technology and of research on computer-based communication (Aschauer; Rickly); computer-based peer response and computer-based instruction that involves gender representations (Burns; Pagnucci and Mauriello); as well as the gendered landscapes of academic cyberspace and other forms of computer-mediated communication environments (Blair and Takayoshi; Guyer and Hagaman; Wolfe; Hawisher and Sullivan).

Representation projects have also focused on identity issues that connect race, class, gender, and sexual orientation (Barber et al.), as well as on computer-based representations of holocaust victims (Salvo); lesbigay populations (Alexander; DeWitt; Comstock and Addison; Regan; Warshauer; Woodland, "I Plan"); and families (Amato; Eldred).

Scholars working in this area have also focused on the increasingly visual nature of communication within computer-based environments and technologically dependent cultures, and they have begun to question both the primacy of alphabetic representation and the conventional relationships between textual and graphical representations within computer-based communication environments (Vielstimmig).[5] As Anne Wysocki and Johndan Johnson-Eilola frame the questions at the heart of this last cluster of projects:

> What are we likely to carry with us when we ask that our relationship with all technologies should be like that we have with the technology of printed words? . . . [W]hat other possibilities might we use for expressing our relationships with and within technologies? (349)

Conclusion

There is a culturally constructed film loop that sometimes plays in our collective memories during those times when we are encouraged to think of technology—and often computers—as the bane of human existence. Sometimes this film loop offers the scene of men pouring from the belly of the Trojan horse, sometimes the "monster" Frankenstein rampaging about the English countryside, sometimes the blinking lights of the recalcitrant computer, Hal, in *2001 Space Odyssey,* and sometimes the philosopher androids from *Bladerunner.* In each case, we see a "technology" involved in the betrayal of human beings. All too often, we forget that it is the humans behind the technology—the designers and makers of the technology—who seek to betray, to dominate, to exert power.

For this reason, we cannot come to know technology by limiting ourselves to science and engineering—to the mechanics or electronics of operation, to the design and manufacture of parts, to the physical study of hardware and software and networks. Technology is not fully constituted by machines. It is, instead, a set of articulated social formations—ideological, economic, political, cultural. And given this fact, the study of technologies must, at its heart, involve the study of the humans who design, make, and use these machines. It is in this realm that many computers and composition scholars locate the exigency of their intellectual work, and for this reason they consider what they do to be important work.

As Anthony Giddens warns, however, even when we have a great deal of knowledge about the social systems for which technologies are designed and in which they are used, the effects of our actions with technology will always overflow our original intentions to generate unanticipated consequences. So, it seems that computers and composition scholars have their work cut out for them in the rest of this century. By continuing to pay attention to technology, by trying to make sure it is used in ways that help people instead of hurt them, these scholars are trying to learn more about what it means to be human.

Notes

1. Especially, for example, Foucault, *Discipline* and *Power;* Ohmann; Olson; Winner.
2. See Bolter; Johnson-Eilola; Joyce; Landow; Lanham; Moulthrop; Sloan.
3. See Coyle; Cockburn; Haraway; Jellison; Kramarae; Plant; Turkle; Wajcman.
4. See Balsamo; Hocks; Takayoshi; Takayoshi et al.; Selfe, "Lest"; and for on the Web, see Hawisher and Sullivan, "Women" and "Fleeting"; Sullivan, "Cyberbabes" and "Wired."
5. See George and Shoos; Handa; Hawisher and Sullivan, "Fleeting"; Kress; Markel; Sullivan, "Cyberbabes."

Works Cited

Alexander, Jonathan. "Out of the Closet and into the Network: Sexual Orientation and the Computerized Classroom." *Computers and Composition* 14 (1997): 207–16.
Amato, Joe. "Family Values, Literacy, Technology, and Uncle Sam." Hawisher and Selfe, *Passions* 369–86.

Aschauer, Anne Brady. "Tinkering with Technological Skill: An Examination of the Gendered Uses of Technologies." *Computers and Composition* 16 (1999): 7–24.

Balsamo, Anne. *Technologies of the Gendered Body: Reading Cyborg Women.* Durham, NC: Duke UP, 1996.

Barber, Margaret, et al., eds. Spec. issue of *Computers and Composition* 14 (1997).

Barker, Thomas T., and Fred O. Kemp. "Network Theory: A Postmodern Pedagogy for the Writing Classroom." *Computers and Community: Teaching Composition in the Twenty-First Century.* Ed. Carolyn Handa. Portsmouth, NH: Boynton/Cook, 1990. 1–27.

Barron, Dennis. "From Pencils to Pixels: The Stages of Literacy Technologies." Hawisher and Selfe, *Passions* 15–33.

Barton, David, and Mary Hamilton. *Local Literacies: Reading and Writing in One Community.* London: Routledge, 1998.

Bennett, Michael, and Kathleen Walsh. "Desperately Seeking Diversity: Going Online to Achieve a Racially Balanced Classroom." *Computers and Composition* 14 (1997): 217–28.

Birkerts, Sven. *The Gutenberg Elegies: The Fate of Reading in an Electronic Age.* New York: Fawcett, 1995.

Blair, Kristine L. "Microethnographies of Electronic Discourse Communities: Establishing Exigency for E-mail in the Professional Writing Classroom." *Computers and Composition* 13 (1996): 85–91.

Blair, Kristine, and Pamela Takayoshi. *Feminist Cyberscapes: Mapping Gendered Academic Spaces.* Stamford, CT: Ablex, 1999.

Bolter, Jay David. *Writing Space: The Computer, Hypertext, and the History of Writing.* Hillsdale, NJ: Erlbaum, 1991.

Brandt, Deborah. "Accumulating Literacy: Writing and Learning to Write in the Twentieth Century." *College English* 57 (1995): 649–68.

———. "Sponsors of Literacy." *College Composition and Communication* 49 (1998): 165–85.

Bruce, Bertram, Joy Kreeft Peyton, and Trenton W. Batson, eds. *Network-based Classrooms: Promises and Realities.* New York: Cambridge UP, 1993.

Buckley, Joanne. "The Invisible Audience and the *Disembodied* Voice: Online Teaching and the Loss of Body Image." *Computers and Composition* 14 (1997): 179–88.

Burns, Hugh. "The Writers We Happen to Teach: An Epilogue." *Computers and Composition* 16 (1999): 167–70.

Castells, Manuel. *End of Millennium.* Cambridge, MA: Blackwell, 1998.

———. *The Power of Identity.* Cambridge, MA: Blackwell, 1997.

———. *The Rise of the Network Society.* Cambridge, MA: Blackwell, 1996.

Castner, Joanna. "The Clash of Social Categories: Egalitarianism in Networked Writing Classrooms." *Computers and Composition* 14 (1997): 257–68.

Cockburn, Cynthia. *Machinery of Dominance: Women, Men, and Technical Know-How.* Boston: Northeastern UP, 1985.

Comstock, Michelle, and Joanne Addison. "Virtual Complexities: Exploring Literacy at the Intersections of Computer-Mediated Social Formations." *Computers and Composition* 14 (1997): 245–56.

Conway, Glenda. "'What Are We Doing Today?' High School Basic Writers Collaborating in a Computer Lab." *Computers and Composition* 12 (1995): 79–95.

Coogan, David. *Electronic Writing Centers: Computing the Field of Composition.* Stamford, CT: Ablex, 1999.

Cooper, Marilyn M. "Postmodern Possibilities in Electronic Conversations." Hawisher and Selfe, *Passions* 140–60.

Coyle, Karen. "How Hard Can It Be?" *Wired Women: Gender and New Realities in Cyberspace.* Ed. Lynn Cherny and Elizabeth Reba Weise. Seattle: Seal P, 1988. 42–55.

Crafton, Robert E. "Promises, Promises: Computer-Assisted Revision and Basic Writers." *Computers and Composition* 13 (1996): 317–26.

Cubbison, Laurie. "Configuring Listserv, Configuring Discourse." *Computers and Composition* 16 (1999): 371–82.

Deibert, Ronald J. *Parchment, Printing, and Hypermedia: Communication in World Order Transformation.* New York: Columbia UP, 1997.

DeWitt, Scott Lloyd. "Out There on the Web: Pedagogy and Identity in the Face of Opposition." *Computers and Composition* 14 (1997): 229–44.

Dragona, Alibi, and Carolyn Handa. "*Genes Glosses:* Literacy and Cultural Implications of the Web for Greece." Hawisher and Selfe, *Global* 52–73.

Duin, Ann Hill, and Craig J. Hansen, eds. *Nonacademic Writing: Social Theory and Technology.* Malibu, NJ: Erlbaum, 1996.

Eagleton, Terry. *Ideology: An Introduction.* London: Versa, 1991.

Eisenstein, Elizabeth. *The Printing Press as an Agent of Change: Communications and Cultural Transformations in Early-Modern Europe.* Vols. 1 and 2. Cambridge: Cambridge UP, 1979.

Eldred, Janet Carey. "Technology's Strange, Familiar Voices." Hawisher and Selfe, *Passions* 387–98.

Faigley, Lester. "Beyond Imagination: The Internet and Global Digital Literacy." Hawisher and Selfe, *Passions* 129–39.

———. *Fragments of Rationality: Postmodernity and the Subject of Composition.* Pittsburgh: U of Pittsburgh P, 1992.

Fey, Marion Harris, and Michael J. Sisson. "Approaching the Information Superhighway: Internet Collaboration among Future Writing Teachers." *Computers and Composition* 13 (1996): 37–47.

Foucault, Michel. *Discipline and Punish: The Birth of the Prison.* 1975. Trans. Alan Sheridan. New York: Random, 1979.

———. *Power/Knowledge: Selected Interviews and Other Writings 1972–1977.* Ed. Colin Gordon. Trans. Colin Gordon, Leo Marshall, John Mepham, and Kate Soper. New York: Pantheon, 1980.

Galin, Jeffrey R., and Joan S. Latchaw. *The Dialogic Classroom: Teachers Integrating Computer Technology, Pedagogy, and Research.* Urbana: NCTE, 1998.

George, Diana. "Wonder of It All: Computers, Writing Centers, and the New World." *Computers and Composition* 12 (1995): 331–34.

George, Diana, and Diane Shoos. "Dropping Bread Crumbs in the Intertextual Forest: Critical Literacy in a Postmodern Age." Hawisher and Selfe, *Passions* 115–26.

Giddens, Anthony. *The Constitution of Society: Outline of a Theory of Structuration.* Berkeley: U of California P, 1984.

Gomez, Mary Louise. "The Equitable Teaching of Composition." *Evolving Perspectives on Computers and Composition Studies: Questions for the 1990s*. Ed. Gail E. Hawisher and Cynthia L. Selfe. Urbana, IL, and Houghton, MI: NCTE and Computers and Composition P, 1991. 318–35.

Grabill, Jeffrey. "Utopic Visions, the Technopoor, and Public Access: Writing Technologies in a Community Literacy Program." *Computers and Composition* 15 (1998): 297–316.

Graff, Harvey J. *The Legacy of Literacy: Continuities and Contradictions in Western Culture and Society*. Bloomington: Indiana UP, 1987.

Gresham, Morgan. "The New Frontier: Conquering the World Wild Web by Mule." *Computers and Composition* 16 (1999): 395–408.

Grimm, Nancy Maloney. "Computer Centers and Writing Centers: An Argument for Ballast." *Computers and Composition* 12 (1995): 323–29.

Gruber, Sibylle, ed. *Weaving a Virtual Web. Practical Approaches to New Information Technologies*. Urbana, IL: NCTE, 2000.

Gurak, Laura J. *Persuasion and Privacy in Cyberspace: The Online Protests over Lotus MarketPlace and Clipper Chip*. New Haven, CT: Yale UP, 1997.

Gurak, Laura, and Johndan Johnson-Eilola, eds. Spec. issue of *Computers and Composition* 15.2 (1998).

Guyer, Carolyn, and Dianne Hagaman. "Into the Next Room." Hawisher and Selfe, *Passions* 323–36.

Haas, Christina. "On the Relationship of Old and New Technologies." *Computers and Composition* 16 (1999): 209–28.

Haefner, Joel. "The Politics of the Code." *Computers and Composition* (1999): 325–40.

Handa, Carolyn, ed. Spec. issue of *Computers and Composition*. 17.1/2 (forthcoming 2001).

Haraway, Donna J. "A Manifesto for Cyborgs: Science, Technology, and Socialist Feminism." *Feminism/postmodernism*. Ed. Linda J. Nicholson. New York: Routledge, 1990. 190–233.

———. *Simians, Cyborgs, and Women: The Reinvention of Nature*. New York: Routledge, 1991.

Harris, Leslie D., and Cynthia A. Wambeam. "The Internet-Based Composition Classroom: A Study in Pedagogy." *Computers and Composition* 13 (1996): 353–72.

Hartley, Cecilia, Ellen Schendel, and Michael R. Neal. "Writing (Online) Space: Composition Webware in Perl." *Computers and Composition* 16 (1999): 359–70.

Hawisher, Gail E., and Paul LeBlanc. *Re-imagining Computers and Composition: Teaching and Research in the Virtual Age*. Portsmouth, NH: Boynton/Cook, 1992.

Hawisher, Gail E., and Charles C. Moran. "Electronic Mail and the Writing Instructor." *College English* 55 (1993): 627–43.

Hawisher, Gail E., and Cynthia Selfe, eds. *Global Literacies and the World-Wide Web*. London: Routledge, 2000.

———, eds. *Passions, Pedagogies, and 21st Century Technologies*. Logan: Utah State UP, 1999.

Hawisher, Gail E., and Patricia A. Sullivan. "Fleeting Images: Women Visually Writing the Web." Hawisher and Selfe, *Passions* 268–91.

———. "Women on the Networks: Searching for E-Spaces of Their Own." *Feminism and Composition Studies: In Other Words.* Ed. Susan C. Jarratt and Lynn Worsham. New York: MLA, 1998. 172–97.

Hawisher, Gail E., et al. *Computers and the Teaching of Writing in American Higher Education, 1979–1994: A History.* Norwood, NJ: Ablex, 1996.

Haynes, Cynthia, and Jan Rune Holmevik, eds. *High Wired: On the Design, Use, and Theory of Educational MOOS.* Ann Arbor: U of Michigan P, 1998.

Herrington, TyAnna K. "The Interdependency of Fair Use and the First Amendment." *Computers and Composition* 15 (1998): 125–44.

Hobson, Eric H., ed. *Wiring the Writing Center.* Logan: Utah State UP, 1998.

Hocks, Mary. "Designing Feminist Multimedia for the United Nations Fourth World Conference on Women." Blair and Takayoshi 285–96.

Hocks, Mary E. "Feminist Interventions in Electronic Environments." *Computers and Composition* 16 (1999): 107–20.

Inman, James A., and Donna N. Sewell. *Taking Flight with OWLs: Examining Electronic Writing Center Work.* Mahwah, NJ: Erlbaum, 2000.

Janangelo, Joseph. "Technopower and Technoppression: Some Abuses of Power and Control in Computer-Assisted Writing Environments." *Computers and Composition* 9 (1991): 47–64.

Jellison, Katherine. *Entitled to Power: Farm Women and Technology, 1913–1963.* Chapel Hill: U of North Carolina P, 1993.

Johnson-Eilola, Johndan. *Nostalgic Angels: Rearticulating Hypertext Writing.* Norwood, NJ: Ablex, 1997.

Joyce, Michael. *Of Two Minds: Hypertext Pedagogy and Poetics.* Ann Arbor: U of Michigan P, 1995.

Kalmbach, James R. *The Computer and the Page: Publishing, Technology, and the Classroom.* Norwood, NJ: Ablex, 1997.

Kent-Drury, Roxanne M. "Finding a Place to Stand: Negotiating the Spatial Configuration of the Networked Computer Classroom." *Computers and Composition* 15 (1998): 387–407.

Kitalong, Karla Saari. "A Web of Symbolic Violence." *Computers and Composition* 15 (1998): 253–63.

Kitalong, Karla Saari, and Tino Kitalong. "Complicating the Tourist Gaze: Literacy and the Internet as Catalysts for Articulating a Postcolonial Palauan Identity." Hawisher and Selfe, *Global* 95–113.

Kolko, Beth E. "Intellectual Property in Synchronous and Collaborative Virtual Space." *Computers and Composition* 15 (1998): 163–84.

Kramarae, Cheris. "Gotta Go, Myrtle, Technology's at the Door." Kramarae 1–14.

———, ed. *Technology and Women's Voices: Keeping in Touch.* New York: Routledge, 1988.

Kress, Gunther. "'English' at the Crossroads: Rethinking Curricula of Communication in the Context of the Turn to the Visual." Hawisher and Selfe, *Passions* 66–88.

Landow, George P. *Hypertext: The Convergence of Contemporary Critical Theory and Technology.* Baltimore: Johns Hopkins UP, 1992.

Lanham, Richard A. *The Electronic Word: Democracy, Technology, and the Arts.* Chicago: U of Chicago P, 1993.

Latchaw, Joan S., and Jeffrey R. Galin. "Shifting Boundaries of Intellectual Property: Authors and Publishers Negotiating the WWW." *Computers and Composition* 15 (1998): 145–62.

LeCourt, Donna. "Critical Pedagogy in the Computer Classroom: Politicizing the Writing Space." *Computers and Composition* 15 (1998): 275–95.

Leverenz, Carrie Shively. "Citing Cybersources: A Challenge to Disciplinary Values." *Computers and Composition* 15 (1998): 185–200.

Logie, John. "Champing at the Bits: Computers, Copyright, and the Computer Classroom." *Computers and Composition* 15 (1998): 201–14.

Markel, Mike. "What Students See: Word Processing and the Perception of Visual Design." *Computers and Composition* 15 (1998): 373–86.

Mauriello, Nicholas, Gian S. Pagnucci, and Tammy Winner. "Reading Between the Code: The Teaching of HTML and the Displacement of Writing Instruction." *Computers and Composition* 16 (1999): 409–19.

Merrifield, Juliet, Mary Beth Bingman, and David Hemphill. *Life at the Margins: Literacy, Language, and Technology in Everyday Life.* New York: Teachers College P, 1997.

Minock, Mary, and Francis Shor. "Crisscrossing Grand Canyon: Bridging the Gaps with Computer Conferencing." *Computers and Composition* 12 (1995): 355–66.

Moran, Charles. "Access: The 'A' Word in Technology Studies." Hawisher and Selfe, *Passions* 205–20.

———. "From a High-tech to a Low-tech Writing Classroom: 'You Can't Go Home Again.'" *Computers and Composition* 15 (1998): 1–10.

———. "Notes Toward a Rhetoric of E-mail." *Computers and Composition* 12 (1994): 15–21.

Moran, Charles, and Cynthia Selfe. "Teaching English across the Technology/Wealth Gap." *English Journal* 88.6 (1999): 48–55.

Moulthrop, Stuart. "Rhizome and Resistance: Hypertext and the Dreams of a New Culture." *Hyper/Text/Theory.* Ed. George Landow. Baltimore: Johns Hopkins UP, 1994. 299–319.

Ohmann, Richard. "Literacy, Technology, and Monopoly Capitalism." *College English* 47 (1985): 675–89.

Olson, C. Paul. "Who Computes?" *Critical Pedagogy and Cultural Power.* Ed. David W. Livingstone. South Hadley, MA: Bergin, 1987. 179–204.

Ong, Walter. *Orality and Literacy: The Technologizing of the Word.* New York: Methuen, 1982.

Pagnucci, Gian S., and Nicholas Mauriello. "The Masquerade: Gender, Identity, and Writing for the Web." *Computers and Composition* 16 (1999): 141–51.

Palmquist, Mike, et al. *Transitions: Teaching Writing in Computer-Supported and Traditional Classrooms.* Greenwich, CT: Ablex, 1998.

Pennington, Martha. *The Computer and the Non-native Writer: A Natural Partnership.* Cresskill, NJ: Hampton, 1996.

Plant, Sadie. *Zeros + Ones : Digital Women + the New Technoculture.* New York: Doubleday, 1997.

Porter, James E. *Rhetorical Ethics and Internetworked Writing.* Greenwich, CT, and Houghton, MI: Ablex and Computers and Composition P, 1998.

Regan, Alison. "'Type Normal Like the Rest of Us': Writing, Power, and Homophobia in the Networked Composition Classroom." *Computers and Composition* 10 (1993): 11–24.

Regan, Alison E., and John D. Zuern. "Community-Service Learning and Computer-Mediated Advanced Composition: The Going to Class, Getting Online, and Giving Back Project." *Computers and Composition* 17 (2000): 177–95.

Reynolds, Thomas J., and Charles R. Lewis. "The Changing Topography of Computer Access for Composition Students." *Computers and Composition* 14 (1997): 269–78.

Richardson, Elaine, and Sean Lewis. "'Flippin' the Script'/'Blowin' Up the Spot': Puttin' Hip-Hop Online in (African) America and South Africa." Hawisher and Selfe, *Global* 251–76.

Rickly, Rebecca. "The Gender Gap in Computers and Composition Research: Must Boys Be Boys?" *Computers and Composition* 16 (1999): 121–40.

Riess, Donna, Dickie Selfe, and Art Young. *Electronic Communication Across the Curriculum.* Urbana, IL: NCTE, 1998.

Romano, Susan. "The Egalitarianism Narrative: Whose Story? Which Yardstick? *Computers and Composition* 10 (1993): 5–28.

Romano, Susan, Barbara Field, and Elizabeth de Huergo. "Web Literacies of the Already Accessed and Technically Inclined: Schooling in Monterrey, Mexico." Hawisher and Selfe, *Global* 189–216.

Salvo, Michael J. "Trauma, Narration, Technology: User-Ordered Representation and the Holocaust." *Computers and Composition* 16 (1999): 283–301.

Sanders, Barry. *A Is for Ox: The Collapse of Literacy and the Rise of Violence in an Electronic Age.* New York: Vintage, 1994.

Selber, Stuart A., ed. *Computers and Technical Communication: Pedagogical and Programmatic Perspectives.* Greenwich, CT: Ablex, 1997.

Selfe, Cynthia L. "Lest We Think the Revolution Is a Revolution: Images of Technology and the Nature of Change." Hawisher and Selfe, *Passions* 292–322.

———. *Technology and Literacy in the Twenty-First Century: The Importance of Paying Attention.* Carbondale: Southern Illinois UP, 1999.

Selfe, Cynthia L., and Paul R. Meyer. "Gender and Electronic Conferences." *Written Communication* 8.2 (1991): 163–92.

Selfe, Cynthia L., and Richard J. Selfe. "The Politics of the Interface: Power and Its Exercise in Electronic Contact Zones." *College Composition and Communication* 45 (1994): 480–504.

Selfe, Dickie. "Surfing the Tsunami: Electronic Environments in the Writing Center." *Computers and Composition* 12 (1995): 311–22.

Shirk, Henrietta Nickels, and Howard Taylor Smith. "Emerging Fair Use Guidelines for Multimedia: Implications for the Writing Classroom." *Computers and Composition* 15 (1998): 229–43.

Sirc, Geoffrey. "'What Is Composition?' After DuChamp (Notes Toward a General Teleintertext)." Hawisher and Selfe, *Passions* 178–204.

Sloan, Sarah. *Digital Fictions: Storytelling in a Material World.* Stamford, CT: Ablex, 2000.

Sosnoski, James J. "Hyper-Readers and Their Reading Engines." Hawisher and Selfe, *Passions* 161–77.

Stacey, David, Sharon Goodman, and Teresa Diane Stubbs. "The New Distance Learn-
    ing: Students, Teachers, and Texts in Cross-Cultural Electronic Communication."
    Computers and Composition 13 (1996): 293–302.
Street, Brian V. *Social Literacies: Critical Approaches to Literacy in Development, Ethnog-
    raphy, and Education.* London: Longman, 1995.
Sugimoto, Taku, and James Levin. "Multiple Literacies and Multimedia: A Comparison
    of Japanese and American Uses of the Internet." Hawisher and Selfe, *Global* 133–53.
Sullivan, Laura L. "Cyberbabes: (Self-) Representation of Women and the Virtual Male
    Gaze." *Computers and Composition* 14 (1997): 189–204.
———. "Wired Women Writing: Towards a Feminist Theorization of Hypertext." *Com-
    puters and Composition* 16 (1999): 25–54.
Sullivan, Laura L., and Victor Fernandez. "CyberCuba.com(munist): Electronic Liter-
    acy, Resistance, and Postrevolutionary Cuba." Hawisher and Selfe, *Global* 217–50.
Sullivan, Patricia, and Jennie Dautermann, eds. *Electronic Literacies in the Workplace:
    Technologies of Writing.* Urbana, IL: NCTE, 1996.
Susser, Bernard. "Networks and Project Work: Alternative Pedagogies for Writing with
    Computers." *Computers and Composition* 10 (1993): 63–89.
Syverson, Margaret A. *The Wealth of Reality: An Ecology of Composition.* Carbondale:
    Southern Illinois UP, 1998.
Takayoshi, Pamela. "Building New Networks from the Old: Women's Experiences with
    Electronic Communications." *Computers and Composition* 11 (1994): 21–36.
Takayoshi, Pamela, et al. "No Boys Allowed: The World Wide Web as a Clubhouse for
    Girls." *Computers and Composition* 16 (1999): 89–106.
Taylor, Todd. "The Persistence of Difference in Networked Classrooms: Non-negotiable
    Difference and the African American Student Body." *Computers and Composition* 14
    (1997): 169–78.
Tu, Thuy Linh, et al. "Communities on the Verge: Intersections and Disjunctures in the
    New Information Order." *Computers and Composition,* 14 (1997): 289–300.
Turkle, Sherry. "Computational Reticence: Why Women Fear the Intimate Machine."
    Kramarae 41–61.
———. *Life on the Screen: Identity in the Age of the Internet.* New York: Simon, 1995.
———. *The Second Self: Computers and the Human Spirit.* London: Granada, 1984.
Vielstimmig, Myka. "Petals on a Wet Black Bough: Textuality, Collaboration, and the
    New Essay." Hawisher and Selfe, *Passions* 89–114.
Wajcman, Judy. *Feminism Confronts Technology.* University Park: Pennsylvania State
    UP, 1991.
Walker, Janice R. "Copyrights and Conversations: Intellectual Property in the Class-
    room." *Computers and Composition* 15 (1998): 243–51.
Warshauer, Susan C. "Rethinking Teacher Authority to Counteract Homophobic Preju-
    dice in the Networked Classroom: A Model of Teacher Response and Overview of
    Classroom Methods." *Computers and Composition* 12 (1995): 97–111.
Whitaker, Elaine, and Elaine N. Hill. "Virtual Voices in 'Letters Across Cultures': Listen-
    ing for Race, Class, and Gender." *Computers and Composition* 15 (1998): 331–46.
Winner, Langdon. *The Whale and the Reactor: A Search for Limits in an Age of High
    Technology.* Chicago: U of Chicago P, 1986.

Wolfe, Joanna L. "Why Do Women Feel Ignored? Gender Differences in Computer-
    Mediated Classroom Interactions." *Computers and Composition* 16 (1999): 153–66.

Woodland, Randal. "'I Plan to Be a 10': Online Literacy and Lesbian, Gay, Bisexual, and
    Transgender Students." *Computers and Composition* 16 (1999): 73–87.

———. "Queer Spaces, Modem Boys and Pagan Statues:Gay/Lesbian Identity and the
    Construction of Cyberspace." *Works and Days* 13.1/2 (1995): 221–40. <http://www.
    iup.edu/en/workdays/Woodland.html> (Dec. 3, 2000).

Wresch, William. *Disconnected: Haves and Have-Nots in the Information Age.* New
    Brunswick, NJ: Rutgers UP, 1996.

Wysocki, Anne Frances, and Johndan Johnson-Eilola. "Blinded by the Letter: Why Are
    We Using Literacy as a Metaphor for Everything Else?" Hawisher and Selfe, *Passions*
    349–68.

Yagelski, Robert P., and Sarah Powley. "Virtual Connections and Real Boundaries:
    Teaching Writing and Preparing Writing Teachers on the Internet." *Computers and
    Composition* 13 (1996): 25–36.

Ziv, Oren. "Writing to Work: How Using E-Mail Can Reflect Technological and Organi-
    zational Change." *Computer-Mediated Communication: Linguistic, Social, and Cross-
    Cultural Perspectives.* Ed. Susan C. Herring. Amsterdam: John Benjamins, 1996.
    243–64.

19

The Eternal Return of Magic-Rhetoric: Carnak Counts Ballots

WILLIAM A. COVINO

M AGIC HAS BEEN an important generative concept in twentieth-century rhetoric and composition, leading primarily to considerations of the relationships between language and power. The compositionist most readily identified with magic is Peter Elbow, whose *Writing with Power* ends with a chapter titled "Writing and Magic," in which he maintains that words and things have a sympathetic and interactive relationship: "The magical view of language, in a nutshell, is that the word is a *part* of the thing it stands for—the word *contains* some of the juice or essence or soul of the *thing* it points to" (358). The material force of words constitutes their power, and realizing this power, Elbow argues, leads writers and teachers to understand that writing is consequential—like a magic spell gone right or wrong.

Pressing the magical view of language into rhetorical analysis, Kenneth Burke argues in *The Philosophy of Literary Form*, "The magical decree is implicit in all language; for the mere act of naming an object or situation decrees that it is to be singled out as such and such rather than as something other." He goes on to propose that, since all acts of language materialize a certain reality, we must take care that our "decrees" are uttered in a dialogic rather than a totalizing spirit, naming the world in a way that maintains its complexity and difference (4).[1]

With Burke, Paulo Freire understands that people can develop a passive relationship to the power of the decrees that govern their lives, resigning themselves to follow social and political regulations as inevitable facts of life. Freire calls such an attitude "magic consciousness" and contrasts it to "critical consciousness," which is the active questioning of what seem to be the governing beliefs in a culture. As representative voices in the application of magic to rhetoric and composition, Elbow, Burke, and Freire continue a longstanding relationship between magic and rhetoric that pervades Western intellectual history, as we see indicated by both Jacqueline de Romilly, in *Magic and Rhetoric in Ancient Greece,* and John Ward, in "Magic and Rhetoric from Antiquity to the Renaissance."

It is not surprising that magic and rhetoric have long been thought of as counterparts, since both are transformative forces aimed at altering material conditions.[2] In premodern thought, persuasive discourse entails the cooperation of cosmic and spiritual forces that can influence the receptivity of an audience. Renaissance philosophers such as Pico della Mirandola and Marsilio Ficino advise orators to observe the positions of the stars and to be mindful of spirits and deities that might affect the power of a speech. In general, the early tendency to accord language magical power—voiced as early as Gorgias's "Encomium of Helen" and continued by both Aristotle and Plato—reflects the belief that words can mediate and change reality. All rhetoric can be understood, then, to have a magical component, and all magic—dependent as it is on spells—is rhetorical. Thus, we can posit the term *magic-rhetoric* as an indicator of their inseparability.

The specifically magical alteration of reality has always promised the transcendence of material conditions and constraints, as well as the creation of new realities. In this connection, magic-rhetoric is the enactment of phantasy or imagination, and phantastic intellection is often associated with people who operate outside of and in defiance of the established order: sorcerers, witches, heretics, artists. Magic-rhetoric that elaborates phantasy-as-subversion can be distinguished from a more rigid and formulaic magic-rhetoric that maintains behavioral conditioning as a kind of "piety." This is the magic that we see practiced by the mesmerizing fascistic figure Cippola in Thomas Mann's "Mario and the Magician," who turns audience members into automatons. Today's pious magic is most apparent in a technoculture that has successfully transformed a tremendous range of human activities and information to hyperlinked Web pages, giving us a virtual reality that is instantaneously responsive, efficient, and peremptory, with great supervisory control over much of everyone's daily life (see Covino, "Cyberpunk").

Magico-rhetorical appeals to phantasy cannot always be easily distinguished from magico-rhetorical appeals to piety, yet we can detect, with reference to these two strains of magic-rhetoric, an ongoing agonistic between "generative" and "conservative" cultural and political forces. This agonistic has developed from antiquity forward as an opposition between two different models of rhetorical invention; it may be summarized as follows: invention and memory, both as interactive canons of rhetoric and as cognitive processes, were widely understood in prescientific literature as involving phantasy, which is the interaction of quasi-spiritual sense impressions (phantasms) that are imprinted on the soul. The moral and ethical quality of phantasy is an issue that occupies Platonic and Christian neo-Platonic philosophy that contributes to the identification of those who practice "unfettered phantasia"—unauthorized by established knowledge, tradition, or law—as dangerous (Watson 71). Unfettered phantasia, or what is also understood as the sin of *curiositas* (what Edward Peters has called "the passion for knowing unnecessary things"), has defined the magician, the witch, and the heretic as outside the sphere of legitimate knowledge (see Covino, "Walt").

At the same time, rhetorical invention is understood in large part as the capacity for phantasy, though it may serve the interests of either "articulate" or "inarticulate" power, as Peter Brown has defined these terms. Those with vested authority, as well as those committed to maintaining such authority, constitute articulate power. Moving beyond Brown's analysis, let me propose that such power may be understood as articulate in two senses: first, it is officially constituted within conventional social and legal structures, and it is thus articulate with other conventional forms of power and authority (the three branches of the U.S. federal government are, in this sense, articulate with one another); second, the language of its operations and communications is generally not regarded as interpretive and is thus articulate in terms of its ostensible clarity. Inarticulate power operates outside the control of conventional institutions and discourses, often adopting modes of expression that are considered irrational or incoherent and is, in this regard, "lawless."

The regulation of such lawlessness is constituted by the regulation of phantasy and extends from Plato's worry that youth will be seduced by false images (accumulating a storehouse of false phantasms) to the motto of Disney World's Twenty-Fifth Anniversary, "It's Time to Remember the Magic." The Disney motto is curiously Wordsworthian, as it asks longtime Disney World fans to associate the park with a magical childhood moment, exerting the power of memory and invention in a fashion not unlike that which Wordsworth describes in "Ode: Intimations of Immortality from Recollections of Early Childhood." The park itself offers thoroughly domesticated, paternalistic phantasy—implying with its motto that parents should initiate their children into the Disney experience, which amounts to the inculcation of conservative American values and the advertisement of corporate benevolence. While both the Platonic/Disneyesque/technocratic version of phantasy and the unfettered phantasia are species of magic, the former is often featured as coincident with legitimate knowledge that supports virtue, reason, and truth, while the latter is associated with illegitimate knowledge that springs from sophistic rhetoric, corruption, madness, and excess emotion.

Magic-Rhetoric in the 2000 Presidential Election

In line with the centuries-old agonistic between legitimate and illegitimate knowledge, understood in terms of magic, the 2000 presidential election provides an illustration of the ways in which the history and theory of magic-rhetoric can be brought to bear on practical examples. The awarding of Florida's twenty-five electoral votes to George W. Bush, which determined his election to the presidency, was finally decided by a U.S. Supreme Court decision that stopped a statewide hand recount of the votes in Florida by local canvassing boards and—in the cases of Palm Beach and Miami-Dade counties—by state judges appointed as counters. The validity of hand recounts was questioned by the Bush campaign throughout the "protest" and "contest" phases of the election, which stretched from November 8 to the Supreme Court's decision on December 12. From the start (a request by the Gore campaign for a hand recount in select Florida counties), the accusation that Gore was resorting to "magic" emerged, and it persisted in day-to-day debates as the process unfolded. One regular charge was that those doing the hand counts were "divining" the intentions of the voters by trying to determine the import of a paper ballot that had not been fully punched through and that instead showed an indentation where a punch-through might have been (a "dimpled chad"), or a partial punch-through (a "hanging" or "swinging" chad). Political cartoons in this connection featured turbaned prognosticators, behaving like Johnny Carson's well-known *Tonight Show* character "Carnak," holding ballots to their heads and announcing the results as if by mind reading. Attempting to understand such characterizations of the hand count brings into focus the conflict between legitimate and illegitimate knowledge that defines the history of Western relationships between magic and rhetoric, which I have summarized above in order to establish a basis for considering our recourse to magic as an organizing concept for rhetorical strategies, and which I will apply below to show some ways that a longstanding lexicon for the agonistic relationship between the discourses of established power and its challengers has emerged yet again.

The hand recounts of votes in Palm Beach, Broward, and Miami-Dade counties involved the visual inspection by an elected canvassing board of every ballot that had not registered a vote when run through the electronic counting machine. The board was charged with determining, in line with Florida statutes, whether marks or perforations on the ballot indicated the intent of the voter. This counting process was immediately vilified in conservative venues, in terms that were widely adopted and repeated:

> However you cut it, with hundreds of chads on the floor after these counts and the county officials taping in chads for Bush and leaving chads punched and the divining of intent of the voters by partisan officials, it's no surprise that Gore is gaining votes! (Dawson)
>
> While granting maximum latitude in divining intentions of Democratic senior citizens on the south Florida Gold Coast, the predominantly Republican votes of young men and women serving their country abroad would be scrutinized with no latitude. (Novak)
>
> Imagine the magic involved in this mysterious mission—to determine the intention of an unknown person, whose behavior has not been observed and of whose belief there is no evidence.
>
> Yet, the ballot counters in Florida would have us believe it is possible, and the presidency of the United States may depend upon their supernatural abilities. (Green)

The charge that hand counts "divine" the intention of voters is complemented by the charge that Democrats were interested in making more votes "appear" through the process of recounts, thus suggesting the materialization out of thin air that we associate with stage magic (see Seifman).[3] Condemning the divination of intention is tied to the belief that the only intentions that "count" are those that are expressed and educed transparently; the metaphor of transparency is literalized by the vote counting machines employed in Palm Beach County and elsewhere, which register an intentional vote as a punch-through that creates a transparent hole that lets light through. In effect, the machine remembers what is transparent or brought to light and forgets what remains in the dark, or occult.[4] The operation of light here as the agency that determines a vote, while it is also a key element of the technological magic that makes high-speed machine counting possible, maintains the opposition between the light (of faith, of reason, of truth) and darkness (of evil, of corruption) that is part of our standard symbolic currency. The light/darkness opposition is not part of any explicit argument against machine counts that I have seen, but it is nonetheless embedded in the machinery itself and part of the cultural psychology that can give the mechanical process symbolic and ethical resonance.[5]

As Peter Brown points out, the sorcerer—and later, the witch—are usually subject to condemning accusations, precisely because the sorcerer is disrupting ascendant power by bringing in, as Brown puts it, "the unseen to redress the balance of the seen" (124). The sorcerer and the witch try to bring to light what has been hidden in the interests of stability, consistency, or tradition. To the extent that the Gore campaign was characterized as doing so by insisting on a hand count, they were regarded as precipitating a "constitutional crisis"—that is, creating a situation unanticipated or unaccounted for by codified processes, thus taking us to the brink of as yet untried, unseen (and thus occult) processes.

In sum, inarticulate power is located in the ambiguation and violation of established constraints, which occurred in this case through the expansion of time limits (extending the election decision well past November 7 and, further, past deadlines established by the Florida secretary of state for certifying the vote); through the practice of unconventional and inconsistent procedures for the reading of ballots, explicitly associated with augury; and through the temporary reversion of authority to small county canvassing boards that were accused of operating outside of state statutes. Articulate power in this case inheres in the vested authority that prevailed: the Florida Secretary of State, the Florida legislature, and the U.S. Supreme Court—all of whom were intent upon containing an opposition that was publicly described in terms of spells and divination.

This review of the 2000 presidential election is, finally, itself an exercise in unfettered phantasia, in speculative analysis that demonstrates some of the intellectual work that alertness to magic-rhetoric can license. I do not finally intend, however, to league the Gore campaign with witches and sorcerers and the Bush campaign with the anti-magical status quo. To do so would be to give the Gore campaign a radical dimension that is far from the case. Rather, I have wished to point out here the extent to which the perceived "challenger" to an established position can be characterized in terms of the opposition between legitimate and illegitimate phantasy, and the ways in which the regulation of a political and rhetorical process can be conceived of in magico-rhetorical terms. In December 2000, the *Miami Herald* published a statistical projection of a complete Florida vote count, showing Gore as the clear winner; the Bush campaign dismissed this analysis as "statistical voodoo," thus continuing the ultimately persuasive and prevailing association of the innovative and inarticulate with dangerous, alien, magic forces (de Gale et al.).

Notes

1. For a more extensive discussion of Elbow and Burke on magic, see Briggs.

2. I present some of the points covered in the first section of this essay more extensively in Covino, *Magic.*

3. The association of the forces of unfettered phantasia with the illegitimate materialization of matter was further apparent in the repeated debates over whether the Florida Supreme Court's decision to allow hand recounts was in conformity with the "rule of law" or was, instead, making new law. As with the question of whether ballots were being "created" through a hand recount, the debate over whether law was being "made" by the (liberal, Democrat) court continued the counterposition of articulate power (represented by the "rule of law") and inarticulate power. Ironically, the inarticulate power in this case is the Florida Supreme Court, an otherwise "articulate" institution that found itself perceived as outside of and thus inarticulate with the Florida legislature, the Florida secretary of state, and the U.S. Supreme Court.

4. There are, however, a number of variables that influence this process. Paterson writes:

> Today's voting systems use cardboard media, with the choices indicated by either a dark mark or an aperture. Photosensors detect a change in either reflection or transmission of light. Accuracy depends jointly on the illumination system, the sensitivity of the photosensors, and the alteration of reflectivity or transmission by the voter's action, whether by choice or accident. Depending on the design and state of maintenance of the equipment, the performance of the illumination system and photosensors may depend on the line voltage, room temperature, time since turned on, and air flow. The voter's effect on the reflectivity or transmission of his ballot depends on his instructions and the nature of the card stock. Card stock varies by manufacturer, batch, and storage conditions.

5. Of course, recourse to the concept of darkness and its coincidence with countercultural power is common. This was especially apparent during the 2000 election contentions, when a group in Boca Raton, Florida, donned black clothes and marched through the downtown with taped mouths in a candlelight vigil protesting the "silencing" of voters in South Florida (Hartnett).

Works Cited

Briggs, John C. "Saving Pluralism from Itself: Peter Elbow, Kenneth Burke, and the Idea of Magic." *JAC* 11 (1991): 363–75.

Brown, Peter. *Religion and Society in the Age of Saint Augustine.* New York: Harper, 1972.

Burke, Kenneth. *The Philosophy of Literary Form: Studies in Symbolic Action.* 3rd ed. Berkeley: U of California P, 1973.

Covino, William A. "Cyberpunk Literacy; or, Piety in the Sky." *Literacy Theory in the Age of the Internet.* Ed. Todd Taylor and Irene Ward. New York: Columbia UP, 1998. 34–46.

———. *Magic, Rhetoric, and Literacy: An Eccentric History of the Composing Imagination.* Albany: State U of New York P, 1994.

———. "Walt Disney Meets Mary Daly: Invention, Imagination, and the Construction of Community." *JAC* 20 (2000): 153–65.

Dawson, A. B. "Vote Fraud Continues in Florida." *Our Nation* 21 Nov. 2000. <http://www.ournation.org/election_2000.htm>.

De Gale, Anabelle, et al. "If the Vote Were Flawless . . ." *Miami Herald* 3 Dec. 2000. <http://miamiherald.com>.

De Romilly, Jacqueline. *Magic and Rhetoric in Ancient Greece.* Cambridge: Harvard UP, 1975.

Elbow, Peter. *Writing with Power: Techniques for Mastering the Writing Process.* New York: Oxford UP, 1981.

Freire, Paulo. *Pedagogy of the Oppressed.* Trans. Myra Bergman Ramos. New York: Penguin, 1972.

Green, Chuck. "Divining Intent of Voters." *Denver Post* 22 Nov. 2000. <http://www.denverpost.com/news/green1122.htm>.

Hartnett, Howie Paul. "Silent Protest in Boca Raton Still Effective." *Palm Beach Post* 30 Nov. 2000: 18A.

Novak, Robert. "A Cooly Crafted Scheme." *Townhall.com* 21 Nov. 2000. <http://www.townhall.com/columnists/robertnovak/rn20001121.shtml>.

Paterson, W. L. "Vote Counting by Machines—and People." *The Idler* 20 Nov. 2000. <http://www.geocities.com/dejarviks/Idler/vIIn147.html>.

Peters, Edward. *The Magician, the Witch, and the Law.* Philadelphia: U of Pennsylvania P, 1978.

Seifman, David. "Vote-Count Flip-Flop Has GOP in Furor." *NY Post.Com* 20 Nov. 2000. <http://www.nypost.com/news/16404.htm>.

Ward, John O. "Magic and Rhetoric from Antiquity to the Renaissance: Some Ruminations." *Rhetorica* 6 (1988): 57–118.

Watson, Gerard. *Phantasia in Classical Thought.* Galway, Ireland: Galway UP, 1988.

Contributors

Charles Bazerman is a professor and the chair of education at the University of California at Santa Barbara. His books include *The Languages of Edison's Light; Constructing Experience; Textual Dynamics of the Professions;* and *Shaping Written Knowledge: The Genre and Activity of the Experimental Article in Science.*

Barbara Couture is the dean of the College of Liberal Arts at Washington State University. Her award-winning books include *Toward a Phenomenological Rhetoric: Writing, Profession and Altruism; Functional Approaches to Writing: Research Perspectives;* and *Cases for Technical and Professional Writing* (with Jone Rymer Goldstein).

William A. Covino is a professor of English and the department chair at Florida Atlantic University. His books include *The Elements of Persuasion, Magic, Rhetoric, and Literacy: An Eccentric History of the Composing Imagination,* and *The Art of Wondering: A Revisionist Return to the History of Rhetoric.*

Sharon Crowley is a professor of English at Arizona State University, where she directs the graduate programs in rhetoric and composition. She is the author of the Winterowd Award–winning *The Methodical Memory: Invention in Current-Traditional Rhetoric* and, most recently, *Composition in the University: Historical and Polemical Essays.*

Tom Fox is a professor of English at California State University at Chico, where he directs the Northern California Writing Project. He is the author of *Social Uses of Writing* and *Defending Access,* and he is coeditor of *Writing With: New Directions in Collaborative Teaching, Learning, and Research* (with Sally Reagan and David Bleich).

Keith Gilyard is a professor of English at Pennsylvania State University and the former chair of the Conference on College Composition and Communication. His books include the award-winning *Voices of the Self: A Study of Language Competence* and *Let's Flip the Script: An African American Discourse on Language, Literature, and Learning*.

Susan C. Jarratt is a professor of English and coordinator of writing at the University of California at Irvine. Her *Rereading the Sophists: Classical Rhetoric Refigured* won Honorable Mention for MLA's Mina Shaughnessy prize. She is coeditor with Lynn Worsham of *Feminism and Composition Studies: In Other Words*.

Thomas Kent is the dean of the School of Graduate Studies and a professor of English at Utah State University. He recently edited *Post-Process Theory: Beyond the Writing-Process Paradigm*.

Steven Mailloux is chancellor's professor of rhetoric at the University of California at Irvine. He is the editor of *Rhetoric, Sophistry, Pragmatism* and the author of *Rhetorical Power* and *Reception Histories: Rhetoric, Pragmatism, and American Cultural Politics*.

Susan Miller is a professor of English and a member of the faculty of the University Writing Program at the University of Utah. She is the author of *Assuming the Positions: Cultural Pedagogy and the Politics of Commonplace Writing* and two award-winning works of scholarship: *Rescuing the Subject: A Critical Introduction to Rhetoric and the Writer* and *Textual Carnivals: The Politics of Composition*.

Jasper Neel is a professor of English and the dean of the College at Southern Methodist University. Among his numerous publications is *Aristotle's Voice: Rhetoric, Theory, and Writing in America*, winner of the 1994 W. Ross Winterowd Award for the most outstanding book on composition theory. He is currently working on a book on Isocrates.

Gary A. Olson is a professor of English at the University of South Florida, where he directs the graduate program in rhetoric and composition and serves as an associate in the Institute for the Study of Social and Political Thought. His most recent book is *The Kinneavy Papers: Theory and the Study of Discourse* (with Lynn Worsham and Sid Dobrin).

Cynthia L. Selfe is a professor of humanities at Michigan Technological University. Her recent publications include *Literacy and Technology in the 21st Century: The Perils of Not Paying Attention* and *Global Literacies and the World-Wide Web* (with Gail Hawisher). Selfe is the first woman and the first English teacher to have won the EDUCOM Award for innovative teaching with technology.

Richard J. Selfe is the director of Computer-Based Instruction in the humanities department at Michigan Technological University. Recent publications include "Traveling the Virtual Terrain: Practical Strategies for Survival in the Electronic Classroom" (with Coffield et al.), "Distance Education: Sites of Political Agency" (with DeVoss, Hayden, and Selfe), and "What Are We Doing to and for Ourselves? (The Material Process of Adapting to Electronic Spaces)."

C. Jan Swearingen is a professor of English at Texas A&M University and immediate past president of the Rhetoric Society of America. She is editor of *Rhetoric, the Polis, and the Global Village* and the author of the award-winning *Rhetoric and Irony: Western Literacy and Western Lies*.

John Trimbur is a professor of writing and rhetoric at Worcester Polytechnic Institute. His recent work includes the edited collection *Popular Literacy: Studies in Cultural Practices and Poetics* and the textbook *The Call to Write*.

Victor J. Vitanza is a professor of English and rhetoric at the University of Texas at Arlington, where he edits *PRE/TEXT* and coedits *PRE/TEXT: Electra(Lite)*. Among his recent publications are *CyberReader* and *Negation, Subjectivity, and the History of Rhetoric*.

Susan Wells is a professor of English at Temple University. Her recent publications include *Sweet Reason: Rhetoric and the Discourses of Modernity* and *Out of the Dead House: Nineteenth-Century Women Physicians and the Writing of Medicine*.

Lynn Worsham is a professor of English at the University of South Florida, where she edits *JAC*, a quarterly journal for the interdisciplinary study of rhetoric, literacy, culture, and politics. Her recent books include *Race, Rhetoric, and the Postcolonial* (with Gary A. Olson) and *Feminism and Composition Studies: In Other Words* (with Susan C. Jarratt).

Index

Adams, Peter Dow: "Basic Writing Reconsidered," 93
Adbusters, 200
Addison, Joanne, 211
affirmative deconstruction, 169
African American English, 116–18, 121
Agamben, Giorgio, 168, 170–72; *The Coming Community,* 166; *Potentialities: Collected Essays in Philosophy,* 170
AIGA Journal of Graphic Design, 193
Alber, Josef, 196
Alexander, Jonathan, 211
allegory, 8
Alphabetic Literacy Narrative, 190–91
Althusser, Louis, 86–87, 92, 112
Amato, Joe, 211
American Bar Association, 121
American Family Association, 81
American pragmatist tradition, 37
American Psychological Association, 121
American Sociological Association, 121
American Speech and Hearing Association, 121
Ames, Susie M.: *Reading, Writing and Arithmetic in Virginia, 1607–1699: Other Cultural Topics,* 49
analytics of space, xiii, 65
anger, 108–9
anthropology, xi–xii, 30, 34, 75; linguistic, 32, 37
anti-ethnocentrism, 146
anti-foundationalism, 20, 137, 139, 144
anti-intellectualism, 113
antiracism, 75
Apollinaire, Guillaume, 197
Arac, Jonathan, 141
archives, xiii, 44–45, 55–64, 132, 157

archontic principle, 57–58
Aristotle, 11, 45, 143, 159, 166, 222; *Metaphysics,* 3; *Nicomachean Ethics,* 170; *Rhetoric,* 68
arrangement, 69
Aschauer, Anne Brady, 211
audience, 73–74, 84
Austin, John, 143

Bacon, Francis, 68
Bakhtin, Mikhail, 18, 20, 37; *Dostoevsky's Poetics,* 20; *Speech Genres and Other Late Essays,* 20
Ball, Arnetha, 123–24
Ballif, Michelle, 24
Balsamo, Anne, 212
Barber, Margaret, 211
Barker, Thomas T., 206
Barnbrook, Jonathan, 200
Barron, Dennis, 210
Barthes, Roland, 181–82
Bartholomae, David: "The Tidy House," 93
Bartky, Sandra Lee, 108–9; *Femininity and Domination: Studies in the Phenomenology of Oppression,* 112
Barton, David, 207
Barton, Ellen, 59
Baruch College, 116
basic writing, 97
Bataille, Georges, 168
Batson, Trenton W., 206
Baudrillard, Jean, 18, 167
Bauhaus movement, 193–95
Bauman, Zygmunt, 208
Bayer, Herbert, 196
Baym, Nina: "Early Histories of American Literature: A Chapter in the Institution of New England," 46